BEING CHINESE,

BECOMING CHINESE AMERICAN

THE ASIAN AMERICAN EXPERIENCE

Series Editor
Roger Daniels, University of Cincinnati

A list of books in the series appears at the end of this book.

SHEHONG CHEN

Being Chinese,
Becoming Chinese American

UNIVERSITY OF ILLINOIS PRESS

URBANA AND CHICAGO

♾ This book is printed on acid-free paper.

Library of Congress Cataloging-in-Publication Data
Chen, Shehong, 1954–
Being Chinese, becoming Chinese American /
Shehong Chen.
p.   cm. — (The Asian American experience)
Includes bibliographical references and index.
ISBN 0-252-02736-1 (cloth : alk. paper)
1. Chinese Americans—Ethnic identity.
2. Chinese Americans—Cultural assimilation.
3. Chinese Americans—Social conditions—20th century.
4. United States—Relations—China.
5. China—Relations—United States.
6. Transnationalism.
I. Title. II. Series.
E184.C5C466   2002
305.895'1073—DC21   2001005762

PAPERBACK ISBN 978-0-252-07389-2

To my parents

Contents

Foreword

Shehong Chen is one of the growing cohort of scholars from the People's Republic of China with American doctorates who are transforming Chinese American studies. In this book she asks the primal question, first asked by the French sojourner Crèvecoeur in 1782, "What then is an American?" And although her research examines only one specific group of people at a particular time—American Chinese in the early twentieth century—her answers have relevance for the whole question of identity and loyalty in an immigrant-based society.

Unlike many of those who came to the United States in the great century of immigration that ran from 1820 to 1924, most Chinese had a clear sense of who they were. They called themselves *gamsanhaak*, or "gold mountain guests." (The Chinese characters for *San Francisco* also mean "gold mountain.") In other words, despite residence in America, they continued to think of themselves as Chinese sojourners in an alien land. By the end of 1920s, Chen argues, this was no longer the case. Her work seeks out evidence for the process by which this fundamental change took place.

She finds her answers chiefly in the faded pages of three Chinese American newspapers published in San Francisco, the cultural center of Chinese America. These publications were not so much commercial enterprises as organs for different sectors of the community. All of the papers were concerned with a modern China; all saw republicanism as the ideal, the only possible future structure of China's government; but each defined it—and China—in a different way. As Chen puts it, "For *Young China*, only a republican form of government could realize the three principles of the people, namely nationalism, democracy, and people's livelihood. For *Chung Sai Yat Po*, only republicanism would guarantee liberty or freedom, equality, and universal love. For *Chinese World*, constitutionalism was the essence of modern China."

But all three newspapers also paid an increasing amount of attention to Chinese in the United States, and what Chen demonstrates most effectively are the ways in which these concerns went hand in hand. Without losing their focus on China—a focus that was heightened during the Sino-Japanese War in the 1930s—American Chinese became increasingly aware that their lives and, perhaps more importantly, the lives of their children were going to be played out in the New World, not in the Old.

This theme resonates throughout the American experience. Contemporary nativists are uneasy about the sometimes intense homeland ties of recent immigrants. They complain that many Mexican Americans pay closer attention to Mexican than to American politics, for example, and that they root for a Mexican soccer team even when (especially if?) it is playing an American opponent. What Chen demonstrates once more is the fatuity of Crèvecoeur's notions about acculturation. Rather than a total and seemingly instant shift from one set of allegiances to another, what usually occurs, as Chen shows us for the Chinese American case, is a gradual, sometimes all but imperceptible accretional change from one set of values and loyalties to another.

Acknowledgments

This study originates from a doctoral dissertation. I thank the supervisory committee members. Peggy Pascoe, with special interests in women's and minority studies, and Sandra Taylor, with special interests in international relations and Japanese American studies, combined to help me find my focus for the dissertation. Peggy Pascoe's constant encouragement, numerous readings of many versions of the dissertation, and thought-provoking questions made my research and writing a process of intellectual growth. Sandra Taylor gave me unwavering intellectual support and friendly mentoring. Anand Yang helped me verbalize the concept of "being Chinese and becoming Chinese American." Alan Coombs was never too busy when I needed somebody to discuss my ideas with. I benefited greatly from his expertise in twentieth-century U.S. history. Wesley Sasaki-Uemura raised challenging questions that pushed me to clarify my arguments.

I would not have had the opportunity for graduate studies without the help of several people. Jeffrey Montague and Annina Mitchell introduced to me the University of Utah and built a bridge for me between Beijing and Salt Lake City. Kent Morrison's recommendation not only got me into the graduate program at the University of Utah but also secured the financial support that enabled me to pursue graduate studies in the United States. Jim Lehning used his wisdom to help me overcome difficulties in the process of pursuing my graduate work.

I would also like to thank the Humanities Center and the Steffensen-Cannon Scholarship Committee at the University of Utah for financial support. The Humanities Center's Graduate Fellowship and the Steffensen-Cannon Scholarship freed me from teaching responsibilities and enabled me to concentrate on researching and writing my dissertation. While at the Humanities Center, I benefited enormously from the friendship, encouragement, and inspiration of the director, Lowell Durham Jr. I also want to thank Lynne Rasmussen for her kindness and secretarial help at the Humanities Center.

I enjoyed my research at the Asian American Studies Library at the University of California at Berkeley. It houses a wonderful collection of Chinese American newspapers and other special collections concerning Chinese American experience, and the library staff provided friendly and helpful service. I especially want to thank the director of the library, Wei Chi Poon, for her direction and guidance at the library and for her friendship and persistent confidence in me.

I am also indebted to those who helped me revise my dissertation for this book. At the University of Massachusetts at Lowell, I thank Charles Carroll, chairman of the History Department, and Nancy Kleniewski, dean of the College of Arts and Sciences, for allowing me to reduce my teaching load for a semester. The staff at the O'Leary Library provided excellent service. In particular, I want to thank Deborah Friedman for her prompt and friendly help in obtaining interlibrary loan items, and Ronald Karr, Helen Jones, and Richard Slapsys for assistance in locating research materials. I thank Mary Kramer, a professor of English, for reading the entire manuscript and for pointing out awkward expressions and logical problems. I also thank Jason Kramer, a computer system analyst, for his technical assistance in word processing.

Thanks also go to my colleagues Mary Blewett, Jonathan Liebowitz, and Donald Mattheisen for sharing their publishing experiences with me and for helping me convert Chinese money to U.S. dollars.

I benefited immensely from consulting with scholars in Chinese American studies. Him Mark Lai answered questions that nobody else could. I thank Judy Yung and Renqiu Yu for their helpful comments on a conference paper that was a part of this study.

I am deeply indebted to Roger Daniels, editor of the Asian American Experience Series at the University of Illinois Press, for his interest in my work and for suggestions to improve the manuscript. I also want to thank the unidentified reader for his or her detailed criticisms and enthusiasm. The staff at the University of Illinois Press gave me prompt and kind help, making my work with the press a wonderful experience. I am especially grateful to Michele May and Theresa L. Sears. I also thank Carol Anne Peschke for her meticulous copyediting.

I want to express my deep gratitude to my parents-in-law for their understanding and support. My father-in-law spent days in Beijing librar-ies helping me look for materials on the Chinese revolution. My deep gratitude also goes to Elizabeth and Keith Montague for acting as my American parents. Friendship from Leslie Thomas, Marilyn Bray, Ed Kim, Lou Tong, Will Louie, Haruko Moriyasu, Gladys Mixco, Paul Johnson, Larry Gerlach, Ray Gunn, Carol Gillmor, Beth Phillips, Melanee Cher-ry, and many others helped to lessen the stress and encourage the intel-lectual process associated with the development of this book.

I express my deepest gratitude to my husband, Zhou Wei. His sup-port and unwavering confidence in my ability helped me to persevere in academic pursuit. Although he is an engineer by profession, his strong interests in social sciences and humanities made our dining table an in-tellectual forum. Numerous conversations and heated debates with him helped me conceptualize, refine, and clarify my arguments.

Finally, I want to thank my sister and brother for taking care of our parents in China. This book is dedicated to my parents.

BEING CHINESE,

BECOMING CHINESE AMERICAN

Introduction

This is a study of the transformation of Chinese identity in the United States between 1911 and 1927. My research interest in this subject matter began when I was a graduate student at the University of Utah. In the early 1990s, I interviewed four Chinese Americans in Salt Lake City for a graduate paper. Three of my interviewees were American-born Chinese, and one came to the United States with her parents when she was a baby. My interviewees showed pride in their Chinese heritage. They told me stories of how they practiced Chinese rituals and celebrated Chinese traditional festivals at home. They also described different encounters of racially oriented prejudice and discrimination and various efforts they had made in fighting for equal rights and opportunities as minority people in the United States.

When I asked them about their thoughts of and connections with China, they became hesitant and worried. One of them said that China could have done better without communism; another asked me whether it was safe to make financial investments in China; still another remembered his experience as an American soldier in the Korean War and how "we were pushed back by them [the Chinese] to the 38th parallel"; and the fourth interviewee expressed disapproval of the Chinese government's action in the 1989 student democracy movement. However, they all expressed their desire to see a strong China and hoped they could do something to help strengthen their ancestral land.[1]

The findings from the interviews were not surprising; they actually reinforced an observation I had been making. I visited Chinatowns, made a few friends among Chinese Americans, and was entertained at Chinese

I

American homes. Having grown up in the People's Republic of China, I sensed that the Chinatown atmosphere and Chinese American homes embodied elements of traditional Chinese culture as well as modern American culture. For instance, Chinatown stores and restaurants publicly displayed offerings to gods and goddesses; Chinese Americans drove hundreds of miles to clean their ancestral graves around the Qing Ming Festival, the traditional Chinese festival to remember the dead; and Chinese American parents would not open letters addressed to their children, for doing so was a violation of their children's right to privacy. Whereas the first two examples reflected Chinese traditional customs, the third was decidedly a reflection of American individualism.

While making such observations, I was wrapping up my Ph.D. coursework with an emphasis on the history of China-U.S. relations. Since the first major wave of Chinese immigration into the United States in the 1850s, China and the United States had encountered two very different fates in the evolutionary history of nation-states. Having just conquered the west coast of the North American continent, the United States began in the 1850s to rise as a world power. For China, the 1840s marked the beginning of humiliation and decline as a nation and a civilization. While the rise of the United States was accompanied by expansionism, industrialization, capitalist democracy, and Christianity, the decline of China was caused partly by Western expansionism and partly by internal struggles over how to cope with challenges posed by the aggressive outside forces in the modern world.

The most intense search for a modern China and modern Chinese identity happened in the first three decades of the twentieth century. The year 1911 witnessed an end to the century-old dynastic system in China and a declaration of the establishment of a modern republic. Such a fundamental change proved not to be an easy matter for China. Western and modern ideas such as capitalism failed to find national capital and an industrial base, thus opening China's market and resources further to outside exploitation. The idea of democracy conflicted with the Confucian hierarchy of social order. Greed for power led to attempts at monarchical restoration and warlords' competition for regional control, pushing China to the verge of disintegration as a unified nation. Intensified search for a way out of China's national crisis led to a cultural movement condemning Confucianism and Chinese tradition, to the embracing of Marxist ideas and formation of the Chinese Communist Party (CCP), and to the height of nationalism against imperialism. It was in early 1923 that the Guomindang (GMD, or the Nationalist Party), which led the 1911 revolution, decided to ally with the Soviet Union and cooperate with the CCP in the national effort for a unified, independent, and modern China.

Knowledge of history and my own observations that being Chinese in the United States carried different meanings from being Chinese in the People's Republic of China combined to form my research questions. How did Chinese in the United States envision a modern China while China as a nation underwent such fundamental changes in the first few decades of the twentieth century? What did they think of the debates and politics in China? Did their experience in the United States affect their vision of a modern China? Did their exposure to American ideology and Christian values shape their sense of Chineseness as the old framework for Chinese identity faced challenges?

The more I think about the dichotomy of Chinese and American history in the modern world, the more aware I am of the interesting position occupied by Chinese in the United States. American Chinese in the early twentieth century were involved in the crosscurrents of conflicting and competing global forces. (Throughout this book I use the term *Chinese Americans* for people of Chinese ancestry who are American citizens; *American Chinese* and *Chinese in the United States* are used interchangeably to refer to any Chinese living in the United States.) As subjects of the dynastic China, they were carriers of traditional Chinese values; as immigrants suffering from discrimination and exclusion in the United States, they were victims of white racism and the weakened Chinese nation. How they survived exclusion and discrimination and how they envisioned and maintained Chineseness and adapted to American society became a much more interesting question for me than diplomatic relations between China and the United States. I decided to make my doctoral dissertation a study of the transformation of Chinese identity in the United States in the early twentieth century.

A review of existing literature on Chinese American studies encouraged my pursuit. Until very recently, Chinese American studies left the first few decades of the twentieth century almost unexamined. According to Sucheng Chan, one of the leading experts on Chinese American studies, the entire period between 1882 and 1943, the "age of exclusion," was "a deplorable lacuna in Chinese American historiography."[2] Students of the period before the passage of the Chinese Exclusion Act of 1882 found materials with which to study the Chinese experience in the United States, many of them in English, including documentation of observations about the Chinese as a different race and debates over and violence against the Chinese presence in the United States. After the passage of the Exclusion Act, Chinese population decreased drastically, and Chinese existence in the United States became much more precarious; as a result, there was little English-language documentation of the Chinese American experience.

Historians of Chinese American studies thus suffered from this lack of source materials for the period between 1882 and 1943. Earlier studies of this period, done mostly by social scientists, whose conclusions do not depend as heavily on first-hand documents as historians do, generally described this period as the "silent years," in which American Chinese scraped together a living by running restaurants, grocery stores, and laundries.[3] For example, Paul Siu's sociological study concluded that the Chinese laundryman remained a sojourner, an immigrant who did not intend to take root in the host society, for more than a hundred years, from the 1850s to the 1950s.[4] Journalists, with very little knowledge of Chinatown life in general, documented sensational stories of Chinese "tong wars" during this period, popularizing and reinforcing the violent and mysterious image of Chinese American experience presented by social scientists.[5] According to these studies, the isolated Chinatown life prevented any contact between Chinese and mainstream American society and encouraged Chinese in the United States to maintain intact their traditional identity.

Meanwhile, on the other side of the Pacific, in mainland China and Taiwan, studies of overseas Chinese, including Chinese in the United States, praised them as "the mother of the Chinese revolution."[6] Before 1949, the Nationalist government in China used this image to solicit support, especially financial support, from Chinese in the United States. Since the establishment of the People's Republic of China, both the government in Beijing and that in Taibei have continued to compete for political loyalty and financial support from Chinese in the United States. To serve the political agendas of their respective governments, scholars on both sides of the Taiwan Straits have claimed that Chinese in the United States maintained political allegiance to China and supported Chinese revolutions. According to Ling-chi Wang, a scholar of Chinese American studies and a political activist, such politically oriented studies resulted in "extraterritorial domination" over Chinese in the United States, whereas Wang Gungwu, a specialist in southeast Asian Chinese studies, maintained that the general statement about overseas Chinese as the mother of Chinese revolution misrepresented the role overseas Chinese played in Chinese revolutions.[7]

With the growing awareness of the existence of Chinese-language source materials and with more Chinese American historians competent in the Chinese language, several studies of the Chinese American experience in the exclusion period appeared. Using Chinese- and English-language source materials, these studies reconstructed various aspects of American Chinese community life and politics and told a more complete story of the Chinese American experience. Yet none of them aimed at a comprehensive understanding of the transformation of Chinese identity in the United States.[8]

Other scholars have been attempting to understand the transformation of Chinese identity in the United States. K. Scott Wong used the concept of transculturation, a process in which "marginal groups select and invent from materials transmitted to them by a dominant . . . culture," to study the American Chinese identity transformation. He concluded that Chinese cultural elites, who had contacts with the United States in the nineteenth and early twentieth century, combined the two worldviews—of traditional China and of the modern United States—to forge a "new and distinctively Chinese American cultural sensibility."[9]

It is in this line of analysis that I attempt to understand Chinese identity transformation in the United States in the context of reforms and revolutions in China between 1911 and 1927. The year 1911 witnessed the climax of the debate between the reformist Baohuanghui (the Society to Protect the Emperor) and the revolutionary Tongmenghui (the Revolutionary Alliance) among Chinese in the United States. The period between 1924 and 1927 witnessed concerted efforts to build permanent Chinese American communities, either by politically and legally fighting for rights to establish families and preserve Chinese cultural practices or by physically constructing community facilities such as the Chinese Hospital.

The study takes a transpacific approach in that it regards reformist and revolutionary programs that aimed to modernize China as the background and impetus for the American Chinese identity transformation. Furthermore, it investigates public debates and community events concerning a modern China among American Chinese to assess the impact of life in the United States and exposure to American culture and ideology on the formation of a Chinese American identity. The study thus moves constantly across the Pacific between events in China and events within American Chinese communities.

Like the most recent studies of the Chinese American experience during the exclusion period, this study relies on American Chinese community newspapers as primary source material. The value of newspapers as primary source material lies in the role these newspapers played in the life of Chinese in the United States in the early twentieth century. According to Leong Gor Yun,[10] author of *Chinatown Inside Out*, published in the 1930s, the influence of Chinese-language newspapers on American Chinese was "incalculable." This is how Leong Gor Yun described the influence of the Chinese language press: "It speaks to the Chinese in a language he understands; it is his only medium for knowing what is happening in his world and the world at large. It gives him a perspective very much needed in a life as narrow as life in Chinatown. Whatever the Chinese do for themselves will therefore probably be taught them through the newspapers."[11]

The influence of Chinese-language newspapers reached beyond those who subscribed to them and those who were educated enough to read them. Chinatown businesses, especially grocery stores, tea houses, restaurants, and Chinatown organization offices usually subscribed to several Chinese-language papers and made them available to shoppers, visitors, or anybody who stopped by to read them. It was also common in American Chinatowns to see newspapers posted on bulletin boards of community centers and to see one person reading aloud from a newspaper with a crowd listening. One study described a general store in San Jose in the first few years of the twentieth century. At the store, Chinese workers "made arrangements for employment and picked up their mail." The store "subscribed to several Chinese newspapers, so that bak [meaning "uncle" in Cantonese and here referring to Chinese adult men in general] would stop to rest, read the Chinese papers, and chat."[12]

Chinese-language newspapers not only served as "the only medium" for American Chinese to obtain information and perspectives but also recorded debates and events taking place among them.[13] Because there are few living witnesses to the 1911–27 period from whom we can take oral histories and because few people left diaries or memoirs behind, Chinese-language papers are invaluable source materials, enabling us to understand the dynamics of social, economic, ideological, and political changes among American Chinese. Judy Yung used American Chinese community newspapers as part of her first-hand materials and stated that scholars of Chinese American studies had yet to tap these valuable sources.[14]

This study investigates three Chinese-language newspapers. They are *Chinese World*, a daily newspaper founded by Kang Youwei and Liang Qichao, reformers from China, that represented the American Chinatown elite in the 1911–27 period; *Young China*, a daily paper founded by Sun Yat-sen that served in the United States as the voice of the Tongmenghui and the GMD; and *Chung Sai Yat Po*, another daily paper founded and managed by Wu Panzhao (Ng Poon Chew), a Chinese Christian minister who advocated reforming and modernizing Chinese cultural practices and adapting to the norms of American mainstream society.

These three papers were selected because they represented a full spectrum of opinions among American Chinese between 1911 and 1927. Although all voiced a desire for a strong and modern China, each envisioned a different way of achieving the goal. This study analyzes the transformation of Chinese identity in the United States through editorial debates, reports of developments in China, and news coverage of American Chinese community events. Because these three papers represented different opinions, they inform us of the process of constructing a Chinese American identity and defining the essential elements that finally made up that identity.

The study is divided into five chapters. Arranged roughly in chronological order, Chapter 1 covers the year 1911. Then, Chinese in the United States offered three different visions for a modern China. Debates over reform and revolution politicized American Chinese communities, challenged traditional Chinese values, and tested boundaries of American Chinese support for revolution. With the establishment of the Republic of China at the beginning of 1912, Chinese identity stood at a crucial crossroads.

Chapter 2 covers the period from 1912 to 1914, in which American Chinese demonstrated the strength of traditional Chinese values, such as opposition to rebellion and willingness to preserve Chinese cultural practices. Meanwhile, the establishment of the Republic of China and the aroused nationalist feelings emboldened American Chinese to stand up for their right to be regarded as an integral part of American society.

Chapter 3 deals with the eventful year of 1915, in which the new Chinese republic faced its first serious external threat from Japan and made its first international appearance at the Panama Pacific International Exposition in San Francisco. In response to Japan's Twenty-one Demands, which encroached on China's territorial integrity and political independence, American Chinese revealed the limit of their Chinese nationalism. Although their organization of a comprehensive anti-Japanese boycott symbolized high-sounding ideals, their failure to implement that boycott revealed the limitations life in the United States had put on most American Chinese. China's presence at the International Exposition stood as testimony that life away from China had made American Chinese idealize Chinese culture and that American Chinese had absorbed certain aspects of Western or American values. The disappointments in China's presence at the exposition and in the Chinese government's acceptance of the Twenty-one Demands served as an impetus for the development of a Chinese American identity, the essence of which was embodied in the formation of the China Mail Steamship Company.

Chapter 4 examines the four essential elements of the Chinese American identity. These four elements became crystallized in the peri-

od from 1916 to 1924, years in which American Chinese supported republicanism against monarchical restoration, tried to preserve the essence
and principles of Confucianism and traditional Chinese culture while the
New Culture Movement in China attacked both, willingly adopted Christianity in constructing a modern Chinese identity while China waged an
anti-Christian movement, and strongly opposed the GMD's alliance with
the Soviet Union and cooperation with the CCP.

Chapter 5 tours an American Chinatown and documents the building of a permanent Chinese American community between 1920 and
1927. American Chinese campaigns against the restrictions put on them
by the 1924 Immigration Act, their efforts to defeat a bill aimed at controlling the practice of Chinese herbal medicine, and their enthusiasm
for building community facilities demonstrated their determination to
live as proud Chinese in the United States and develop a material base
for the new Chinese American identity. A glimpse of some American
Chinatown activities in this period reveals that Chinese in the United
States had developed their own culture, which drew on both traditional
China and modern America.

The findings of this project fill a gap in the study of the Chinese experience in the United States. Chinese were not as inassimilable as they
are usually portrayed, nor were they unqualified supporters of Chinese
revolutions. The way in which American Chinese envisioned a modern
China in the 1911–27 period provides a framework for understanding the
worries and confusions my interviewees revealed in their relationship
with China. The transcultural identity formed in the process of searching for a modern sense of Chineseness in the same period explains the
mixed cultural identity American Chinatowns and American Chinese
families represented in the early 1990s.

As a comprehensive attempt to understand the transformation of
Chinese identity in the United States, the findings shed light on the forces
that shape ethnic identities. The study answers the call of pioneering
Asian American scholars such as Roger Daniels and Him Mark Lai not
to study the Chinese in the United States in terms of "what has happened
to them"[15] but "to fully probe and understand the processes governing
the development of Chinese American communities."[16] Finally, I hope
this study reveals the variety of information community newspapers can
provide to scholars in their attempt to reimagine life among Chinese in
the United States in the first few decades of the twentieth century.

1 A Search for a Modern China and Challenges to Traditional Chinese Identity, 1911

Before 1910, Sun Yat-sen, leader of the Chinese republican revolution, was regarded as a rebel by most Chinese in the United States. When he visited Chinatowns in the United States to solicit support for his revolutionary cause, he had to act covertly. One relative of a leader of the Tongmenghui, or the Revolutionary Alliance, remembered that as a child she had witnessed Sun hiding in her house and that she, her mother, and her sisters had acted as guards at the door and windows while Sun lived in the house.[1] The strangers and suspicious people they feared were not Westerners;[2] the child and her mother were guarding Sun Yat-sen from other Chinese.

In traditional China, being a rebel was one of the most dangerous traits. As a scholar of Chinese studies has stated, the cultural psychology in traditional China was characterized by "social conformity, consensus, collective responsibility, and . . . almost pathological fear of disorder."[3] This cultural psychology rested on a reward and punishment system in which all people were to obey a heaven-ordained emperor and behave according to the hierarchical order prescribed by Confucianism. In the Confucian hierarchical order, subjects should obey rulers, sons should obey fathers, and wives should obey husbands. This cultural psychology set the authoritarian tone for the political and social order of

Chinese society and the Chinese family. Disobedience to or rebellion against authority was punishable at both family and state levels.

Even as late as December 1910, this traditional Chinese cultural psychology was still prevalent among Chinese in the United States. After much effort, the Tongmenghui, founded in Tokyo, Japan in 1905, finally established its branch organization in the United States and started to publish its own newspaper, *Young China*, in October 1910. Yet this revolutionary organization attracted only a few members, mostly Chinese students attending American universities, American-born Chinese who had been active in fighting for their citizenship rights in the United States, and laborers with a daring and rebellious spirit. Tongmenghui members became known among Chinese in the United States as "the lost youngsters," recalled Huang Boyao, English secretary of the Native Sons of the Golden State, the forerunner of the Chinese American Citizens Alliance, and an early member of the American Tongmenghui.[4] Apparently because of the prevailing antirebellious mass psychology among Chinese in the United States, some of these early Tongmenghui members publicly announced their withdrawal from the revolutionary organization.[5]

Yet by the end of 1911, most Chinese in the United States had committed themselves to supporting the revolutionary cause. As a result of a rebellion led by the revolutionary Tongmenghui against the Qing court, China's millennia-old dynastic system crumbled and was replaced by the Republic of China, with Sun Yat-sen as the first president. Chinese throughout the United States held parades and meetings to celebrate the founding of the new Republic. They organized local fundraising activities and enthusiastically bought military bonds issued by the National Relief Bureau.[6] Chinatown organizations, particularly the Chinese Consolidated Benevolent Association (CCBA) and the Chinese Chamber of Commerce of San Francisco, the overall organization for all Chinese businesses in the United States, sent cables to congratulate Sun Yat-sen as China's first president.[7]

From fear of rebellion to support of revolution characterized the dynamics of American Chinatown politics and transformation of traditional Chinese identity in the year 1911. Driving the dynamics and serving as the impetus for transformation was "the search for modern China."[8] The search for a modern China evoked debates over fundamental issues that shook the foundation of Chinese traditions and culture. Therefore, the search was a complicated process, and scholars of Chinese studies believe that Chinese identity, or a modern sense of Chineseness, is problematic.[9] If Chinese identity in China was problematic after the imperial system in China ended, then Chinese identity in the United States was even more complicated. In his study of diasporic cultures and identities, James Clifford theorized that diaspora peoples were involved in "the political ambivalence, the utopia/dystopic tension, of diaspora visions that are always entangled in powerful global histories."[10]

Living in diaspora and being discriminated against for their racial and cultural identity, American Chinese longed for a strong and powerful China to stand up for and protect them. Yet China was being weakened by internal turmoil and external encroachment. What did American Chinese think was the way to rescue China from its problems? Why was Kang Youwei's reform program more attractive to them than Sun's revolutionary alternative? What roles did traditional mentality and mechanisms of social control play in the gradual change of their attitude toward the revolution? What undermined the foundation of traditional Chinese identity? Did diasporic experience and environment have an impact on the change?

Chinese American Communities in 1911

Large-scale Chinese migration to the United States started at the end of the 1840s. Widespread economic dislocation, caused mainly by Western expansionism, served as the "push" factor, and the discovery of gold in California served as the "pull" factor. Most Chinese who came to the United States in the nineteenth century were searching for economic advancement. Chinese usually called the United States "the Gold Mountains," and going to the Gold Mountains meant a chance to get rich.

This hope of getting rich contributed to a difference between the traditional Chinese society and Chinese communities in the United States. This difference lay in the fact that whereas in traditional Chinese society merchants or businessmen were given low status—in fact, those who traded with foreigners were regarded as treacherous and therefore deserving heavy punishment—in Chinese communities in the United States big merchants or businessmen were admired and shared the highest social status with Confucian scholars.

Anti–Chinese immigration legislation and practices had also helped shape the Chinese American population, which, by the first decade of the twentieth century, had turned out to be "predominantly petite bourgeois."[11] The 1882 Chinese Exclusion Act barred Chinese laborers from entering the United States for ten years. The 1888 Scott Act prevented Chinese laborers who were on temporary visits in China from returning to the United States. The 1892 Geary Act extended the exclusion of Chinese laborers for another ten years. The exclusion was extended indefinitely in 1904. The Exclusion Act effectively reduced the American Chinese population from the highest figure of 107,488 in 1890 to 71,531 in 1910.[12] In addition, economic depressions and white labor unions' pressure on capitalists against hiring "cheap Chinese labor" had limited the growth of a Chinese working class. Racial discrimination had also limited opportunities for American Chinese capital accumulation, making it impossible for the few Chinese capitalists to provide support for the growth of an American Chinese working class.[13]

Chinese who remained in the United States in the first few decades of the twentieth century were thus driven into urban areas where they formed "gilded ghettos."[14] It was within these "gilded ghettos" that many Chinese found a way to make a living. Many of them ran laundries and restaurants, and others had to rely on Chinatown businesses for employment. Only a small number of American Chinese worked as farm laborers, miners, railroad workers, and workers in cigar and shoe manufacturing industries. Another small number of American Chinese worked as domestic servants for white families. Laundries and restaurants, together with other Chinatown retail businesses that helped sustain Chinese lifestyle and culture in the United States, usually were managed as partnerships. As a result, Chinese businessmen and professionals such as medical doctors, translators, and priests, who belonged to "exempt classes" under the exclusion laws, made up more than 40 percent of the declining Chinese American population by 1910.[15] The term *businessman* was broadly used to include employees who owned shares in the businesses they worked in, such as laundries, grocery and drug stores, and restaurants.[16]

The large percentage of American Chinese who were related to businesses and the determination to pursue wealth shaped the social and political hierarchy of the Chinese communities in the United States. The two major organizations for all Chinese in the United States were the Jinshan Zhonghua Huiguan, or the Chinese Consolidated Benevolent Association (CCBA) of San Francisco, known to the mainstream society as the Chinese Six Companies, and the Jinshan Huashang Zhonghui, or the General Chinese Chamber of Commerce of San Francisco.[17] These two organizations made up the American Chinatown elite.

The CCBA was founded in 1882, the year the Chinese Exclusion Act was passed, under the instructions of the Chinese Consul General in San Francisco in hopes of challenging anti-Chinese legislation. The CCBA was a confederation of district associations numbering between six and eight at different times. Its popular name, Chinese Six Companies, derived from the fact that the CCBA started with six district associations under it. The majority of Chinese in the United States came from six geographic districts in Guangdong. The six associations were formed to take care of people from their respective districts. Presiding presidents of these district associations were gentry-directors on the board of the CCBA and took turns being president of the CCBA. These district association presidents were titled scholars from China, who came with diplomatic passports and as members of the Chinese consular staff. These gentry-directors worked closely with the Chinese Consul General, who represented the Chinese government in the United States.

The other half of the board of the CCBA was made up of merchant-directors, Chinese businessmen who had succeeded in getting rich in the United States. Regarded by the mainstream society as "the government within the government," the CCBA, together with the district associations under it, maintained control over the life of all Chinese in the United States. The CCBA, or a relevant district association, usually managed by businessmen, sent representatives to meet arriving Chinese at the wharf and took them to the association headquarters to be registered. Before Chinese returned to China, they had to report to their district associations or the CCBA to get clearance on any possible debts and to obtain exit permits by paying a few dollars. These associations had agreements with transpacific shipping companies that all Chinese had to present an association's exit permit to purchase tickets.

The other important American Chinatown organization was the Chinese Chamber of Commerce. Established in 1908, this chamber of commerce was formed "to connect business relations, to consolidate unity, to promote constructive competition, to explore opportunities and rid obstacles, and to arbitrate and solve disputes" between Chinese businesses. The role of this chamber in the general life of all Chinese in the United States was to help promote relations with the mainstream society and to cooperate with the CCBA in organizing activities concerning affairs in China.[18] No Confucian scholars from China served as leaders. Instead, the Chinese Chamber of Commerce was presided over by successful and well-established Chinese businessmen who, like their peers in the CCBA, had vested interests in the existing hierarchy of Chinese communities in the United States and whose vision of a modern China included both laissez-faire capitalist ideology and opposition to radical revolutions.

Besides this business-oriented mentality and the community norm against rebellions or revolutions, another characteristic prevalent among Chinese in the United States in the early twentieth century was the close connection with China. First, the fact that 79.1 percent of American

Chinese in 1910 were born in China[19] spoke to their close feelings to the home country. Second, the laws that deprived Chinese of the right to become naturalized citizens made Chinese participation in American politics impossible. Third, both American legislation that prevented wives of Chinese laborers from coming into the United States and Chinese tradition, which discouraged Chinese women from traveling far, meant that most American Chinese kept families in China. It is difficult to get an exact figure of how many Chinese in 1911 had their complete nuclear family with them. The number of Chinese females, which was 4,675 in 1910, or 6.5 percent of the total American Chinese population, and included married women as well as minor girls, tells us that the majority of Chinese at this time still had families in China.[20] With families in China, American Chinese were as concerned about China's well-being as their counterparts in China were.

This close connection fostered strong nationalistic feelings among Chinese in the United States. They admitted that China as a country had become weak in the face of the industrialized West. China's weakness as a nation in the world was always mentioned in the same breath with the United States' anti–Chinese immigration laws and practices. One of the poems written on the walls of Angel Island Immigration Station by detained Chinese reads, "For what reason must I sit in jail? It is only because my country is weak and my family poor." Another one reads, "If my country had contrived to make herself strong, this [banishment to Angel Island] never would have happened."[21]

This acute awareness made most Chinese in the United States supporters of modernization programs in China. One of the modernization programs they supported was Kang Youwei's reform movement. Kang Youwei, a Confucian scholar, had witnessed China's repeated humiliations and failures at the hands of foreign powers and had come to accept the social Darwinism of the 1890s. His belief in the survival of the fittest among nations and his Confucian education made him a reform-oriented nationalist. According to Kang, the West could claim no superiority over China in moral development, and there was no better science of government than what could be found in the Six Classics. But China was lagging behind the West in the development of science and technology, he warned. His prescription for a modern China was to catch up with the West in scientific and technological development while preserving China's own principles, institutions, and moral tradition, Confucianism.[22]

Kang Youwei was joined by his student, Liang Qichao, in the early 1890s in promoting the idea of a gradual and nonviolent reform for a strong and modern China.[23] With Kang Youwei providing the theoretical guidance, the reform of the 1890s was centered around the effort to transform the existing absolute monarchy into a constitutional monarchy.[24] Their reform movement, which lasted for only a hundred days and thus became known as the Hundred Days' Reform, aimed at modernizing the administrative, economic, educational, and military system of the existing Qing dynasty through the consent and cooperation of Emperor Guang Xu, was suppressed in China in 1898 by the conservative Empress Dowager Ci Xi. Kang and Liang escaped persecution and fled to North America, hoping to find support for their reform programs.

This reform-oriented modernization program fit well with the mentality of most Chinese in the United States. In 1899, to get the widest support possible, Kang and Liang suggested that a Baoshanghui, a Society to Protect Commerce, be organized to push for reforms in China. However, American Chinese community leaders suggested naming the organization a Baohuanghui, a Society to Protect the Emperor. This suggestion reflected their willingness to recognize the sacred position of the Chinese emperor and their acceptance of the imminent need for reforms in China.

The Baohuanghui enjoyed wide support among Chinese in North America. The society was first established in Canada, yet the reform leaders quickly recognized the importance of the larger Chinese population in the United States. Almost immediately, they sought support from Chinese in the United States to establish an influential newspaper, *China Reform News*, which was soon renamed *Chinese World*. Because its leaders showed respect for traditional Chinese values and advocated a moderate program to make China a strong and modern nation, the Baohuanghui commanded the loyalty of most Chinese in the United States in the early 1900s. Most Chinatown organizations cooperated with the Baohuanghui, and many American Chinatown businesses invested in Baohuanghui-sponsored banking and investment programs aimed at developing China's natural resources and commerce and financing the society's reform movement in China.[25] The most impressive feature of Baohuanghui's success among the Chinese in the United States was that it won the support of the Zhigongtang, a secret society[26] to which many Chinese laborers in the United States belonged, and of Wu Panzhao (Ng Poon Chew), the most respected person among Chinese Christians, who numbered between 2,000 and 3,000 by 1910.[27] The Baohuanghui managed the Zhigongtang newspaper *Ta Tung Yat Po* until 1904, and Wu Panzhao was a Baohuanghui stalwart until 1903.[28]

The popularity of this reform program among Chinese in the United States decreased as China continued its decline as a nation in the world and as Chinese in the United States continued to suffer discrimination and exclusion.[29] The failure of the reform program to make China a strong and modern nation opened doors for other, more radical suggestions for the salvation and modernization of China.

Sharply contradicting the reform-oriented program was Sun Yat-sen's radical revolutionary program, aimed at overthrowing the existing Qing ruling court and changing China's century-old dynastic system to a modern democratic republic. Unlike Kang Youwei and Liang Qichao, Sun received most of his education in Hawaii and Hong Kong.[30] His exposure to Western philosophies and his observation of Western political systems influenced his ideological orientation.[31] Although he tried in 1894 to suggest political reforms within the existing system in China, he abandoned his reform attempts, when his petition failed to get much attention, and organized a secret society in Hawaii to overthrow the Qing dynasty and establish a republic later that year.[32]

His revolutionary ideas were further developed into what became known as the three principles of the people. These principles were *minzu zhuyi* (nationalism), *minquan zhuyi* (democracy), and *minsheng zhuyi* (people's livelihood), which Sun believed were the basis of the evolution of modern Europe and the United States as well as "an ideological basis for the new China."[33] The Tongmenghui made these three principles the political platform of the organization. The Tongmenghui bylaws interpreted the principle of nationalism to mean "overthrowing the Manchu barbarians and restoring China to the Chinese," the principle of democracy to mean "creating a republic" with democratic institutions like those practiced in Europe and the United States, and the principle of people's livelihood to mean "distributing the land equally."[34] The third principle caused some debate among initial members in Tokyo. Sun's explanation of this principle at this stage was vague, but he persisted, and it was accepted into the bylaws of the Tongmenghui.[35]

However, the three principles of the people were only narrowly accepted by the American branch of the Tongmenghui, established in 1910, five years after the founding of the organization in Japan. Realizing the distance between this radical revolutionary platform and the mentality of Chinese in the United States while writing the bylaws for the branch, Sun and several of his followers in the United States avoided the explicit phrase "distributing the land equally," substituting instead the more theoretical phrase, "the principle of people's livelihood."[36] Only after Sun's patient explanation and persistence did the three principles become the essence of the oath that all American Tongmenghui members had to pledge. In reality, the majority of Tongmenghui members in the United

States simply concentrated on overthrowing the Manchus as the task of the organization. The editorial of the first issue of the American Tong-menghui newspaper, *Young China Morning Paper*, made the following declaration:

> We Chinese trying to make a living abroad have suffered all kinds of discrimination. . . . The United States has established special laws excluding Chinese laborers, which was a non-humanitarian act. Yet that was not enough. There have been increasing strict regulations and meticulous fault-finding practices, which intended to wipe all Chinese from the American continent. . . . If we Chinese wish to defend ourselves against such discrimination, we must first of all restore our national independence. In order to restore our national independence, we must first restore the Chinese nation. In order to restore the Chinese nation, we must drive the barbarian Manchus back to the Changbai Mountains.[37] In order to get rid of the barbarians, we must first overthrow the present tyrannical, dictatorial, ugly, and corrupt Qing government. Fellow countrymen, a revolution is the only means to overthrow the Qing government.[38]

This simple and narrow concentration on anti-Manchuism still failed to gain much support at the beginning from Chinese in the United States. The Tongmenghui's focus on regarding the Manchus as foreign and on overthrowing the Qing dynasty as its principal goal fit well with the Zhigongtang's political aim of *fanqing fuming,* or overthrowing the Qing and restoring the Ming. Yet life in the United States had played down the political nature of the Zhigongtang. Being a member of the organization was more for protection, employment opportunities, or mutual aid for business purposes. In addition, the mass psychology favoring obedience and discouraging rebellion limited the popularity of Sun's revolutionary program in American Chinatowns.

Ineffectiveness of the reform program and incompatibility of Sun's revolutionary program with the prevailing mentality of Chinese in the United States provided ground for a third vision for a modern China. Expressing this third vision was Wu Panzhao and his newspaper, *Chung Sai Yat Po,* which could be translated literally as *Chinese and Western Daily.*

Wu Panzhao's personal history and ambitions anticipated the emerging complex transnational identity of Chinese in the United States. Arriving in the United States as a Guangdong peasant boy of fifteen in 1881, a year before the passage of the Chinese Exclusion Act, Wu very quickly learned about the discrimination Chinese suffered in the United States. He was educated in a Presbyterian church school and went on to the San Francisco Theological Seminary. In 1892, the year the Geary Act was passed,[39] Wu was ordained as the first Chinese Presbyterian minister on the Pacific coast. Wearing Western clothes and having his queue cut off, Wu intended "to teach the Chinese to be at home in America" and "to teach Americans to appreciate the fine qualities of the precious and ancient civilization that had nurtured him"[40] through his position as a church minister.

What was emerging in Wu was a new identity formed in the cross-currents of Chinese and American history. Wu apparently no longer intended to return to China. To him, being Chinese no longer meant donning traditional Chinese clothes or observing Chinese customs such as growing a queue. His devotion to Christianity showed that he had selectively adopted values from the mainstream American culture. Yet his intention to help his compatriots and to spread the fine qualities of Chinese culture revealed his Chinese identity.

Wu's pride in "the precious and ancient" Chinese civilization was challenged not only by Western expansionism but also by Chinese resistance to new ideas symbolized by the suppression of the 1898 Hundred Days' Reform. Political developments in China and anti-Chinese discrimination in the United States made Wu realize that his original goals of teaching Chinese to be at home in America and teaching Americans to appreciate Chinese culture and civilization were no longer enough if he wanted to help China and the Chinese in the United States. Living in the era in which yellow journalism was exerting significant influence on the American public, Wu decided to publish a Chinese-language daily newspaper that would rally support from Chinese in the United States for the reform programs in China and alert them to "the dangers of American immigration laws and the fight for civil rights and citizenship."[41]

Greeting the Chinese public on the first Chinese New Year's Day of the twentieth century, Wu Panzhao's *Chung Sai Yat Po*[42] announced that it was fighting for "a modern strong Chinese nation and equal rights for Chinese both in immigrating to America and in settling there."[43] Wu's recognition of the necessity of reform and modernization in China made him a strong supporter of the Baohuanghui reform programs. Yet his particular background and vision shaped his unique ideas for salvation and modernization of China and for his fellow Chinese in the United States. *Chung Sai Yat Po* was thus born with a diasporic vision and would serve, in the years to come, as a strong American Chinese community voice in the search for a modern China and a powerful guide in transforming the Chinese identity in the United States.

By 1911, three different visions for salvation and modernization of China had appeared among Chinese in the United States. We now turn to the nationalist discourse carried in the three Chinese-language newspapers representing these three visions to examine the essence of Chinese American nationalism and the development of the Chinese American identity.

A Nationalist Discourse, 1911

Representing the reformist Baohuanghui, *Chinese World* was a major voice in the nationalist discourse among Chinese in the United States. The central argument of the paper in 1910 continued to be that the best road for a modern and strong China was through reform of the existing absolute monarchy into a constitutional monarchy.

This argument seemed plausible when the Qing court showed some willingness to implement reforms. Japan's victory in the Russo-Japanese War of 1904–5 (Japan being a constitutional monarchy and Russia being ruled by an absolute monarch) and the increasing clamor for reform through the popular press in China apparently motivated the Qing court's new decision to accept the reform package proposed by the 1898 reformers led by Kang Youwei. By 1910, the Qing court had launched such political and constitutional programs as reforms in education, which included setting up modern schools and sending students to study abroad, and in the military, which included training a new army with invited German and Japanese instructors. Prominent in the reform programs was the promulgation of constitutional principles, with the promise to realize full constitutional government by the end of 1913. At the same time, the court issued a series of electoral laws and established Provincial Assemblies and the Central Legislative Council. The electoral laws stipulated that the Provincial Assemblies would be elected by those with Confucian education or with property or by government office holders and that the Central Legislative Council would be partially elected by and from the Provincial Assemblies and partially appointed by the emperor.

Cheered by such gestures, *Chinese World* argued that China's salvation now lay in the immediate reinstatement of the exiled reformers Kang Youwei and Liang Qichao. The paper further specified that Kang and Liang must participate in the drafting of a constitution and serve as leaders in the parliament.[44] The reform programs the paper endorsed and the argument that only the reinstatement of Kang and Liang could save China demonstrated that the paper represented the belief in elite rule in China. In fact, it explicitly argued that the reform party, now under the new formal name of the Constitutionalist Party (although it was still better known among Chinese in the United States as Baohuanghui) gathered the cream of Chinese society and represented the prevailing opinion in China. It was this elite, the paper pointed out, on which all Chinese people should fix their hope.[45]

Thus, *Chinese World* represented one form of Chinese nationalism. It regarded China as a nation-state with interests that needed to be protected in the community of nation-states. Central to this vision of Chinese nationalism was the idea of a constitutional government, with the preservation of the monarch as a unifying symbol of the Chinese nation and the maintenance of the existing social and cultural framework. Although *Chinese World* attacked the corruption and impotence of the existing government and complained about its slowness in realizing the constitutional government, it did not see the monarchical system as the root of China's problems. The paper believed that the reform programs adopted by the Qing court had already made China a constitutional monarchy. The paper therefore called upon all Chinese in the United States to join the Constitutionalist Party to make the voice louder and the push harder for forming a parliament. The paper believed that to join the party and to push for a parliamentary system where people's voices would be heard was the only way to be a patriot.[46]

Unlike Sun and his followers, who argued that Manchus were aliens in China, *Chinese World* and the Constitutionalists never regarded the Qing court as aliens ruling over Chinese.[47] In fact, in 1907, in the name of the overseas Chinese members of the Constitutionalist Party, Kang wrote a manifesto addressed to the Qing court. One of the ten requests made in this manifesto was to end the distinction between Han Chinese and Manchus and to adopt the term *Zhonghua* as the name of China.[48] The Chinese character *hua*, meaning "Chinese," connotes culture and civilization, and the *guo* in *Zhongguo* ("China") connotes a nation. By suggesting *Zhonghua* as the name for China, the Constitutionalists wanted to include the Manchus, the Mongolians, and other nationalities living within the territorial boundaries of China at the time as Chinese.

What confronted the Chinese people at the time were imperialism and the task for political reforms, the Constitutionalists argued. Liang Qichao believed that anti-Manchuism would only harm the long-term goal of Chinese nationalism, which was to build a unified, strong, and modern country. The main enemy of Chinese nationalism at that time, according to Liang, was foreign imperialism, which had been threatening China's dismemberment since the mid-nineteenth century.[49] Xu Shiqin, a prominent Constitutionalist Party leader in the United States, dismissed Sun's theory that the Manchus were alien rulers as a fallacy and pointed out that China's problem was political in nature and that the solution to it was full realization of a constitutional government.[50]

The establishment of a constitutional government with a monarch had to be accompanied by the preservation of Confucianism, reformers believed. The essence of Confucianism, narrowly defined, was a social, moral, and political order in which an emperor ruled over subjects, fathers controlled sons, and husbands dominated wives. Confucianism further dictated that for a society to keep order and enjoy harmony, those who ruled and controlled carry out their duties with benevolence and those who were ruled and controlled obeyed as duty and obligation. In a constitutional monarchy, the educated elite would make decisions for the uneducated masses, and the power of the monarch, the emperor, would be limited by a parliament made up of Confucian scholars such as Kang and Liang. In a constitutional monarchy, the essential moral principles, embodied in Confucianism, would still be governing the life of the Chinese people. To keep Confucianism alive and to celebrate it as the essence of Chinese culture, *Chinese World*, around the time of the Wuchang Uprising, which marked the beginning of the 1911 Revolution, carried editorials and articles commemorating the birthday of Confucius and referred to Confucius as China's "Arch Bishop."[51]

Chinese World, representing the reform-oriented nationalism, naturally argued against revolutions as a way for China to attain salvation. After the failure of the Guangzhou Uprising in the spring of 1911, the paper editorialized about the damage done by the revolutionary rebellion. Then it pointed out that Guangdong was too remote to have any impact on the central government. It predicted that even if revolutionaries succeeded in taking over the province from the Manchus, the chaotic situation would lead to interventions by foreign governments that had interests in China. Guangdong would become the ground for bloody battles, and China would further lose sovereignty and suffer humiliations.[52]

Believing that most Chinese in the United States feared chaos and mob rule in China, *Chinese World* reminded its readers of what had happened in France after the French Revolution. Arguing that Napoleon's dictatorship was brought about by a revolution that aimed at liberty and equality by abolishing the old system, the paper implied that revolutions would produce the same result in China.[53] Therefore, it was wise for China to avoid a radical revolution. Reform of the existing system was the only way to save China from extinction and to build a strong and modern China.

In contrast to this reform-oriented and antirevolutionary argument in the nationalist discourse was the argument for a radical revolution as the necessary road to a modern Chinese nation. Expressing this argument was the Tongmenghui paper, *Young China*. At the beginning of 1911,

Young China launched an all-out attack on the Qing court. It insisted that Manchus and Han Chinese were not of the same race; it blamed the Manchus for China's weak international status, noting that the Qing court had made repeated concessions to foreign powers;[54] it pointed out that the so-called reforms launched by the Qing court were only a smokescreen, for there was no sincere effort at convening the parliament, the cabinet posts were all appointed by the Qing court, and all positions of power were in the hands of the royal family;[55] and it denounced the Manchus for having enslaved the Chinese as beasts of burden during the last 200 years.[56] That Manchus and Han Chinese were of different races was a shaky argument, but it was not difficult for *Young China* to blame the Qing court for the problems China was facing at the time.

In addition to offering the argument that the Qing court was an alien government in China, *Young China* challenged *Chinese World*'s prediction that revolution would lead to foreign intervention, which would, in turn, cause the disintegration of China. It pointed out that the repeated diplomatic concessions made by the Qing court to foreign powers had already brought China to the verge of national disintegration. Furthermore, the paper carried editorials, one after another, warning against the imminent danger of China being carved up by various foreign powers. At the time, Russia was pressing for more rights and privileges in, and sending troops to, China's northern Manchuria, Mongolia, and Xinjiang; Japan was pressing for more control and sending troops to China's southern Manchuria; Britain was sending troops to China's Yunnan Province; and even the small and weak Portugal was bullying Chinese in Macao. The paper thus concluded that the Qing court was too corrupt and too weak to stand up against foreign aggression, and revolution aimed at overthrowing the Qing court was the only way to save China from the danger of dismemberment.[57]

The paper also defended the revolutionary plan by pointing out that the bloodshed a revolution might bring was nothing compared with the deaths of ordinary Chinese people under the Manchu dictatorship, either by cruel punishment or natural disasters. Revolutionaries were benevolent and strictly disciplined: Rather than killing blindly, they would target only enemies and traitors. The paper thus urged people not to resist revolutionaries to avoid becoming victims.

The paper also served as a publicity medium for the revolutionary cause in China. After the Guangzhou Uprising in the spring of 1911 failed in China, there was widespread doubt among Chinese in the United States as to whether there was enough support for the revolutionary cause in China. Recognizing such doubt and detecting the increasingly strong desire for change in China, *Young China* carried a series of editorials informing its readers that the failure of the Guangzhou Uprising resulted from insufficient preparation and that the revolutionary current was getting stronger daily in China.[58] The paper thus suggested that the general trend in China was no longer for reforms but had turned toward revolution.

Young China exploited small incidents to excite Chinese in the United States to support its revolutionary platform. In the spring of 1911, Russians drove about 3,000 Chinese laborers away from a work site in Haishenwei (Vladivostok) because they suspected the Chinese of carrying a contagious disease. When the Chinese laborers arrived in Shandong, China on their way to their respective homes, they were refused shelter by the officials. The paper regarded these local officials in Shandong as part of the Qing government and asked why Chinese people should support a government that refused to protect and take care of its own people. The paper also reported more local incidents in which Chinese were badly treated at the United States Customs because American customs officers reportedly said that all Chinese were "prisoners of the Manchus" and were not entitled to freedom and happiness.[59]

Young China was given a better opportunity to attack the Qing government when several provinces in China suffered severe floods in the spring of 1911. The paper reported that people in the flooded areas were homeless and starving, that local bandits were taking advantage of the natural disasters and looting people's property, and that government officials were doing nothing to control the situation.[60] The paper further asserted that in China, while millions of people were homeless and starving, Manchu princes and princesses were living decadent lives, and the court was building an expensive palace and organizing grand birthday parties. Even though China was in imminent danger of being carved up by foreign powers, the Naval Department of the Qing court was filled with opium smokers, and the Grand Marshal of China's Navy was the little boy emperor, Pu Yi.[61]

Young China also used historical references to arouse the Chinese people's hatred against the ruling Qing court. The paper commemorated the death of the last emperor of the Ming dynasty, the one replaced by the Qing dynasty, and called on all Chinese to mourn the death of the Chinese nation. Those who refused to support the revolution aimed at restoring the Chinese nation were not loyal and patriotic Chinese, the paper insisted.[62] Being accused of not being Chinese was shameful and a serious insult.

Young China in this period only superficially addressed the principle of democracy, which it interpreted to mean liberty and equality for all people. Competing against *Chinese World,* which represented the more popular and better-established Baohuanghui at the time, for the support of poor Chinese and Chinese women in the United States, *Young China* gave distinctive female names to editorial writers and commentators, such as "Female Historian of Truth," "Sword Sharpening Lady," and "Sword Loving Lady."[63] Such provocative pen names revealed the radical nature of the editorial staff. On one hand, the Chinese nation under the rule of the Manchus was compared with the oppressed female gender, which was finally rising up against oppression. On the other, it was a challenge to Chinese men to say that Chinese women, the weaker half of the nation, were speaking out and rising up in arms. However, the paper betrayed its limited understanding of liberty and equality for women when it reasoned that it was important for women to have a good education because only educated mothers could bring up young republican citizens, which meant that the woman's place was still at home.[64]

Further addressing the concepts of liberty and equality, the paper compared China under Manchu rule with colonial status in Annam (today's Vietnam) and Korea. It said that in Annam, the French limited how far local people could travel and punished people at home if a relative fled. In Korea, the Japanese imposed restrictions on socialization, checked private mail, and ruled that three to five families share a kitchen knife. The paper implied that such a fate was in store for all Chinese if the Qing government were not overthrown. All Chinese in the United States, the paper argued, should give financial support to the revolutionary cause to save China from such a fate.[65]

By presenting such a radical vision, *Young China* tried to fit in with the political goal of the Zhigongtang, which was to overthrow the Qing dynasty and to connect the low status and discrimination Chinese suffered in the United States to the incompetence of the national government in China. To get support from the Zhigongtang, which appealed to Chinese laborers and small businessmen, the paper avoided clear definitions of the concepts of democracy, equality, and liberty and narrowly defined Chinese nationalism as anti-Manchuism. The paper did not expound on the principle of people's livelihood or the principle of equal distribution of land, for advocates of this revolutionary vision of Chinese nationalism were aware that very few Chinese in the United States at the time understood or embraced such principles.

Neither the Baohuanghui nor Tongmenghui originated in the United States. The indigenous Chinese-language newspaper taking part in this nationalist discourse in the United States was *Chung Sai Yat Po.* By the beginning of 1911, *Chung Sai Yat Po* had become an influential newspaper. It stayed neutral between the Baohuanghui and Tongmeng-hui and expressed its own opinions concerning China's salvation and modernization. Believing in Christian love, this paper did not support the radical revolutionary means advocated by *Young China* in early 1911. It still regarded the Qing court as the legitimate government of China. Whereas *Young China* was advising Chinese men to cut off their queues as an act of rebellion against the Qing court, *Chung Sai Yat Po* reported in detail how the Qing government debated and finally passed a law allowing the queue to be cut off.[66] However, *Chung Sai Yat Po* did not think that the Qing court's constitutional reforms and the reinstatement of Kang Youwei and Liang Qichao could save China. It argued that the internal and external problems besetting China at the time could be solved only by a united Chinese nation aimed at comprehensive reforms. It explicitly argued that the reforms, which the Qing court promised to carry out and on which the Constitutionalists pinned all their hopes, were doomed in China.[67]

Chung Sai Yat Po's road to China's modernization may have been idealistic for the situation in China, but it was representative of the paper's overall vision, which was to develop a form of Chinese capitalism modeled on the United States. It argued that the fundamental way to build a modern and strong China was to develop its industry and commerce. China's present status was caused partly by lack of economic development. Western expansionism exposed China's backwardness and caused economic dislocation for millions of Chinese. Dislocation and heavy government taxation in turn caused internal turmoil, challenging the Qing government. It was such internal turmoil that exposed China's weakness to the industrialized West and to Japan. Therefore, the paper concluded, the development of industry and commerce was the only way to relieve China of the internal turmoil and external humiliation.[68]

The paper encouraged Chinese in the United States to explore business opportunities as Chinese while living in the United States. It pointed out that Chinese, especially Chinese merchants, in the United States could contribute to the economic development of China by organizing a transpacific business association. The paper predicted the twentieth century to be the Pacific century. Because China was a country of vast land, rich resources, and a huge market, it was inevitable that it would become the focus of international trade competition. Chinese in the United States should grasp this opportunity to gain some benefits. To compete with other foreign nations in developing the resources and tapping the market of China, the paper concluded, Chinese in the United States ought to be organized.[69]

Besides its emphasis on economic development, *Chung Sai Yat Po* also advocated religious freedom and humanitarian morals for a modern and strong China. It celebrated the endorsement of religious freedom by the Provincial Assembly in Fujian as a starting point for all China.[70] Whereas *Young China* mourned the death of the last Ming emperor to arouse anti-Manchuism, *Chung Sai Yat Po* commemorated the emperor for his humanitarianism. The paper said that before he committed suicide, the emperor instructed that he would rather have his body torn into pieces than to have any civilians hurt. On Abraham Lincoln's birthday, the paper praised his humanitarianism.[71] In commemorating the death of a humanitarian emperor in Chinese history and the birth of a humanitarian president in U.S. history, the paper advocated a modern China whose moral codes were based on universal love between the ruler and the ruled and on harmony in society.

As a locally originated and community-based paper, *Chung Sai Yat Po* was more concerned than the other two papers about the direction of American Chinese community development. While voicing its own vision for a modern China, the paper also urged Chinese in the United States to support popular education and to reform certain Chinese customs and practices. It argued that Chinese suffered discrimination in the United States mainly because most Chinese had no education. To combat laws excluding and discriminating against Chinese in the United States, Chinese first of all had to send their children to school.[72] The paper regarded Chinese practices such as idol worshipping and kowtowing for blessings as signs of ignorance and practices "civilized Americans" could use to ridicule and despise the Chinese.[73] This apparently was a reaction to the host society's opinions, and it demonstrated the paper's advocacy for selectively integrating American values in constructing a Chinese American identity.

The discourse on a modern China carried in these three newspapers exerted tremendous influence on the development of the Chinese identity in the United States. Whereas *Chinese World*'s vision encouraged maintaining the fundamental elements of traditional Chinese identity, *Young China* advocated radical revolution against China's dynastic system, which implied challenges to the fundamental values governing traditional Chinese society. If we see *Chinese World* as defending the existing identity and *Young China* as destroying it, then *Chung Sai Yat Po* was pointing out a way to construct a new identity.

From 1899 to 1911, debates over China's future served as catalysts for the politicization of Chinese communities in the United States.[74] The fact that both the Baohuanghui and Tongmenghui found footholds in American Chinatowns demonstrated the close identification Chinese in the United States felt with China. On the other hand, *Chung Sai Yat Po*'s vision of a future China and its prescription for a relationship between American Chinese communities and China showed the diasporic dimensions of Chinese American nationalism and new meanings of Chineseness.

The nationalist discourse carried in the three Chinese-language newspapers both guided development of opinions and reflected the prevailing mentality of Chinese in the United States. One of the first studies of community life in American Chinatowns stated that the influence of the Chinese press on Chinatown life was "incalculable." It was the only medium for Chinatown Chinese to know what was happening in their own world and the world at large,[75] but more importantly, these papers reflected the changing as well as the prevailing mentality of Chinese in the United States. The fact that *Young China* was able to advocate openly its radical revolutionary ideas in 1911 demonstrated that the traditional Chinese identity had come into question. The visions expressed by the most popular Chinese-language paper, *Chung Sai Yat Po*, revealed a direction in which the identity among Chinese in the United States might change.

Challenges to Traditional Chinese Identity

Three events that took place in early 1911 revealed that the foundation of the traditional Chinese identity was being shaken. One was the controversy between *Chinese World* and *Chung Sai Yat Po* that began with a debate over Confucianism versus Christianity and ended with *Chung Sai Yat Po*, representing Christian beliefs, as the actual winner. Another one was the debate over whether Wen Shencai, a young man who killed a Manchu official in Guangdong, was a murderer or a revolutionary hero. The third was about what caused the deaths of more than 300 Chinese in Mexico.

In traditional China, Christianity was an alien belief system. Nineteenth-century Chinese history had witnessed a number of conflicts between Chinese and Christian missionaries in China.[76] Among Chinese in the United States, however, Christian churches had attracted 2,000 to 3,000 members by 1910. Through church activities, Chinese Christians had regular contacts with mainstream society. Leaders of Chinese Christian churches, such as Wu Panzhao, had been working hard at bridging the gap between Chinese and mainstream society and earned special respect among non-Christian Chinese in the United States.[77]

Chung Sai Yat Po's increasing pessimism about the reform movement in China and its promotion of Christian values made the Baohuanghui unhappy and uneasy. *Chinese World*, the Baohuanghui newspaper, carried an editorial attacking Christianity as an anarchist religion. The editorial argued that Christianity made the Jewish state and the Roman Empire perish and confined the European Continent to darkness for more than 700 years.[78] In response, *Chung Sai Yat Po* pointed out that the Confucianism that the reformers were advocating was not a religion and that those who despised Christianity in the past were all "ignorant social scum." It further argued that refusal to accept Christianity meant "stubborn conservatism."[79] Liang Chaojie, the writer of this editorial in *Chinese World*, was from Xinning in Guangdong, where a lot of taro, a starchy root vegetable, was grown. Cui Tongyue, the writer of *Chung Sai Yat Po*'s editorial, in an angry response to terms such as "son of a thief" and "shameless scum" who had "betrayed his own religion of Confucianism,"[80] said that conservatism made people so ignorant that they regarded taro as the best food in the world. As a result, they had eaten too much of it and were suffering from indigestion. Yet they still refused to take the doctor's advice, so their days were numbered.[81]

Cui made a mistake by not explicitly mentioning Liang's name in his counterattack. The editorial aroused indignation among Xinning people in the United States. The Ningyang District Association, the organization for all Xinning people in the United States, first demanded a public apology from *Chung Sai Yat Po* to all Xinning people and then demanded that the paper fire Cui Tongyue and its acting manager (Wu Panzhao, the manager, was on a trip to China at the time) and that the paper stop publication for ninety days.[82] *Chung Sai Yat Po* apologized, although it said that the editorial was not aimed at Xinning people and declared that it was illogical for the paper to insult Xinning people as a whole, for the manager and most of the stockholders of the newspaper company were themselves from Xinning.[83] Cui Tongyue resigned from the paper. The paper refused to fire the acting manager or to stop its publication. The Ningyang District Association then declared a Xinning people's collective boycott of *Chung Sai Yat Po*.[84]

It was quite clear that *Chinese World* was behind this chain reaction. First, *Chinese World* published excerpts of Cui's editorial, making it sound like a direct attack on all Xinning people. The first response from the Ningyang District Association was only a demand for an apology from *Chung Sai Yat Po*. The association seemed to regard an apology as the way to end the dispute. Yet *Chinese World* did not think it was enough. It published an unsigned public letter from Xinning people, suggesting a boycott of *Chung Sai Yat Po*. Under such instigation, when representatives from *Chung Sai Yat Po* apologized to the Ningyang District Association, the association's gentry-directors and merchant-directors declined to give a prompt response. A delayed written response demanded that the paper stop publication for ninety days, or Xinning people would boycott the paper.

Chinese World did excite the Xinning people as a collective body for a short while. An angry crowd of about 250 people gathered at their District Association building. They packed the meeting hall, occupied the stairs leading to the meeting hall, and spilled onto the street outside the building. Some of the agitated people demanded violence against *Chung Sai Yat Po*, and others proposed a boycott. After several inflammatory speeches were made, some proposed to storm the *Chung Sai Yat Po* office, which would have ended in bloodshed. However, the gathering crowd attracted police. The police dispersed the crowd and arrested eight people. The event was reported by *Chinese World*[85] and the *San Francisco Chronicle.*[86]

Chinese World's tactics were based on the assumption that the Chinese in the United States still identified closely with their native districts and that Xinning people, the largest group of Chinese in the United States at the time, would all be united against their common enemy, *Chung Sai Yat Po*. By 1911, the foundation for such assumptions had been undermined by the intervention of political parties into American Chinatown politics as well as by the increasing concerns for China as a nation. When Chinese first arrived in the United States, people with the same surnames and originating from the same districts gathered together and formed protective organizations. In the 1890s, people from Siyi, four districts in Guangdong, boycotted businesses run by people from Sanyi, three districts in Guangdong.[87] Since the arrival of Kang Youwei and Liang Qichao in the United States, such narrow identities as Sanyi or Siyi had been replaced by a broader identity as Chinese in a world of nations. American Chinese-language newspapers, most of them starting publication around the turn of the century, had been engaged in discussions on China's future as a nation and on the rights and interests of Chinese in the United States as an ethnic group. Such discussions had also helped foster a broad sense of Chineseness and undermine earlier regional identities.

Under such circumstances, the boycott against *Chung Sai Yat Po* did not get full support from all Xinning people. According to the boycott rules, all Xinning people should stop all business dealings with *Chung Sai Yat Po*, all Xinning households should publicly sign the boycott agreement, and any violation would be punished.[88] Yet a reading of *Chung Sai Yat Po* demonstrates that even after the boycott went into effect, the paper still carried advertisements from Xinning businesses and published many signed letters from Xinning people. In public letters against the boycott, many Xinning people pointed out that the boycott was the result of a sinister scheme projected by Liang Chaojie and that obeying the boycott would only show a serious lack of independent judgment on the part of Xinning people. Other letter writers called on all Xinning people to rise above their narrow district identification to strive for prosperity and equality for all Chinese in the United States. Still others pointed out that the boycott was instigated by the Baohuanghui and aimed at destroying *Chung Sai Yat Po,* the popular paper that was becoming increasingly critical of the reform programs and had voiced opposition to the reinstatement of Kang and Liang. These letter writers pointed out that following such a boycott would mean supporting the Baohuanghui.[89]

Such expressions of independent thinking and broader identity as Chinese and such encouragement for opposition against the Baohuanghui indicated that the traditional Chinese identity was being questioned, and the long-time defender of that identity was no longer respected. As a result of this dispute, more and more Chinese, Christians and non-Christians, seemed to identify with what *Chung Sai Yat Po* was advocating.

Besides public letters from Xinning people, *Chung Sai Yat Po* also enjoyed support from Chinese organizations. The San Francisco Chinese Christian Church Alliance advised its members, especially members originally from Xinning, not to participate in the boycott and to do their part in enlightening their fellow Xinning people to the truth of the matter, which was that *Chung Sai Yat Po* had no intention of insulting Xinning people.[90] The Chinese Chamber of Commerce pointed out that the dispute between *Chung Sai Yat Po* and Xinning people evolved from something trivial, and it hoped to see a peaceful end to the dispute. The chamber also reasoned that all Chinese should be united to promote business and advised all Chinese businesses to uphold justice by not participating in the boycott.[91]

Meanwhile, *Young China* saw this as an opportunity to make an ally of *Chung Sai Yat Po.* It published Xinning people's letters against the boycott day after day.[92] It also carried editorials advising Xinning people to end the boycott. One of these editorials said that the boycott showed that Chinese lacked unity among themselves and that it would only provide reason for outsiders to laugh at Chinese.[93] The paper praised *Chung Sai Yat Po* for its long history of publication, its principles of peace and harmony, and its credibility among Chinese in the United States. It further said that the boycott was not hurting *Chung Sai Yat Po* at all. Instead, it made the paper even more popular, for some American businesses, which supported *Chung Sai Yat Po*'s refusal to accede to unreasonable demands, began to advertise in the paper.[94]

Advising readers to follow "the truth of the matter," "promote business," "uphold justice," and don't "provide reasons for outsiders to laugh at us Chinese" and evoking American business support as a measure of popularity demonstrated that these were values being promoted among the Chinese in the United States at the time. These values, together with encouragement of independent thinking, a broad Chinese identity, and open opposition against the Baohuanghui, indicated that traditional Chinese identity was being undermined.

The second event that shook the foundation of traditional Chinese identity began when a young man named Wen Shencai murdered a Manchu official in Guangdong. *Young China* reported the event by declaring that Wen was a devoted revolutionary whose action was aimed at driving the Manchus out of China and establishing a republic in China.[95] Later, the paper further reported that Wen's action was the result of having listened to Sun Yat-sen's speeches, which had convinced him that all Manchu officials were rotten to the core and were the Chinese people's enemies.[96] Wen was thus a hero working for the Chinese nation against the barbarian Manchus.

Chinese World also reported the event, but of course it did so in an effort to discredit Wen Shencai. It called Wen a killer and reported that the reason behind the murder was nothing more than a "woman issue." Fu Qi, the Manchu official killed by Wen, had insulted Wen's wife. Wen was outraged but could not expose Fu Qi's action, for Wen himself would have to "wear a green hat" according to Chinese conventional values.[97] Wen thus resorted to killing Fu Qi, the paper concluded.[98] By making the root cause of the killing "a woman issue," the paper tried to disassociate Wen's action from the rising tide of anti-Manchuism in China and to discredit so-called revolutionaries as "unruly social scum" taking vengeance against their personal enemies. The *Chinese World*'s story was groundless, yet it was clear that the paper told the story in a familiar Chinese way to downplay the significance of the incident.

Ever since its dispute with *Chinese World, Chung Sai Yat Po* had been voicing a mildly prorevolutionary opinion. China's revolutionary party, it argued, originated from the tyrannical nature of the present system.[99] The paper's opinion on the Wen Shencai incident was that it was the dictatorial system itself that led to such a murder. The paper interpreted the murder as an expression of the people's opinion and further pointed out that there would be more such murders in China until the tyrannical government was replaced by a government that truly represented the people.[100]

Young China's exaltation of Wen Shencai as a hero and *Chung Sai Yat Po*'s interpretation of Wen's action as the result of an oppressive system in China sent out an important message to the Zhigongtang, an extension of the anti-Manchu secret society in China. In China's history, secret societies usually were formed and joined by people who were at the bottom of society, and secret society members were regarded as outlaws or social outcasts. That Wen was a hero and Wen's action was politically and socially acceptable amounted to an endorsement or support of anti-establishment activities in which secret societies such as Zhigongtang were engaged.

The recognition of Wen Shencai as a hero and Wen's action as politically and socially acceptable came just as Sun Yat-sen visited the Chinese community in New York. Sun was publicly welcomed by the Zhigongtang branch there. At the time, because Sun was still regarded as a rebel and his followers as troublemakers by the government in China and by the Chinatown leadership, all CCBA meeting halls were closed to Sun and his revolutionary activities. Yet in New York, the Zhigongtang arranged a meeting between Sun and local Chinese at the CCBA meeting hall there. The New York CCBA's president and other officials did not dare to stop the meeting, for they realized that it was better to have revolutionary propaganda than to have a violent fight.[101] In early May 1911, the New York Zhigongtang publicly announced its support for Sun and his program to overthrow the Qing dynasty.[102]

The recognition of Wen's killing of a Manchu official as heroic and socially acceptable played only a minor role in the Tongmenghui's winning of the New York Zhigongtang's support. Sun Yat-sen himself had worked hard to win support from this Chinese secret organization, whose members usually were poor had low social status both in China and in American Chinatowns. Yet open debate over Wen's action marked an important step in challenging the traditional values held by American Chinese. Although rebelling against authorities, especially against the supreme power in the imperial court, was taboo according to Chinese traditional values, those who joined the anti-Manchu revolutionary ranks in the United States were now regarded as normal Chinese people, albeit with a more daring spirit.

The victory of *Chung Sai Yat Po* over *Chinese World* and the acceptance of Wen Shencai as a hero were important indicators that the traditional Chinese values were experiencing challenges and changes. These indicators by no means showed that the Chinese in the United States identified with the radical revolutionary ideology propagated by the Tong-menghui and *Young China*. There was still no formal alliance between the Tongmenghui and the Zhigongtang, for the Zhigongtang general authorities in San Francisco were not yet giving endorsement. At this crucial moment, however, *Young China* committed an almost suicidal mistake in its effort to win support. This mistake demonstrated clearly the existing gap between the radicalism expounded by *Young China* and the prevailing mentality of the Chinese in the United States at the time.

The incident started in Mexico, where a war was in progress between the Porfirian government and the Maderista revolutionaries. There were about 500 Chinese living in a town called Torreon in northern Mexico. Most of these Chinese were in business, importing and marketing merchandise from China and running restaurants and grocery stores. Chinese businesses in Mexico were estimated to have a total value of more than $3 million at the time. In mid-May, the Maderista revolutionary army defeated the government forces and occupied the town, then killed more than 300 Chinese and plundered and destroyed all Chinese businesses.

The Baohuanghui had strong influence in Torreon. In 1906, Kang Youwei and his Baohuanghui had invested in real estate businesses in Torreon and founded the Chinese-Mexican Bank there to take care of the investment and financial matters of other party-run businesses in Asia and the Americas. Standing out as one of the large financial institutions in the region, this bank had won the bid for the construction of Torreon's trolley lines.[103] Although by 1911 the Baohuanghui business network in general had collapsed, its control and influence over the Chinese in Torreon were still strong. Unlike other towns and cities where there were CCBAs representing and protecting Chinese, in Torreon there were only the Baohuanghui branch office and the Chinese Merchant-Laborer Association. With business-related Chinese as community leaders and with Baohuanghui still wielding strong influence, the Tongmenghui had made few inroads among the Chinese in Torreon.

Chinese in the United States had divided opinions about the Mexican revolutionaries.[104] To the reform-minded, Mexican rebels were troublemakers vying for power. A letter to *Chinese World* asserted that Mexican rebels were by no means revolutionaries, for Mexico had been a democracy "for a hundred years" and there was no need for another revolution.[105] Yet *Young China* saw Mexican revolutionaries as counterparts of Chinese revolutionaries and had been reporting on their "victories" and on how warmly Mexican people had welcomed the "disciplined" revolutionary army.[106] After the killing of more than 300 Chinese, *Young China* reported that the Chinese in Torreon had been supporting the government army in defending the town from the revolutionary army. On the night of May 16, the government army gave up its defense and fled the town. The next morning, the Chinese there continued to resist, not knowing that the government army had already given up. It was this effort to resist the Mexican revolutionary army, the paper concluded, that led to the death of so many Chinese.[107]

Young China saw the tragedy as an opportunity to expose the Bao-huanghui, whose conservatism, the paper said, was the root cause of the tragedy in Torreon. The paper pointed out that the Mexican revolutionary army hated the Chinese in Torreon for their support of the government forces. The Chinese there sent congratulatory cables when the government forces won a battle; they sent food to retreating troops when the government forces lost a battle. Furthermore, the Chinese in Torreon were told by Baohuanghui members that Mexican revolutionaries were just like the Chinese revolutionaries wanting to rebel against the existing government. Therefore, they were social outcasts and rebels. The Chinese in Torreon were so poisoned that they died as victims of the antirevolutionary Baohuanghui. The paper then concluded that the Chinese deaths in Torreon were "lighter than feather," whereas the deaths in the Spring Uprising in Guangdong were "heavier than Mount Tai."[108]

Such an attack attracted fierce rebuttals from the surviving Chinese in Torreon. One Chinese said in his public letter that *Young China* was fooled by rumors created by the Mexican revolutionary army to defend itself in light of international protest against such cruel killings of innocent civilians and to pave the way for diplomatic negotiations with the Chinese government. The letter said that *Young China*'s editorial writer was a heartless, brainless, and shameless Chinese and that the paper was dumping its hatred against the Baohuanghui onto innocent Chinese. The letter further pointed out that the paper had ruined the negotiating position of the Chinese government against the Mexican government, making the already weak China even weaker.[109]

The reality of the tragedy was that the Chinese in Torreon had been aware of a strong anti-Chinese element in the Maderista revolutionary party's political platform. As the Maderistas approached Torreon, the Chinese Merchant-Laborer Association circulated a statement to the Chinese living in Torreon and its vicinity. The statement said, "Brothers, Attention! Attention! This is serious. Many unjust acts have happened during the revolution. Notice has been received that before ten o'clock today the revolutionists will unite their forces and attack the city. It is very probable that during the battle a mob will spring up and sack the stores. For this reason we advise all our people, when the crowds assemble, to close your door and hide yourselves and under no circumstances open your places for business or go outside to see the fighting. And, if any of your stores are broken into, offer no resistance but allow them to take what they please, since otherwise you might endanger your lives. *This is important.* After the trouble is over, we will try to arrange a settlement."[110]

The Chinese in Torreon heeded the association's caution and did not resist. Yet the anti-Chinese mob, consisting of Maderista soldiers and local civilians and with more than 4,000 participants, systematically wrecked Chinese businesses and slaughtered Chinese men, women, and children. According to one witness, the mob entered the Chinese Bank Building and threw "Chinamen" out the windows, and their friends below "finished them." "Little children were stood up against the wall and shot down, crying 'No me matten' (Don't kill me)." The mob did not ignore Chinese living on the outskirts of the city. "Mounted troopers . . . dragged Chinamen in to the plaza by the hair to execution."[111]

More letters from Chinese in Mexico and in the United States were published in *Chinese World.* These letters said that the surviving Chinese in Mexico were so angered by the editorial in *Young China* that they were talking about boycotting the paper. The letters also pointed out that many Chinese in Mexico belonged to the Zhigongtang. Out of the 303 who died in the massacre, about 180 were Zhigongtang members and only about 40 belonged to the Constitutionalist Party, or the Baohuanghui.[112]

Young China, apparently realizing that it had made a huge mistake, quickly changed its tone and started to blame the Manchus and the Constitutionalist Party for the deaths of the Chinese in Torreon. It put blame on a few Baohuangdang Chinese who had been supporting the Mexican government army.[113] These few Chinese fired first at the Mexican revolutionary army.[114] The Mexican revolutionary army therefore killed all the Chinese they encountered, for they could not distinguish Baohuangdang Chinese from other Chinese. Thus it was the Baohuangdang that led to the killing of the innocent Chinese and destruction of Chinese property there. By publicizing the inside story, the paper was thus crying out on behalf of the innocent victims.[115] Still later, *Young China* shifted its blame onto the Manchus, arguing that the Qing government had always treated overseas Chinese as "wicked people" and had refused to protect them. It was this lack of protection by their home government that led to the tragedy.[116]

In its account of the incident, *Young China* showed its political and ideological sympathy with the Mexican revolutionaries and its strong opposition to the conservative Baohuanghui. The mistake lay in the insensitivity of the editors toward the essential needs of an ethnic group. Persistent ethnic group identities reveal that human behavior cannot be detached from primordial sentiments that include kinship, language, religious beliefs, historical memories, and cultural practices. In an attempt to theorize an explanatory model of ethnic solidarity, George Scott stated that primordial sentiments are aroused "when members of an ethnic group face opposition from another group on the basis of their ethnic, or ethno-religious, distinctiveness."[117] What happened to 303 Chinese in Mexico undoubtedly was based on ethnic difference. It was impossible to expect Chinese in the United States to respond sympathetically toward the Mexican revolutionaries who brutally killed Chinese.

Young China failed to reach Chinese in the United States also because it did not tap into their primary concerns. So eager to expose the conservative Baohuanghui and so disappointed that American Chinese were slow in shifting their support to the radical revolutionary cause, the paper forgot that American Chinese wanted a strong China to stand up for and protect Chinese overseas and were more interested in living a peaceful life, protecting their rights, and accumulating wealth than making revolutions.

These three events outlined the dimensions and limitations of the emerging Chinese identity. Chinese nationalism provided the impetus for these debates and controversies. In turn, the conflicts revealed that the traditional identity among Chinese in the United States was being challenged, and the emerging identity contained dimensions of their diasporic experience and environment. In the latter half of 1911, Chinese in the United States faced more concrete challenges, and Chinese identity was thrown into a crisis.

Chinese Identity at a Crossroads

By mid-1911, all three of these Chinese-language newspapers painted a dismal picture of the situation in China to Chinese in the United States. China was becoming weaker and weaker in the international system, the Qing court was getting more and more corrupt and impotent, and there was no sincerity in promised constitutional reforms. In the United States, too, things looked bleak. In addition to strictly enforcing the Chinese Exclusion Act of 1882, American immigration officials continued to exercise their right to search Chinese living quarters randomly and to arrest Chinese who did not carry registration certificates with them. In 1911, American Chinatown authorities of various organizations appealed to the Qing government several times to negotiate for an end to the search practices. All those efforts failed. The fact that the government in China was weak and impotent was thus a constant sore spot in the lives of all Chinese in the United States. Capitalizing on the rising nationalist sentiment, Sun Yat-sen, having been publicly welcomed in New York by the Zhigongtang, visited Chinese all over the United States and gave anti-Manchu public speeches. He was welcomed by local Zhigongtang lodges.

Yet moral and financial support for the Tongmenghui from Chinese in the United States was still disappointing. Sun decided in late June to merge the Tongmenghui with the Zhigongtang to get support from the Zhigongtang leaders, who commanded a large number of Chinese in the United States. At the time, other Tongmenghui leaders and major Zhigongtang leaders still saw many differences in terms of ideals and political goals. Sun worked with both sets of leaders, who finally accepted the merger. This merger favored the Zhigongtang leaders' long-held ambitions, which were to get recognition and legitimacy for their organization in a future China. All Tongmenghui members were to join the Zhigongtang. A day was set for Sun Yat-sen, who had personally joined the Zhigongtang in 1904 in Hawaii, to lead all Tongmenghui members in San Francisco, where the Zhigongtang Grand Lodge was located, in a simplified ceremony to join the Zhigongtang.[118]

After the merger, the National Relief Bureau was organized in the United States to raise money for the grand cause of overthrowing the Qing dynasty and establishing a republic in China. The Zhigongtang's Grand Lodge in San Francisco distributed flyers to lodges in the United States and then sent out four representatives to give speeches aimed at raising funds for the grand cause. The Grand Lodge asked all lodges and members to donate generously and to provide room and board for the speakers. Among the four speakers was Sun Yat-sen.[119]

This expedient compromise with the Zhigongtang did not result in an immediate success for the fundraising effort for the revolutionary cause, however. Huang Xing, a principal leader in China of the 1911 Revolution, complained in mid-October 1911, four and half months after the establishment of the bureau, that the bureau "had only remitted 20,000 (Chinese) yuan," roughly U.S.$12,600.[120] Although most Chinese wanted to see a strong and modern China and had accepted the fact that reform had failed and some sort of a revolution was necessary, they did not see how it was going to happen. Most Chinese at this time still had their families or part of their families in China. They might no longer be worried about whether it was against Chinese traditional values to be rebellious, but they did not want to see chaos or bloodshed in their homeland.

The lack of enthusiastic support from the Chinese in the United States was also related to the attitude of the Chinatown elite and the popular and nonpartisan *Chung Sai Yat Po*. The CCBA and the Chinese Chamber of Commerce, the American Chinatown elite at the time, refused to endorse the bureau or the fundraising effort, and *Chung Sai Yat Po* kept silent on the matter. The CCBA and the chamber were officially registered organizations that worked closely with the Qing government's diplomatic corps in the United States. This Chinatown leadership depended on the existing government for legitimacy and authority. Only by preserving the existing system and government could they preserve their own power and position.

As late as July 1911, Chinese communities in the United States, under the conservative elite leadership, still publicly recognized the Qing court as the government in China and shunned the Zhigongtang and Tongmenghui as rebels. Even though the National Relief Bureau's speakers were touring the United States to raise money among the Chinese, the CCBA in New York City organized a big welcome ceremony for a Qing naval vessel that stopped at New York on its tour of the world. The CCBA rejected the New York Tongmenghui's proposal to send a representative to the welcoming team, for it was afraid that sending such a representative might create embarrassment on the spot.[121] The Chinese Consul General in San Francisco, a representative of the Qing government, celebrated his birthday with several dinner parties, sponsored by him and held in his honor. Among those present at the parties were big merchants, the CCBA president and presidents of district associations, a famous Christian minister, a student representative, and social celebrities such as Wu Panzhao.[122] No representative from the Tongmenghui or Zhigongtang was invited.

The successful October 10 Wuchang Uprising changed the political atmosphere in the United States Chinese communities, however. After the uprising, *Chung Sai Yat Po* gave full support to the revolution in China. The paper called on all Chinese to support the emerging government, for it represented democracy and happiness for all Chinese.[123] *Chinese World*, although still referring to the uprising as rebels creating disorder, reported that the Qing government was in great danger, for most people in China hated the corrupt government and were ready to aid antigovernment rebellions. Even government officials in Beijing tended to support the rebelling forces, *Chinese World* reported.[124]

This change in the political situation in China and in the attitude of the two newspapers gave ordinary Chinese confidence in the revolutionary cause. Chinese in Chicago, Los Angeles, New York, and other American cities and towns enthusiastically bought military bonds issued by the National Relief Bureau.[125] Chinese women organized to sew clothes for soldiers on the battlefields in China.[126] One man was said to have contributed all his savings to the revolutionary cause.[127] Chinese Christian churches organized fundraising activities for China's Red Cross and wrote letters to the U.S. government and governments around the world, asking them to recognize the Republic of China. They also cabled the Prince Regent of the Qing court, asking him to abdicate.[128]

All these activities were carried out without the leadership of the CCBA, which demonstrated the impact of the revolution on the American Chinese community structure and on the identity transformation. Because the CCBA was commissioned by the Qing government in Beijing, it did not recognize the revolutionaries until the new republic was firmly established at the end of the year. Even when it assumed the responsibility, in early December 1911, for collecting money on behalf of the revolutionary government in Guangdong under the leadership of Hu Han-min, the CCBA declared that assuming the responsibility did not mean that it had "taken part with the revolutionists or voiced any sentiment in their behalf."[129] It took the responsibility because local Chinese merchants, most of whom were from Guangdong Province, had been receiving telegrams from home indicating "deplorable" financial conditions in the province and therefore urged the collection of money. The revolution thus broke the usual pattern of social control in American Chinatowns. The CCBA had to bend toward public sentiment and pressure. The revolution also led to an expression of discontent from Chinatown laborers. In New York City, 400 Chinese restaurant employees signed an agreement on November 30 to stage a collective strike unless their employers raised wages, guaranteed weekly payments, reduced daily working hours to twelve, and provided a place to sleep.[130]

By the end of 1911, when the CCBA and Chinese Chamber of Commerce recognized Sun Yat-sen as the first president of the Republic of China, a new collective identity among Chinese in the United States had emerged. However, this new identity was formed on quicksand. The Republic of China brought the centuries-old imperial system in China to an end, but it did not bring with it an all-encompassing framework to replace the old one. Chinese identity after 1911 thus faced problems. For Chinese in the United States, it was even more problematic because there were diasporic forces influencing the shaping of a Chinese identity. We have already seen such forces at work while Chinese in the United States were discussing and debating the competing visions of a strong and modern China.

The emerging new identity among the Chinese in the United States rested on competing visions of what the Republic of China should represent. After the revolutionary situation in China had declared the virtual death of the dynastic system, *Chinese World* still stressed the importance of Confucius and Confucianism in the building of a new China. Editorials exalted Confucius as China's Jesus Christ and Confucianism as China's state religion. The paper made Confucius's birthday a major event, calling on Chinese in the United States to hold commemorative meetings and suggesting that all Chinese businesses and offices make it a holiday, just as Christians celebrate Christmas. It argued that all Chinese should worship Confucius; those who did not should feel shameful.[131] It implied that the Republic of China should still follow Confucian principles and declare Confucianism the official state religion.

Chung Sai Yat Po argued that the new China must allow religious freedom, for all true democratic governments in the present world allowed it, and should encourage Christianity in China, for Christian morals would help develop spiritual life and bring harmony to the new society.[132] For the Chinese in the United States, the paper hoped that as new Chinese republican citizens, officials would be selfless, civilians would be generous in supporting patriotic causes, and Chinese schools would produce qualified citizens. It also believed that, along with the death of the monarchical system, the Chinese should get rid of the Chinese lunar calendar, end tong wars, and reform bad habits. It even suggested that all Chinatown businesses, including retail stores, should be closed on Sundays.[133]

As for the revolutionary supporters, they were arguing among themselves. The alliance between the Zhigongtang and the Tongmenghui was based on different expectations, with the former wanting to obtain legitimacy and recognition and the latter desiring support of its revolutionary programs. There was little common ground as to what a new China should be like except that the Manchus should not be in control. Even during the short-lived alliance, cracks appeared. Some Tongmenghui leaders, who had initially objected to the merger, thought of the Zhigongtang as an out-of-date secret society joined only by uneducated people who engaged in unlawful activities. Because of these attitudes, the Tongmenghui often ignored the Zhigongtang on public occasions. For example, in early November 1911, the Tongmenghui, which had used the name of the Zhigongtang in raising money for the revolution in China, held a banquet to celebrate the establishment of the republic. Invited to the banquet were American politicians, American big businessmen, and American social celebrities. At the banquet and in the invitations, the Zhigongtang was not mentioned at all, either as a co-host or as an ally.[134]

Apparently angered by such treatment, the Zhigongtang held its own banquet in honor of the new Chinese republic three days later, inviting both Chinese and American dignitaries.[135] In early January 1912, a proposal was made that the Tongmenghui and Zhigongtang become one single organization by merging *Young China* and *Ta Tung Yat Po*, the Zhigongtang paper, into one newspaper and incorporating Zhigongtang property with Tongmenghui property. Although Zhigongtang leaders accepted the proposal, Tongmenghui leaders rejected it.[136] The two papers were never merged.

This alliance fell apart completely in early 1912 when Tongmenghui leaders in China ignored the Zhigongtang leaders' request for official recognition of their organization and the role their organization played in the founding of the Republic of China. The Zhigongtang, still representing a large number of the Chinese in the United States, quickly turned against the Tongmenghui.

Sun Yat-sen's three principles of the people, which were supposed to be the bedrock for the new republic, were never explained to the Chinese in the United States. Therefore, there was no understanding among most American Chinese of what these principles meant and how they could be achieved, except for superficial notions such as liberty, freedom, or happiness for all Chinese.

The year 1911 witnessed a fundamental challenge to the traditional Chinese values prevailing among Chinese in the United States. The debates carried in the three different newspapers and community activities in 1911 revealed tensions between forces of Chinese traditional values and the influence of diasporic consciousness and environment. Although many historians of overseas Chinese studies have portrayed the Chinese in the United States as enthusiastic supporters of the revolution,[137] the debates in 1911 over reform and revolution demonstrated that most Chinese in the United States did not support violent revolution as a means for change, nor did radical ideas such as socialism fit their ideology.

The Chinese in the United States had come to identify themselves with the newly established Republic of China, but this did not end the tensions between Chinese traditional values and diasporic consciousness and environment. The three visions, expressed by the three Chinese-language papers at the end of 1911, anticipated further debates over the future of China and further transformation of identity among Chinese in the United States.

The events that occurred in 1911 in American Chinese communities had done enough to destroy the framework on which the traditional Chinese identity was built, but there was no consensus for a set of ideas or values that would serve as the core for a new Chinese identity. Thus, at the official founding of the Republic of China, identity among the Chinese in the United States stood at a crossroads.

2   Defending Chinese Republicanism and Debating Chineseness in the United States, 1912–14

In 1913, the Chinese Consolidated Benevolent Association (CCBA) in San Francisco, the most important organization for Chinese in the United States, took down the portrait of Sun Yat-sen from the central wall of its meeting hall, leaving the portrait of Yuan Shikai, president of the Republic of China, standing alone.[1] This small but significant event showed that Chinese communities in the United States had retained the traditional Chinese habit of hanging portraits of revered national leaders in a community's most symbolically prominent place. This event also revealed that American Chinese support for Sun Yat-sen, leader of the 1911 Revolution and advocate of the three principles of the people, was limited. Sun and his party actually became targets of attacks in American Chinatowns when they waged another revolution against the increasingly despotic Yuan government in China.

The debate over whether Yuan or Sun was a more appropriate leader for China can be analyzed as a reflection of diasporic nationalism,[2] by which different interest groups in diaspora competed for local control. The 1911 Revolution brought into question the legitimacy of the traditional power structure and social hierarchy. The impact was very much felt in American Chinatowns. The Tongmenghui, which became Guomindang (GMD) in 1912, tried to claim not only its legitimacy but also its leading position in Chinatown life and politics as its counterparts held the na-

43

tional power in China. The Chinatown elite, Confucian scholars and successful merchants holding important positions as gentry-directors and merchant-directors of umbrella community organizations, had to find legitimacy by supporting a party in China that shared ideology and interests with them.

Besides concerns over power and control, there were also debates over whether "state power" (*guoquan*) was more important than "people power" (*minquan*). This debate brought into prominence the conflict between traditional Chinese belief in elite rule and the Western concept of democracy and rule by the people. Together with this debate were arguments about gender equality and equality between different ages and groups of different socioeconomic, religious, and educational backgrounds. The debates among Chinese in this period reflected not only the conflicts between Chinese traditional and Western values but also the special circumstances confronted by Chinese diaspora.

Diasporic nationalism has another side: the nonelite people's interests. Whether they had families in China or were in the process of bringing families into the United States, most Chinese wanted to see a stable, prosperous, and strong China. They believed that the Yuan government, which was able to unite all of China without further bloodshed, was more conducive to unity and stability in China. The Second Revolution,[3] they thought, was only prolonging suffering for Chinese people. Given their tradition of following the elite, it was natural that they favored the conservative Chinatown elite and the Yuan government. Despite the geographic distance, American Chinese were still tied to politics in China between 1912 and 1914.

However, living in diaspora provided space for the development of a new cultural sensitivity. How important were Chinese traditional values and customs in constructing their new cultural identity? How much should they adopt Western values and adhere to norms of American mainstream society? Decisions over such fundamental issues represented their diasporic experience and environment. Accepting Christianity would give the Chinese access to the larger society and establish bridges for non-Chinese to better understand Chinese. Other decisions were made according to economic considerations such as business opportunities created by celebrating the Chinese New Year for Chinatown business owners. Thus, the emergent cultural identity was Chinese American in nature, for it retained Chinese traditional values and customs while encompassing Christian values and norms of American mainstream society.

The impact of the 1911 Revolution on American Chinatowns was significant. Despite the restoration of conservative control, a spirit of independence and democracy gradually took hold of Chinatown life. Chinese American leaders resorted to the American way of lobbying against U.S. legislation and questioned the constitutionality of anti-Chinese administrative measures. The American-born Chinese used their citizenship rights to thwart a California legislative attempt at disenfranchising American citizens of Chinese ancestry and organized themselves politically. Chinese in the United States were positioning themselves as an ethnic minority group in the tapestry of American society.

A New Nationalist Discourse, 1912

The Republic of China, declared on January 2, 1912, included only seventeen provinces that had achieved independence from the Qing government. The rest of China was still under the control of the Qing court. To unify China without further bloodshed, Sun Yat-sen gave up the presidency to Yuan Shikai, who was then premier in the Qing government and was in control of the Qing army. Although Yuan agreed to adopt the republican form of government and to demand the abdication of the Qing court, he believed that conservative forces still prevailed in China. Before taking the office of president, he said to a London *Times* reporter that "70 percent of the Chinese people are conservatives" and that after the Qing court was overthrown, "the conservatives must, before long, try to restore the monarchical system."[4] Although Yuan did not attempt to restore the monarchical system in China between 1912 and 1914, his firm belief that this was the desire of the people combined with his desire to become emperor one day to pave the way for the rise of conservative forces in China.

The unsettled nature of the new Republic of China provided ground for further contention among the three Chinese-language newspapers in the United States. Because it represented the voice of the revolutionaries whose actions had led to the republic, *Young China* believed that its vision of the republic should predominate. It deeply resented the appointment of Yuan Shikai. When Sun Yat-sen was negotiating a deal with Yuan for the unification of China, the paper carried cables sent by Tongmenghui members to China, asking Sun and his government in Nanjing not to give the presidential post to Yuan. The paper and the cables instead supported the idea of a northern expedition to unify all China under the republican government. "Dare-to-die" teams were organized, standing ready to join the northern expedition. The paper called on all Chinese in the United States to support the teams financially.[5] Only Sun's personal cables stopped the dispatching of these teams.[6]

Young China's resentment against Yuan was based on its fear that Yuan would ruin the fruit of the 1911 Revolution. During the revolution, the paper pointed out, Yuan had acted as an enemy to the Chinese people by leading the Qing army in killing Chinese. Right after Yuan assumed the presidential post, the paper informed its readers that Yuan had decided to keep the diplomatic envoys sent by the Qing court to foreign countries and had appointed figures with inclinations toward a monarchical system to important government posts. In *Young China*'s opinion, this was evidence that Yuan harbored an ambition to restore the monarchical system in China and to become emperor himself.[7]

According to *Young China*, Yuan's assumption of the presidency in China endangered the future of the new Chinese Republic. To defend the republic, the paper supported the idea of turning the Tongmenghui into a political party, named the Nationalist Party, or Guomindang (GMD). The paper assumed that, as in modern democracies such as the United States, the GMD would serve as a political force in politics and government in China in general and as a check against Yuan's monarchical ambitions in particular.[8]

Having established a republic in China, *Young China* argued, the main task of the revolutionary party was to realize the principle of people's livelihood.[9] This principle, the paper explained, meant that the power of the state should be used to develop China's economy and that state socialism should be practiced. Such state socialism included abolishing private land ownership and rights of inheritance, imposing progressive taxation, confiscating property from people who had gone overseas and from national traitors, and nationalizing banking and financing institutions and means of transportation. The paper emphasized the importance of this central task of the GMD and pointed out that the future of the new Chinese republic hinged on taking such steps toward equality.[10]

Besides economic equality, *Young China* also advocated abolishing practices that showed social inequality in traditional Chinese society. At New York CCBA, a reporter from the paper observed a debate over the use of the term *daren* (your excellency). One side argued that as republican citizens, Chinese should stop using the term *daren* when addressing the Chinese consul in New York.[11] The argument continued that everyone was equal in a republic and that the consul was only a servant of the Chinese people. However, the other side regarded the term as a way to express courtesy and respect. *Young China* then commented that insistence on using the term showed that some Chinese still suffered from the profound servility that Chinese tradition had imprinted on them. Because such servile practice could only stain the quality of republican citizens, the paper advised all Chinese to keep their personal integrity to qualify as republican citizens.[12]

Besides economic and social equality, *Young China* believed that civic participation in national and community politics was another quality that republican citizens should develop. The paper encouraged all Chinese people, in China and overseas, to be politically involved and to exercise their rights as citizens of the republic. The Tongmenghui, for which the paper was the voice, had already set an example of political participation by writing a public letter to China's president and the senate of the provisional government. The letter requested that the new Chinese government appoint a strong ambassador to negotiate with the U.S. government for an end to all anti-Chinese discriminatory laws and practices and for new treaties guaranteeing equal treatment of Chinese in the future.[13]

Young China apparently was advocating fundamental changes in the traditional Chinese identity. The conservative result of the 1911 Revolution undercut the possibilities for change by helping to keep the American Chinatown elite in power. Therefore, in real life, there was no incentive to question authority and participate in politics. The fact that most Chinese in the United States had come there looking for economic betterment for themselves and their families, combined with their exposure to the laissez-faire capitalist system, made them suspicious of socialist equality, especially the ideas of abolishing private land ownership and confiscating personal property.[14] *Young China* therefore was advocating ideas beyond the ideology and social milieu of many Chinese in the United States.

In contrast to *Young China, Chinese World*, the paper that had advocated reforms as a way to modernize China and had defended Confucianism as the essence of Chinese civilization, welcomed Yuan as president. At the beginning of 1912, when the revolutionaries were negotiating with the Qing court for the unification of China, the paper carried on its editorial page a manifesto promulgated by a reform-oriented association in China. The manifesto called attention to the dangers of a divided China and advocated reconciliation between the North and the South. It argued that the fundamental difference between the North and the South was that between democratic constitutionalism and monarchical constitutionalism. Instead of prolonging the military conflict to determine which would prevail, the manifesto suggested that a decision should be made through a national assembly representing both the North and the South.[15]

When the Qing emperor abdicated and Yuan was elected president by the senate of the provisional government, *Chinese World* accepted

Yuan as the legitimate leader for all China and committed its full support to Yuan's government as the sole legitimate government of China. The paper praised Sun for his contributions to the establishment of the republic and his selfless decision to give up the presidential post in the interest of a peaceful unification of China.[16]

However, the unification of China did not bring peace, prosperity, and happiness to the Chinese people. *Chinese World* attributed continuing chaos in China to the destruction of order caused by the revolution. The paper reported and commented especially on the misery and chaos in Guangdong, the native province for most Chinese in the United States. Xinning, the native district for the largest section of Chinese in the United States, had become "a world of bandits and thieves," the paper said.[17] It also carried detailed reports of military skirmishes in Guangdong and in other provinces. Such chaos made business and commerce impossible.[18] Chinese in the United States sent weapons home to defend their businesses and homes from looting bandits, but the military government in Guangdong refused to allow the weapons to be imported. The government army even looted homes and searched travelers for weapons. These, the paper reported, were the results of the revolution.[19]

Reports of such chaotic situations laid the foundation for *Chinese World* to propose its own recipe for restoring order, which was to reinstate the gentry class at all levels of government and to govern society with Confucianism.[20] It believed that in China, where the majority of people were uneducated, too much liberty and democracy would lead only to chaos. Confucianism, on the other hand, prescribed who should govern and who should be governed, who should be respected and who should respect, and who should be obeyed and who should obey. In essence, there were different categories of people, and when each category minded its own duty, there would be order in society.

In accord with its firm belief that Confucianism could save China from disorder, *Chinese World* gave loud support to making Confucianism the official state religion in China. The paper noted that the 1911 Revolution had destroyed the traditional Chinese value system. Revolutionary advocacy of rebellion, liberty, and equality had made the Chinese society a world of robbers, thieves, and bandits. Revolutionary concepts had also destroyed the moral codes of Chinese society. Sons now could threaten fathers with knives, and students could walk out of school examinations. A society with neither order nor values appeared weak to the outside world. Therefore, the Russians dared to cut Mongolia away from China.[21] According to *Chinese World*, all this resulted from the abandonment of Confucianism. Because it was Confucianism that had sustained the great Chinese civilization for thousands of years, the only way for China to restore its greatness in the world now, the paper stated, was to make Confucianism China's state religion.[22]

In addition to its attacks on the general idea of equality, *Chinese World* specifically opposed gender equality. It believed that women's participation in politics would only do harm to the political process.[23] According to Confucianism, a virtuous woman should not be talented. A person with no talent could only muddle the political process. The paper also used a story to show how troubling the idea of liberty and equality for women was. A Chinese woman in the United States wanted to enjoy liberty and equality. Against her parents' wishes, she got engaged to a man and eloped with him, only to find that the man already had a wife in China.[24] The paper explicitly pointed out that liberty and equality for women were in direct opposition to the criteria for "good women." Liberty and equality should not be taught to women.[25]

Echoing its equation of revolution with terror, *Chinese World* once again used the French Revolution as an example to warn the Chinese people against another revolution. Demonstrating its belief in elite rule, the paper pointed out that the destruction of social order and the abandonment of traditional values would lead to mob rule. When a society was ruled by ignorant masses, people with education, people who owned property, and people who believed in religion often were killed. That was the situation in France, and it would happen in China, too, if the so-called revolutionaries in the southern part of China launched another revolution against the Beijing government in the name of building a true republic with liberty and equality.[26]

Besides these descriptions of terrors and chaos associated with revolution and accompanying prescriptions for moral and social order, *Chinese World* also directly attacked the fundamental principle of the GMD. The paper argued that the principle of people's livelihood should be interpreted as the "principle of people's death" (*minsi zhuyi*). In Guangdong, where the government was still controlled by the revolutionaries, popular religious practices such as ancestor worship, the worship of various gods, and the practice of employing house servants were arbitrarily abolished, and there were inflationary policies and high taxes. There was no social or moral order, and life in general was dangerous and miserable. The paper claimed that such was the concrete result of the so-called principle of people's livelihood.[27]

Although the problems in Guangdong could not be attributed to the *minsheng* principle,[28] what *Chinese World* described touched many Chinese in the United States directly. Fong Chow, who came from Guangdong and was superintendent of a gold mine in northern California, lost a son to bandits in Guangdong during this period. The bandits kidnapped his son and demanded "25,000 in American gold dollars." Fong Chow failed to send that amount of money back, and his son was never returned to him.[29]

What contributed to the "dangerous and miserable" life in Guangdong was chronic poverty and lack of established law and order. Poverty had been a characteristic of life in Guangdong and served as a main impetus for emigration to the United States since the Opium Wars and Taiping Rebellion. The 1911 Revolution destroyed the established social, political, and legal orders of society. Local bandits and other criminals took advantage of the disorderly situation and robbed poor as well as rich homes and disrupted businesses. Particularly vulnerable were homes whose men were in the United States. To make the situation even worse, the Guangdong government, with Hu Hanmin, a close associate of Sun Yat-sen, as governor, had to collect taxes to keep the government afloat because the Beijing government itself was having serious financial problems and could not be expected to provide support.

After much discussion of the harmfulness of revolution and revolutionary ideas, *Chinese World* offered its remedy for China. In the wake of the failed Second Revolution, led by the GMD against the Yuan government, the paper editorialized that it was now "state's power" (*guoquan*), not "people's power" (*minquan*), that China needed to consolidate. The editorial compared a country to a business corporation in which the people were shareholders and the government was the executive. When shareholders supported the executive and worked for the profit of the corporation, the business flourished; when shareholders scrambled for selfish benefits, no matter how competent the executive was, the business declined and would eventually lose its ability to compete. The state of affairs in China was just like a poorly managed company in which militarists and rebels fought for their own power with slogans of liberty and equality and claims for individual rights overwhelmed moral duties for public benefits. This state of affairs led to a weak China in the international system. Only by shifting the emphasis from people's power to the building of state's power could Chinese in the United States expect to see a strong China. The editorial finally concluded that it was this weak China that led to exclusion, discrimination, deportations, killings, and other kinds of problems that Chinese in the United States suffered.[30]

This argument simplified the political situation in China and appealed to the mentality of many Chinese in the United States. Using the management of a business as an example made *Chinese World*'s conservative theory against democracy reasonable, although the editorial neglected to mention that shareholders should have the right to participate in the decision-making process. Who would want to see selfish scrambles for individual power? It was against traditional Chinese values to emphasize individual needs, let alone fight for power at the expense of public safety and social stability, as leaders of the Second Revolution were portrayed as doing. Most American Chinese had longed for a strong China that could bring happiness and prosperity to their families and protect diasporic Chinese. Why would they support selfish rebels who could only bring chaos to China and make China weaker in the international system?

Chinese World's argument for state's power reflected the Chinatown elite's desire to preserve their power. American Chinatown elite relied on the conservative regime in Beijing for their power and status. Between 1912 and 1914, there were still close connections between the Chinese diplomatic corps in the United States and main Chinatown organizations such as CCBAs and other district associations.[31] Support for the Yuan government thus amounted to protection of their own powers and positions. Because the search for a modern China had provided a forum where ideas of democracy, equality, and representative government were discussed together with Confucian ideas of social order and the role of government, *Chinese World* was downplaying the idea of democracy and stressing the virtue of behaving as obedient followers. When Confucius was asked about government, he replied that there is good government "when the emperor is emperor, the minister is minister, the father is father, and the son is son."[32] Although Confucius talked about duties for both the ruler and the ruled, *Chinese World* emphasized the duty for the ruled to be obedient to maintain social order and harmony. This was the essence of the argument for *guoquan,* or state's power.

Thus, after its short-lived support for the establishment of a Chinese republic, *Chinese World* once again became the defender of Confucianism and the advocate of Chinese traditional values among Chinese in the United States. Representing the opinion of the Chinatown elite and riding on the resurgence of the conservative forces in China, this paper played an important role in shaping a new Chinese identity in the United States between 1912 and 1914.

These two diametrically opposed visions for the building of a strong and modern China did not cover the entire spectrum of opinions among Chinese in the United States. Hopes among American Chinese for a prosperous homeland and desires to represent a great and modern China to the world were expressed by the nonpartisan, pro-reform *Chung Sai Yat Po.* Believing in nonviolence and opposing partisan politics, *Chung Sai Yat Po* welcomed Yuan as president of the Chinese republic and praised Sun's yielding the presidency to Yuan as "an unprecedented great act."[33] However, the paper spoke loudly against the proposal of making Confucianism China's state religion. It argued that making Confucianism China's state religion would lead to national disintegration, for there were non-Han nationalities with different belief systems in China. Also, Confucianism as China's state religion would not only threaten the development of liberty, freedom, and equality, which were essential principles of a republic, but would also lead inevitably to the restoration of the monarchy.[34]

Chung Sai Yat Po believed that the establishment of the Chinese republic provided an opportunity to develop Christianity in China. It believed that because Christianity advocated equality among all peoples as God's children and universal love, its popularization in China would cure social problems, end political scuffles and factional differences, and build China into a strong and modern republic.[35] The paper also argued that Christianity in China would reassure the world that there would be no more anti-Christian uprisings in China and that Chinese people were no longer godless, making China a respected equal in the international community.[36]

Chung Sai Yat Po opposed Sun's challenges to President Yuan's power. The paper accepted Yuan as China's president and Yuan's government as China's legitimate government and so considered Sun Yat-sen's anti-Yuan propaganda and actions rebellious, troublemaking activities.[37] The paper believed that a republic needed morals as well as laws that all citizens had to obey. Sun's effort to overthrow Yuan, who was elected president by the Chinese Parliament, was unlawful and immoral. The paper compared Sun's anti-Yuan campaign to students' disobeying school rules; both actions warranted reprimands.[38]

Chung Sai Yat Po promoted its own version of freedom and equality, and it argued against Sun Yat-sen's principle of people's livelihood. It pointed out that Sun's radical theories of equality caused social turmoil in China when lower-class masses staged strikes to demand equality.[39] The paper also argued that socialism would harm China. Socialism promoted class solidarity beyond national boundaries, but what China needed was to develop its nationalism or patriotism to save it from extinction. Instead of socialist principles, what China needed was family values and Christian morals to act as a check against political corruption and social evils.[40]

Chung Sai Yat Po argued that the Republic of China should develop laissez-faire capitalism. Right after the establishment of the Chinese republic, the paper called on all Chinese capitalists to pool their money to develop China's wool industry.[41] It was assumed that republican citizens would discard the traditional long gowns made of silk and adopt Western-style clothes that had to be made from wool. Because most of the wool consumed in China at the time was imported, China should develop its own wool industry to be self-sufficient. Later on, the paper complained that China's market was still filled with foreign goods because Chinese capitalists were too conservative to invest in the development of their own national industry. It called on all Chinese with money to help build China's modern economy.[42] Helping to develop China's national industry was one of the important ways to show patriotism. The paper explicitly pointed out that patriotism started with efforts to develop national industry and consume national products.[43]

Besides encouraging China's development by appealing to its readers' patriotism, the paper saw a direct relationship between the lack of economic development and the image American mainstream society had of Chinese in the United States. Because China did not have a developed manufacturing industry to produce high-quality products, Chinese in the United States could display and sell only unrefined products in their stores. Such goods made Chinese appear backward and uncivilized.[44]

Chung Sai Yat Po also believed that as part of the process of developing laissez-faire capitalism, China needed to develop a modern educational system. In traditional China, schools put emphasis on reading and memorizing classics and on bringing up an educated elite while keeping the majority ignorant and obedient. A modern educational system should not only teach children to be responsible citizens but also teach general knowledge to all citizens. The system should include schools that would train people to be professionals and businessmen fit for the modern world.[45]

Representing a growing consciousness as modern Chinese or American Chinese, *Chung Sai Yat Po* advocated reforming certain Chinese cultural practices and encouraged a degree of accommodation to American mainstream society. It criticized traditional Chinese wedding ceremonies, which involved wasteful banquets that often put sponsoring families deeply in debt. Instead, the paper encouraged wedding ceremonies performed in churches, where newlyweds received blessings from church ministers.[46] It also argued against early and arranged marriages on the grounds that those outdated practices allowed Chinese women to be treated as chattels. Such practices should be discarded in the modern republic.[47] The paper even insisted on getting rid of the Chinese lunar calendar and Chinese New Year celebrations.[48]

Advocating Chinese "assimilation"[49] in the United States, *Chung Sai Yat Po* encouraged American Chinese to try to get closer to the American mainstream society. It argued that the fact that many Chinese did not speak English and still wore traditional Chinese clothing created a gap between the mainstream society and Chinese communities. To the

American mainstream society, tong wars, opium dens, and gambling houses were distinctive features of American Chinese communities. Lack of family life and lack of religious faith made the Chinese appear unwilling to be assimilated.[50] All these problems should be remedied to turn the Chinese into republican citizens and to present the Chinese to the mainstream society as people of a great civilization. The paper argued that the assimilation of different nationalities in a country would bring peace to that country, and the assimilation of different races would bring peace to the world.[51]

Unlike the other two papers, which represented opposite visions of a new China and a new Chinese identity, *Chung Sai Yat Po* reflected a vision shaped by diasporic experience and environment as well as by Chinese cultural heritage. *Chung Sai Yat Po*'s vision pointed out the way in which a distinctive Chinese American identity was taking shape. Yet in the short run this diasporic vision ran against the prevailing value placed on preserving Chinese cultural practices among Chinese in the United States.[52] However, *Chung Sai Yat Po*'s opposition to radical theories and to continuing revolution coincided with the opinions of *Chinese World* and the desire for peace and order prevalent among Chinese in the United States.

Political Identifications

In mid-1913, *Young China* issued an editorial analyzing why most Chinese in the United States supported Yuan Shikai while the GMD waged the anti-Yuan Second Revolution. According to this editorial, some Chinese supported Yuan because they lionized him as an omnipotent person for China, some mistook all GMD members as selfish seekers of benefits and power, many suffered from lack of education and were thus followers and worshipers of Confucian scholars and of people of age and fame, and still others thought that Yuan's violation of the laws should be punished through legal channels and that there was no need to resort to military means.[53]

Young China obviously was disappointed, yet it made an accurate assessment of the majority of the Chinese in the United States. Most of the Chinese in the United States came from China as adults, carrying with them a complete set of Chinese traditions and cultural values. The American Chinatowns they had been living in, which were isolated from American mainstream society and run by Confucian scholars and conservative Chinese business leaders, reinforced these traditions and values. Their support of the 1911 Revolution was, as one scholar argued, the result of "a taught nationalism"[54] rather than a fundamental change in outlook or a break with their traditional identity. They were told by nationalist leaders from China that only a strong China could protect them and that only by overthrowing the Manchus could the Chinese nation be saved and become strong. After the successful Wuchang Uprising in China, which led to the death of the Qing dynasty, most Chinese celebrated the establishment of the Republic of China, hoping it would restore China's greatness, bring peace and happiness to their families in China, and extend protection to Chinese in the United States.

What American Chinese hoped for did not materialize. The new Republic of China was quickly plunged into domestic turmoil, and it failed to extend protection to the Chinese in the United States. Furthermore, the conservative result of the 1911 Revolution enabled American Chinatown elite to maintain their social control. In traditional Chinese society, members of the elite class were cultural models whose behaviors were to be emulated and whose opinions were to be followed. The fact that the elite of the American Chinatowns identified with the Yuan government therefore influenced the opinion of the majority of the Chinese in the United States in the period between 1912 and 1914.

Although *Young China*'s analysis of the lack of support for the Second Revolution from Chinese in the United States was generally accurate, it lacked perception. The principle of people's livelihood, or socialism, advocated by the revolutionary GMD and expounded by *Young China*, did not speak to the needs and desires of most Chinese in the United States. Whether or not they were successful businessmen, most of them aimed for a better life for themselves and for their families. The concept of private ownership of property was essential to securing their goals. They longed for peace and stability in China, where many of their families lived, and refused to support the violence and destruction another antigovernment revolution would bring.

Most Chinese in the United States quickly shifted their support from Sun Yat-sen to Yuan Shikai. The Chinese Chamber of Commerce in San Francisco, which had been among the last to express support for Sun and the 1911 Revolution, was the first organization to cable to Yuan, after Sun yielded the presidential position to him in order to unify China without further military conflict, recognizing him as China's president.[55] At the same time, the CCBA issued an official notice to all Chinese communities in the United States to celebrate the unification of China.[56] Responding to the CCBA's notice, Chinese throughout the United States ignored *Young China*'s rejection of Yuan as president and celebrated the unified Republic of China. Even the Tongyuanhui, the Native Sons of the Golden State, the organization for American-born Chinese who at that time generally were young and had received or were receiving an American education, celebrated the unification of China with a banquet.[57]

The Zhigongtang, which had turned against the Tongmenghui, changed the name of their organization to the Chinese Republic Association. By mid-1912, the new organization had openly committed its support to the Chinese community leadership in the United States for the common interest of all Chinese. It had also declared its support to the Yuan government in China.[58]

The shift of support from Sun to Yuan was accelerated by the Tongmenghui's own actions and problems. According to Chinese traditional values, competing for power and position was shameful. When the revolutionary government was established in Nanjing, many Tongmenghui members in the United States went back to China, and some of them were appointed to positions in the new government.[59] By the end of January 1912, so many leaders had gone to China that the Tongmenghui in the United States was struggling to fill its vacant positions with new people.[60] When the Chinatown elite and Zhigongtang leaders pointed out that the new government was not being fair by appointing only Tongmenghui members to government positions, *Young China* carried an editorial reasoning that because Tongmenghui members had rendered their services to the establishment of the new government, they deserved the rewards offered to them.[61] Such an argument went against the grain of Chinese traditional ethics that emphasized living and working for the good of society, not for individual gratification.[62]

The Tongmenghui lost support not only among ordinary Chinese in the United States but also among its former enthusiastic supporters. Wu Yiping, a Tongmenghui leader and an important editor of *Young China* in 1911, disappeared from the paper as an editorial writer. He later explained in the newspaper that he was engaged in organizing a business enterprise and did not have time to work for the Tongmenghui.[63] Li Shinan, one of the founders of *Young China* and of the Tongmenghui, resigned from his editorial position at the paper.[64] Wang Chaowu, another founder and the managing editor of the paper, died of gas poison inhalation at home at age 36 in August 1912.[65] *Young China* was so weakened that the Tongmenghui had to send Ma Lixiang from China to act as editor-in-chief.[66] Earlier in 1912, *Young China* had had to require all Tongmenghui members to pay a $4 "newspaper fee" to help tide the paper over.[67] Apparently the paper as a business enterprise was not getting enough support from Chinese businesses.

Then the exposure of a Tongmenghui leader's embezzlement further accelerated the decline of credibility of the Tongmenghui among Chinese in the United States. Tan Yuelou was the former Tongmenghui secretary and cashier. Tongmenghui members had to pay "a two-dollar basic membership fee," "a four-dollar newspaper fee," "a ten-dollar military fee," and "a certain amount of monthly dues."[68] There were also donations and contributions from members, supporters, and sympathizers. In September 1912, it was revealed that Tan, who was secretary and cashier from June 15 to August 17, had embezzled an estimated $5,000 from the money collected by the Tongmenghui. When he refused to return the money, the police were called, a warrant was issued, and he was arrested.[69] An announcement was made in *Young China*, calling all those who had given money to Tan to report to the Tongmenghui with their receipts to determine the exact amount Tan had embezzled.[70]

While the Tongmenghui was losing supporters, a new political party was introduced to the Chinese in the United States. Named the People's Society, this new party was initiated by some former Tongmenghui members who disagreed with Sun over the party's political platforms. Headed by Li Yuanhong, vice president of the Republic of China, with the stated purpose of consolidating and building the republic, the People's Society attracted immediate attention from Chinese in the United States. Both *Chinese World* and *Chung Sai Yat Po* praised the society as "the political party for the new China" and a party organized by "men of noble characters" and "for the common good of all Chinese people."[71] An American branch of the People's Society was organized immediately, with the Chinese Consul General in San Francisco as president and Wu Panzhao, owner of *Chung Sai Yat Po*, as vice president.

It must be pointed out that the selection of the president and vice president of the People's Society was very important. The Consul General was considered the official representative of all Chinese in the United States and the liaison between the Chinese government and the American Chinese. His selection meant that the society was a legitimate organization endorsed by the Chinese government. Wu Panzhao, a representative of all Chinese Christians, was more importantly one of the few people widely respected among all Chinese in the United States. His selection meant that the People's Society was an association that respectable and knowledgeable Chinese with good morals and patriotic feelings could join. The People's Society, established and supported by many Chinese while the revolutionary Tongmenghui/GMD was losing its support as a political party, signified that most Chinese in the United States at the time identified with Yuan as China's leader and considered Sun and his party troublemakers.

The close identification of American Chinese communities with the new Chinese republic was highlighted by the fact that these communities sent representatives to the parliament in China. In 1909 the Qing court approved a nationality law that declared that Chinese residing overseas would be considered Chinese nationals.[72] The new Chinese government not only kept this law but also allowed Chinese on the American continent and Hawaii to send six representatives to Beijing, where three would be elected parliamentary senators. The process of selecting six representatives attracted much attention among Chinese in the United States. *Chinese World* editorialized that such a representative should have political and legal knowledge, should be familiar with the conditions in which overseas Chinese lived and with the situation in China, and should be a learned man who spoke the official language in China.[73] By listing such qualities, *Chinese World* was campaigning for Liang Chaojie, a Confucian scholar who was one of the best students of Kang Youwei[74] and also the writer of the editorial that gave rise to the Ningyang–*Chung Sai Yat Po* dispute of early 1911.

Chinese World's list of qualities obviously reflected its emphasis on Confucianism and its role as a defender of a more traditional Chinese identity. *Chung Sai Yat Po* did not agree. According to *Chung Sai Yat Po*, a representative should have a good knowledge of American laws, be familiar with conditions of Chinese in the United States, speak good English, be a good diplomat and a humanitarian, live in the United States, and be of extraordinary character.[75] This paper apparently was recommending somebody like Wu Panzhao. Yet there was no evidence that Wu ran as a candidate. The qualities listed by the paper signified the changed criteria for being Chinese among some American Chinese.

Young China did not come up with any criteria for such a representative, nor did the Tongmenghui recommend any of its members for candidacy. American Chinese businessmen in San Francisco, through the Chinese Chamber of Commerce, elected Kuang Yaojie, president of the CCBA in San Francisco; in New York, Zhu Zhaoxin, a student from China, was elected.[76] The Zhigongtang, under the new name *Chinese Republic Association*, sent its own representative, Tang Qiongchang, to Beijing. Tang was the managing editor of *Ta Tung Yat Po*, the newspaper of the Chinese Republic Association. Chinese in Canada, Cuba, and Hawaii also elected representatives. In Beijing, Tang, the Zhigongtang representative, Zhu, the student from New York, and Lu Xin, the representative from Hawaii, were finally selected as senators representing all Chinese in the Americas and Hawaii.[77]

Thus, by the end of 1912, the identification of most Chinese in the

United States with the new China under Yuan Shikai was complete. This identification showed the strength of Chinese traditional identity and the political commitment of Chinese in the United States to the republic as the best hope for building a modern China. The combination promised something to everyone. For the gentry elite, Yuan represented a less dramatic break from Chinese traditional culture than Sun. For the business elite, Yuan promised to develop China's economy as the nation's first priority.[78] For people such as Wu Panzhao, who had accepted laissez-faire capitalism and American middle-class ideology, Yuan represented a unified China. Peace and unity were of utmost importance for the new China to develop capitalism and a modern society with a middle-class backbone. And for most ordinary Chinese, although their Chinese traditional values determined that they would follow the elite, their desire for peace in China and their belief in the evils of socialism distanced them from the radical Tongmenghui/GMD.

For all these reasons, most Chinese in the United States opposed the Second Revolution Sun Yat-sen led against the Yuan government. *Chinese World* and *Chung Sai Yat Po*, serving as opinion leaders and sources of information for Chinese in the United States, spoke loudly against the Second Revolution, advised readers to stand behind the Yuan government, and reported opposition to the Revolution in China and among Chinese in diaspora. Both papers believed that a second revolution would only divide China.[79] *Chinese World* even claimed that Huang Xing, who took command of the anti-Yuan armies in the South, was fanning rebellion to achieve his selfish ambition of becoming China's president. The paper thus urged the Yuan government to take actions to suppress such a rebellion in its embryonic stage and called on all patriotic Chinese in the United States to stand up against revolutionaries who had become "common enemies of the four hundred million Chinese."[80] On the other hand, *Chung Sai Yat Po* pointed out that Sun was an idealist and Yuan was a practical leader for China.[81] Because most of Sun's ideas, such as his radical notion of absolute equality embodied in the principle of people's livelihood, could not be implemented in China, Yuan was a more suitable person for China at the time. It advised all Chinese to support Yuan and his government.[82]

The two papers also defended Yuan's actions as being in the interests of the Chinese republic. According to *Chinese World*, Yuan's loan of approximately $100 million from a consortium of foreign banks was the only way to help tide China over its financial difficulties.[83] Chinese businessmen throughout the world, from Canton to Honolulu, from Tokyo to Hanoi, from North America to South America, had all cabled support to the Yuan government, *Chung Sai Yat Po* reported. Yet, the paper added, businessmen were not the only Chinese supporting the government. Overseas Chinese workers, through organizations such as the Zhigongtang, also expressed support to the Yuan government. Many nonradical Chinese people in the media and many young Chinese students also stood firmly behind the government.[84]

Whereas Yuan got overwhelming support, Sun was portrayed by *Chinese World* as a "corrupt traitor" to the Chinese nation. This conservative newspaper accused Sun of having printed military bonds through which he made 400,000 Chinese yuan, roughly U.S.$252,000, for himself.[85] He then used the money to buy Western-style mansions in Macao and luxurious houses with gardens in Kowloon, Hong Kong for himself and his new wife; the bonds in the hands of many ordinary Chinese people were only scraps of paper.[86] Even more damaging was this paper's story of Sun's "traitorous action." When Sun was provisional president of the Nanjing government, the story said, he gave the Japanese the privilege of running a national bank in China.[87] Whereas the first accusation aroused anger among Chinese who still held the bonds they bought to support the 1911 Revolution, the second accusation tapped into the American Chinese fear of China being controlled by foreigners.

Despite *Young China*'s argument that there was enough evidence to prove that Yuan was the instigator of Song Jiaoren's murder and that Yuan had become a dictator by ignoring the parliament in obtaining the loan,[88] the majority of Chinese in the United States did not support the Second Revolution.[89] The few Chinese in the United States who supported the Second Revolution apparently realized that ordinary fundraising for the military action in China would not be fruitful. They came up with the idea of collecting money through a game sponsored by the National Salvation Society, an organization not explicitly aimed at supporting the revolution but at saving China. Organizers and enthusiasts would donate articles, and the society would sell 10,000 tickets for a dollar each. When all 10,000 tickets were sold, a drawing of lots would be held. Two hundred fifty lucky people would be rewarded with the donated articles, which included rings, pins, watches, pens, books, and ties. The $10,000 then would be sent to China to support the anti-Yuan military effort.[90] The society had a hard time selling tickets, for the drawing of lots was not held until September, and Yuan had suppressed the rebellion in China in August.

The lack of support for the Second Revolution was also revealed by the fact that even former Tongmenghui members both in the United States and in China spoke out against it. Ma Xiaojin, a former Tongmenghui member and editorial writer for *Young China* in 1911, and other former revolutionaries believed that the GMD committed political suicide by waging the Second Revolution.[91] When a new political party, the Progressive Party, was organized in China with China's vice president Li Yuanhong and Constitutionalist leader Liang Qichao as leaders for the purpose of defending republicanism from conservative bureaucratic forces and rebellious radicals,[92] many GMD branches throughout the United States cabled Beijing to join the Progressive Party or simply to change their present organizational name to the new party name.[93] *Young China* was dismayed that within two weeks of its organization, the new party established offices in San Francisco.[94]

The response to the Second Revolution revealed that most Chinese in the United States preferred to see a unified and peaceful China. Many Chinatown organizations in the United States cabled the Beijing government, asking it to suppress the secessionists in Guangdong and preserve the republic in China,[95] to restore order to China after the military defeat of the rebellious forces,[96] and to execute, on behalf of all people under heaven, the leaders of the Second Revolution, who "were currying favor with Japan and dividing up China."[97]

Supporting China's unification was one way Chinese in the United States showed their continuing close identification with their home country. Another way was through their commitment to defending China's independence and sovereignty. When President Yuan approached foreign banks for a loan to tide the new republic over its financial difficulties, the foreign banks demanded in return the right to oversee China's financial matters. Because this would encroach on the new republic's independence, Chinese in the United States immediately supported a proposal to collect money directly from Chinese citizens. All three papers carried supportive editorials advising their readers to donate or lend money to the Chinese government.[98] The Tongmenghui, the Zhigongtang, all Chinese churches, and *Chinese World* immediately started to collect donations from Chinese in the United States.[99] When the Citizen Donation Bureau, organized by the CCBA, opened its office, all the money collected by different organizations was given to the bureau. Two CCBA directors, Li Baozhan and Kuang Renrui, were awarded "medals of patriotism" for supporting the citizen donation by the Chinese government in Beijing.[100]

When, in the latter part of 1912, Russia formally committed itself to the defense of Mongolian autonomy, Chinese in the United States were again united in demanding government action against foreign encroachment. A proposal was made among American Chinese to raise funds for military preparedness against the Russians. This proposal was supported by the three Chinese-language newspapers.[101] The CCBA again set up an office to collect money. This time the CCBA required all adult Chinese to donate at least U.S.$10. Those returning to China had to give the $10 donation before they could leave.[102] However, the Yuan government made compromises with Russia for a peaceful settlement of the Mongolia question.[103] In July 1913, the CCBA announced that the money collected for military preparedness against Russia in Mongolia would be kept in a bank for later emergencies in Mongolia.[104]

Identification with different political forces in China and with China as a nation revealed the political ideology, the strength of traditional Chinese values, and the commitment to an independent and peaceful China among Chinese in the United States. After the establishment of the Republic of China, Chinese in the United States strongly desired peace and development in China. With no fundamental break from the framework of traditional Chinese identity, most Chinese, after a brief period of supporting the Revolution of 1911, continued to accept social and political control exercised by the gentry-business elite. This combination of prevailing mentality and continued elite control shaped the political orientation of American Chinatown politics, which opposed radical ideas such as socialism and antiestablishment actions such as the Second Revolution. Although debates over politics in China revealed overwhelming opposition among most Chinese in the United States to radical ideas and rebellious actions, financial support for the defense of China's independence and sovereignty went beyond factional politics, demonstrating the breadth of American Chinese identification with China as a nation in the period between 1912 and 1914.

Cultural Identifications

James Clifford has argued that "diasporic cultural forms can never, in practice, be exclusively nationalist"; instead, they practice accommodation with and resistance to norms of their host countries.[105] This applies to Chinese in the United States between 1912 and 1914. Although Chinese in the United States kept close identification with the government in China and supported efforts to defend China's sovereignty and independence, they made accommodations to the norms of American mainstream society. However, accommodation did not mean abandoning traditional Chinese cultural values and practices. Instead, accommodation to norms of American mainstream society was combined with the continuation of traditional Chinese cultural practices to form a transnational cultural identity among Chinese in the United States.

It was the Chinese Christians, represented by *Chung Sai Yat Po*, who served as a bridge between the mainstream culture and American Chinatown culture. Before the 1911 Revolution, Chinese Christians were unable to play such a role. In China's history, Christianity had been regarded as part of Western imperialism, and there had been many antiforeign uprisings that involved attacks on missionaries, churches, and Christian converts. However, the establishment of the Republic of China made Chinese Christians both bold and proud in their identity as Christians.[106] They believed that the adoption of Christian beliefs not only would make Western powers accept and respect China as an equal[107] but would also help end prejudice and discrimination against Chinese in the United States, for prejudice and discrimination were believed to be derived mainly from unfamiliar Chinese beliefs and customs.[108]

Although *Chung Sai Yat Po* argued that China should popularize Christianity, it obviously realized the limitations of its impact on China as a nation. However, the paper believed that Chinese in the United States were windows through which the American mainstream society viewed China. Out of patriotism and a sense of mission to improve the Chinese image, in the period between 1912 and 1914, *Chung Sai Yat Po* and Chinese Christians took several actions; some were welcomed by all Chinese in the United States, and others were rejected. These events inform us of the process underlying the formation of a transnational Chinese culture in the United States.

Motivated by the new republic's constitutional guarantee of religious freedom in China, Chinese Christian leaders in the United States proposed to organize a Chinese Young Men's Christian Association (YMCA) in San Francisco, the city with the largest concentration of American Chinese at the time and the port of entry and departure for all Chinese in the United States. According to the proposal, the association would help young Chinese learn the morals and skills they needed to contribute to their mother country and would provide recreational facilities to Chinese, who did not have access to such facilities because of racial prejudice and segregation. The proposal also mentioned that the association would teach American-born Chinese the Chinese language and Chinese culture to bring up a generation with both Chinese and English language skills.[109]

This proposal received support from all groups of Chinese in the United States. Within half a year, the first Chinese YMCA was officially opened in San Francisco. *Chinese World*, representing the Confucian-traditionalists and the Chinatown elite, congratulated the association on its official opening, hoping that it would provide facilities for all Chinese to receive some education, but more importantly, the paper encouraged the association to educate the younger generation so that they might grow up willing and able to contribute to the development of a modern and strong China.[110] The Tongmenghui also sent congratulations to the association on its official opening.[111]

Encouraged by the enthusiastic support expressed by various groups, Chinese churches immediately sent representatives to other Chinese communities in the United States to raise funds to construct a YMCA building. The Chinese consul general in San Francisco issued an announcement asking all Chinese in the United States to donate money for the building. In the announcement, the consul general said that the YMCA was organized to promote general interests and that the completed building would bring "unlimited benefits" to young Chinese.[112]

Chung Sai Yat Po saw even more significance in the establishment of the YMCA. The paper argued that Chinese suffered discrimination in the United States partly because they lacked education, looked sick, and lived immoral and filthy lives. It then concluded that the Chinese YMCA would help remedy these problems and improve the Chinese image and status.[113] Such a negative portrayal revealed that stereotypes prevailing among the mainstream society had affected the paper.[114] At the same time, the actions advocated by the paper demonstrated a willingness to accommodate to the norms of the mainstream society.

It is difficult to say whether most Chinese in the United States accepted *Chung Sai Yat Po*'s opinion, but no Chinese rejected the idea of creating educational and recreational opportunities. The idea of improving moral education through Christian beliefs evidently was not as acceptable, for there was no sudden increase of Chinese Christians in the United States around this time.

The Chinese YMCA, which drew financial support from churches and from Chinese businessmen who had converted to Christianity, sponsored all kinds of activities aimed at bringing Chinese closer to American mainstream society. Such activities included lectures introducing American ways of life, such as cooking and housekeeping, and plays advocating valor, martial spirit, civil rights, and patriotism. Together with the Customs Reform Society (*Gailiang fengsu hui*), a church-sponsored organization, the association put on plays encouraging Chinese to get rid of "bad habits," such as opium smoking and gambling, and to learn "good habits," such as keeping a clean and tidy appearance.[115]

The establishment of the Chinese YMCA, whose activities were supported as well as attended by various groups of Chinese, signified some Chinese accommodation to the norms of the mainstream society. However, such accommodation was highly selective. Most Chinese seemed willing to accept new norms and practices in addition to but not instead of their own fundamental Chinese values.

One of the most important identifiers of being true Chinese around 1910 was the knowledge of Chinese rituals and traditional festivals. Myron Cohen, a scholar of Chinese anthropology, observed that Chinese tend to put emphasis on "proper behavior rather than on proper ideas" when they judge whether someone is truly Chinese.[116] Many Chinese rituals, such as remembering the dead and making offerings to the Kitchen God, and all Chinese traditional festivals were based on the Chinese lunar calendar. Although the Republic of China declared the observance of the Western calendar for official businesses and political activities, the lunar calendar continued to be the record of time for Chinese to carry on Chinese cultural traditions.

Thus, the debate between *Chung Sai Yat Po* and the Recreational Society for Reading Couplets,[117] an association of China-educated people who wanted to preserve traditional Chinese culture, over the observation of the lunar calendar tested the extent to which the majority of American Chinese were willing to abandon Chinese traditions. Continuing its advocacy for reforming Chinese traditional practices and customs, *Chung Sai Yat Po* argued that the lunar calendar was no longer fit for modern life in the United States. The paper pointed out that the lunar calendar was designed with superstitious ideas about so-called predetermined fate, thus providing grounds for superstitious practices such as fortune telling and witchcraft. Such superstitions caused a nation of people to depend on various gods and goddesses and to suffer from lack of motivation for a better life. The paper also noted that the lunar calendar marked many holidays that kept people from work. The celebration of the Spring Festival, known more commonly as the Chinese New Year, was attacked as the worst example. For twelve days, everything ground to a halt, *Chung Sai Yat Po* asserted. Such celebrations bred laziness and contributed to the slow pace of life among Chinese, the paper concluded. The paper argued that the lunar calendar, which was at the root of China's backwardness, should be abandoned and Chinese in the United States, who had been "living in a civilized country and breathing in civilized air," should be the first to stop observing it.[118]

This was quite an attack on Chinese traditional culture. The language used in this editorial resembled that used by iconoclastic nationalists in movements such as the May Fourth Movement, the Superstition Destruction Movement (1928–29), and the Cultural Revolution (1966–76) in China. What *Chung Sai Yat Po* attacked as superstition—popular religious activities such as fortune telling, worshipping various gods and goddesses, and ancestral cults—was an essential component of the traditional cultural framework with which all Chinese identified. What *Chung Sai Yat Po* described as laziness-breeding traditional festivals was a significant element of Chinese cultural heritage.

In response to *Chung Sai Yat Po*'s attacks, *Chinese World* carried a series of articles written by the Recreational Society for Reading Couplets. The Recreational Society argued that the lunar calendar reflected the wisdom of Chinese culture and civilization and so could not be dismissed as outdated. The society pointed out that the way the Chinese lunar calendar marked the movements of the universe and seasonal changes on the earth remained an unsurpassed miracle. It favored the observation of both the Western calendar and the Chinese lunar calendar.[119] The society dismissed the accusation that the lunar calendar reflected superstitious ideas. It pointed out that such accusers were "slaves of western countries and dogs of westerners."[120]

Chung Sai Yat Po apparently did not want to be accused of attacking Chinese culture and civilization. It made a rather weak counterargument by pointing out that the so-called Chinese culture and civilization the Recreational Society tried to defend included Manchu rule over China. By favoring the observation of the lunar calendar, the society was in essence advocating the restoration of Manchu rule in China, the paper said.[121]

In this debate, the Recreational Society spoke for more Chinese than *Chung Sai Yat Po*. Chinese throughout the United States expressed support for the society by making donations. The names of the donors and the amounts were published in *Chinese World*. The society in turn gave all the donations to the Chinese government via the CCBA as financial contributions to the building and consolidation of the Chinese republic.[122] The society came out of the debate not only as a defender of Chinese culture and civilization but also as patriotic to the Chinese republic. *Chung Sai Yat Po* lost this debate but also made enemies among Chinese businessmen.[123] In the end, Wu Panzhao, the owner of *Chung Sai Yat Po*, went to a representative of the Recreational Society seeking a peaceful end to the debate.[124]

Chung Sai Yat Po's failure to abolish the lunar calendar not only demonstrated American Chinese willingness to preserve Chinese cultural heritage but also reflected the business orientation of American Chinese communities. Most Chinese business owners in the United States insisted on preserving the Chinese lunar calendar and observing Chinese traditional festivals. Not only was it part of their cultural heritage, but Chinese traditional festivals also brought them business. For instance, for the Qing Ming Festival, or the day to remember the dead, Chinese families bought food, incense, paper money, and other related items as offerings. The Mid-Autumn Festival was an occasion for family reunions with abundant good food and a seasonal gift exchange of moon cakes. Standing above all other festivals was the Chinese New Year, which was celebrated with many gift exchanges, visits between relatives and friends, entertainment, and banquets. It had been the American Chinatown tradition to ask local police and authorities for permission to hold street fairs and set off firecrackers and fireworks to celebrate the Chinese New Year.

The willingness to preserve the Chinese cultural heritage and the interests of businessmen led to continued observance of the lunar calendar and celebration of Chinese traditional festivals. Despite an ambivalent decision made by the Chinese Chamber of Commerce, the general organization for Chinese businesses in the United States, about whether the Chinese New Year should be observed,[125] the Chinese New Year of 1913 was celebrated in American Chinatowns. The CCBA publicly announced that the Chinese New Year would be observed and celebrated in all American Chinatowns, whereas the Chinese Christian churches announced a decision not to observe or celebrate it.[126] Yet as *Ta Tung Yat Po*, the newspaper of the Chinese Republic Association, reported, both consumers and business owners in Chinatowns demanded the observation of the festival, and the CCBA was only promoting the common interest.[127]

Chung Sai Yat Po's failure to stop the observation of the Chinese lunar calendar and traditional Chinese festivals indicated that most Chinese in the United States did not see Chinese traditional culture as a barrier to progress or modernization. Yet as a people living in diaspora, they were willing to learn to accommodate to some norms of the mainstream society. However, they would not make such accommodation at the expense of their own cultural heritage. Their refusal to abandon the lunar calendar and the Chinese traditional festivals showed the strength of Chinese cultural identity among most Chinese in the United States. As will be seen later, this strong Chinese cultural identity was maintained even when China itself waged anti-Confucius and antitradition political movements.[128]

Emergence of an Ethnic Minority Consciousness

Accommodation to the norms of American mainstream society and continued observation of the lunar calendar and traditional Chinese festivals demonstrated both "routes and roots" in the construction of a transnational cultural identity.[129] This cultural identity formed in an environment of racial discrimination. American Chinese in 1912–14 fought against legislative and administrative attempts to further limit Chinese immigration into the United States. By evoking the democratic institutions of a republican system and the American Constitution to protect their rights and by organizing for the protection of American citizenship privileges, Chinese demonstrated their consciousness as an integral part of the American nation. The appearance of this ethnic minority consciousness also lay in the development of family-oriented communities and in the scale of involvement in activities for Chinese American rights.

Recent studies show that Chinese in the United States struggled against discriminatory immigration laws and practices in the nineteenth and early twentieth centuries and contributed to the formation of American immigration policy.[130] Most such studies detailed Chinese efforts in the American court system against racist practices within the framework of laws already enacted by the federal and state legislatures. Between 1912 and 1914, Chinese fought to prevent anti-Chinese bills from becoming laws. This change marked the beginning of an endeavor aimed at forming families in the United States and acting as viable participants in the American political system under the Chinese exclusion laws.

The Chinese American population after 1910 began to take on a new look. Being mostly urban-based and with many engaged in businesses, American Chinese communities witnessed the growth of two other significant characteristics: an increasing number of Chinese women and the appearance of a second generation. According to U.S. Census data, while the total American Chinese population dropped from 71,531 in 1910 to 61,639 in 1920, the female number grew from 4,675 to 7,748 within the decade. Those under age 24 made up 24.4 percent of the total Chinese population in the United States in 1920. By 1930, the American Chinese female population had reached 15,152, having almost doubled the figure in 1920 and more than tripled that of 1910. The number of American Chinese under age 24 was 34.6 percent of the total Chinese American population in 1930.[131]

The growth of the Chinese American population resulted in part from an opportunity created by the San Francisco earthquake and the ensuing fire. The exclusion law of 1882 not only prevented Chinese laborers from entering but also denied the right of entry to wives and children of Chinese laborers remaining in the United States. The earthquake and the fire destroyed almost all records of the San Francisco population, giving Chinese residents the opportunity to claim American birth. As American citizens, they were entitled to bring their wives over, and their children born in China were derivative American citizens according to American laws and were therefore entitled to enter the United States.

In addition, because children and wives of Chinese merchants, who belonged to the exempt classes, were allowed to enter, some Chinese also resorted to deceptive ways of forging business connections. Some bribed merchants to list them as partners or bought shares in order to be listed as partners; others presented authorities with false papers, thus becoming "paper merchants." According to one immigration commissioner, "A number of the stores in the cities are organized . . . just to give the Chinese a chance to be a merchant."[132]

The unstable situation in the wake of the 1911 Revolution and the changed view of woman's position in China also helped create a new push factor for immigration to the United States. Political, social, and economic disorders in China threatened everyday life of family members who were still in China and dimmed the future for their children. The search for a modern China in general and the 1911 Revolution in particular undermined the traditional framework for Chinese society, which restricted women to their homes. "New women" were expected to be "educated mothers and productive citizens" in the development of a modern China.[133] More and more Chinese American men tried to bring their wives to the United States, where they helped raise children and assisted in family businesses.

As a result of the rising number of women and the opportunity for China-born children to enter the United States as American citizens, the makeup of the Chinese American population changed greatly in the first three decades of the twentieth century. In the years between 1908 and 1924, the year in which the passage of another immigration act stopped wives of American citizens of Chinese ancestry from entering the United States, 6,623 Chinese women and girls entered the United States.[134] While the total Chinese population in the United States dropped from 89,863 in 1900 to 74,954 in 1930, the number of American citizens of Chinese ancestry more than tripled, from 9,010 to 30,868.[135] The quick increase of the number of American citizens of Chinese ancestry stemmed from two sources: the presence of Chinese wives and the entrance of children born in China.

The number of Chinese children and wives entering the United States concerned American immigration officers and lawmakers. Immigration authorities noted in 1909 that "the second generation . . . is coming forward in such numbers the matter becomes more grave than ever."[136] They suspected that some Chinese who claimed to be children of American citizens of Chinese ancestry and of merchants in the United States for immigration purposes forged the connection. Their suspicion was well founded, for some Chinese claimed having fathered more children than they actually had and then sold the empty slots for a profit, and others entered the United States by forging merchant status or claiming to be sons of merchants.[137] As an effort to stop "paper sons," a term referring to Chinese who used the name on the document they purchased to enter the United States, from coming in, detailed interrogations were conducted before a Chinese was permitted to land in hopes of finding discrepancies between narratives given by the father and the incoming child, in most cases a son. Although interrogations prevented some from entering, most Chinese were well prepared and survived the long and detailed interrogations.

The administrative measure was then aided by an attempt to further legislate against Chinese immigration. In August 1911, William P. Dillingham, a senator from Vermont, introduced a bill "to regulate the immigration of aliens and the residence of aliens in the United States" in the Senate Committee on Immigration. Better known as "the literacy bill" aimed at preventing unwanted immigrants, it specified that for Chinese, only the exempt categories, which included merchants and their legal wives and children, were admissible. The bill then inserted the following phrase: "But such persons or their legal wives and foreign-born children who fail to maintain in the United States a status or occupation placing them within the excepted classes, shall be deemed to be in the United States contrary to law, and shall be subject to deportation."[138] The bill was passed in the Senate on April 19, 1912.

The particular provision of the Dillingham Bill apparently was designed to keep American Chinese under surveillance after entrance and to give immigration authorities the right to search and check Chinese residents in the United States. The specific language of the provision targeted the merchant class, which had been the main pillar in sustaining Chinese presence and had started to form families in the United States. If the bill became law, the effect would be devastating to American Chinese communities. Some would fail to prove or to sustain merchant status in real life. In case of a divorce or the death of a merchant, the entire family would be deported.

Reaction to the bill from Chinese in the United States was strong. Both *Chinese World* and *Chung Sai Yat Po* reported that the Senate had passed a bill aimed at "preventing Chinese from changing status after their arrival in the United States and deporting all dependents of a Chinese merchant in the United States once the merchant dies."[139] All Chinese rose above their subidentities, such as Christian, GMD, or Confucianist, and demonstrated ethnic solidarity in their efforts to stop the bill. Chinese businessmen sent representatives to Washington, D.C. to see

China's diplomatic envoy (there was not yet an ambassador from the newly established republic) and decided to hire a special lawyer to prevent the bill from becoming law. They cabled President Yuan, the Beijing Parliament, and even the governor of Guangdong, asking them to negotiate with the U.S. government to stop the bill. The CCBA, the Chinese Chamber of Commerce, and the Native Sons of the Golden State (NSGS) cabled the American president and the speaker of the U.S. House of Representatives. All Chinese in the United States helped to prevent the bill from passing by donating money to cover the expenses of the effort. The NSGS, whose members had the right to vote in the United States, contacted congressional representatives of their respective districts, persuading them to vote against the bill.[140]

To the relief of Chinese in the United States, the Dillingham Bill failed to pass the House of Representatives. The House proposed its own literacy test bill. The House bill struck out all forty sections of the Senate bill, which was written as a comprehensive bill restating American immigration policy, and replaced it with a brief four-section bill concentrating only on the issue of a literacy test. During the deliberations on the House bill, Congressman John E. Raker from California proposed an amendment to further limit immigrants from Asia. The amendment read, "All aliens, natives of any part of Asia or the islands adjacent to Asia or in Asiatic seas and the descendants of such natives, who can not read in some European language (should be excluded)."[141] The Raker amendment, which caused worries among Chinese,[142] was not accepted. The House passed the brief bill on December 18, 1912. Because the Senate would not accept the House bill, the issue was finally resolved in conference. The literacy test bill, without the particular language against Chinese, was vetoed by President Taft on February 14, 1913. The bill ultimately died when the House failed to get enough votes to override the veto, although the Senate did.

This concerted effort to stop the bill from becoming law reflected the growing Chinese consciousness as a minority group in the United States. They resorted to various means within the American political system to stop a bill. In addition to lobbying Congress, they also cabled the U.S. president, asking him to exercise his veto power in the interest of healthy Sino-American relations.[143] American-born Chinese used their citizenship rights and fought against discriminatory legislation on behalf of their ethnic group.

This consciousness was also expressed in a publication of the Chinese American Association.[144] The publication pointed out that the Chinese were enterprising and intelligent people, that they were not barbarians refusing to accommodate to the norms of the mainstream society, and that they were in the United States not to compete for jobs but to develop and promote business and commercial relations between China and the United States.[145] Therefore, they were liaisons between China, a modern republic with a huge market and rich natural resources, and the United States, a modern industrialized republic looking for overseas markets and resources. As liaisons, Chinese in the United States had been contributing to the development of the United States.

Despite these clear indications of a willingness to be an integral part of American society, anti-Chinese practices persisted. In early 1914, the immigration authorities approached San Francisco CCBA's attorney, John McNab, for an agreement to register all Chinese residents in the United States. When McNab refused to cooperate, the immigration authorities then turned to the attorney for the San Francisco Chinese Chamber of Commerce, O. P. Stidger, on the matter. Stidger agreed and tried to persuade Chinese merchants to support the registration measure by arguing that the registration proposal actually protected the Chinese merchants' rights in the United States. According to the details worked out by Stidger, all Chinese residents, legal or illegal at the time, would be registered and obtain certificates of residence. After the registration was completed, immigration authorities would conduct random searches among Chinese for illegal immigrants.[146]

The CCBA and the Chinese Chamber of Commerce responded to Stidger's proposal quickly and negatively. They had the following worries. First, although the proposal said that all Chinese already in the United States would be considered legal residents, they believed that Chinese who did not belong to the exempt categories and Chinese who did not already have legal documents to present would be deported in the process of registration. Second, after the registration was over, Chinese would have to carry their certificates all the time; homes and businesses could be searched any time of the day or night. Third, those who somehow missed the opportunity to register would be deported. More importantly, the two Chinese organizations very perceptively argued that the measure was discriminatory because of all the immigrant groups in the United States, only the Chinese were required to register. Moreover, because the proposed registration required all Chinese, including American citizens of Chinese ancestry, to register, it was a violation of the U.S. Constitution.[147]

The analysis of consequences and argument about the inherent discrimination and the questionable constitutionality of the registration measure further reinforced the theme that American Chinese as a whole

were consciously defending themselves as an ethnic minority group. Studies have shown that some Chinese did enter the United States in ways
defined by the immigration laws as illegal.[148] Yet the registration measure
had singled out the Chinese as a collective body, creating a confrontation
that easily aroused ethnic solidarity. This need to defend themselves as a
collective body fueled the emerging ethnic minority consciousness. As
an integral part of the American nation, the Chinese now believed that
they were under protection of American laws and the Constitution. Just
as they knew how to lobby Congress against potential legislation in 1912,
they were demonstrating now that they knew how to argue against government measures by using ideas and principles of equality and justice
in a democratic polity.

Reinforcing their consciousness as an ethnic minority group, the
Chinese in the United States followed their initial analysis of the consequences of registration with a public letter to the immigration authorities, reasoning against the proposed registration measure. The letter said
that the registration proposal made all Chinese merchants, both in China and in the United States, unhappy, which could only hinder further
development of commercial relations between the two countries; that it
was not the Chinese choice to be cooks, gardeners, or laundrymen (they
were eager to learn professional skills); and that immigration officers had
been violating American laws as well as basic principles of humanitarianism by bullying and humiliating Chinese.[149]

The analysis and reasoning against the registration proposal, together
with the actions taken in 1912 to block the anti-Chinese provision in a
Congressional bill, marked a fundamental difference from the defense
Chinese presented in the nineteenth century. In 1877, in the midst of anti-
Chinese violence and cries for Chinese exclusion legislation, the CCBA
presented a "Memorial" to Congress. In the Memorial, the CCBA depicted the Chinese as guests, appealed to the concepts of reciprocity and international justice under bilateral treaties, and used various kinds of
evidence to show that Chinese were not immoral, filthy, and dishonest
people.[150] In 1912 and 1914, American Chinese were no longer guests;
they were American citizens or legal residents in the United States. They
did not present a memorial; instead, they directly sent representatives and
hired lawyers to Capitol Hill. Chinese with American citizenship rights
directly contacted their own district representatives. It was no longer
bilateral treaties under which they claimed protection; instead, they
evoked the concept of equal protection under the law and challenged the
constitutionality of the registration measure. Being aware of America's
commercial and trade interests in China, they argued that their presence

promoted American relations with China. Instead of citing evidence to prove the good character of the Chinese people, they pointed out that Chinese had been driven into the laundry, the restaurant, and other low and humble businesses.

The Chinese refusal to accept the registration proposal prevented federal authorities from implementing a nationwide registration in 1914. Yet harassment of American Chinese did not stop. Random searches of Chinese businesses and residences for illegal immigrants continued. In fact, in the same month that the registration proposal was made, immigration officers in the greater Los Angeles area arrested about twenty Chinese and accused them of being illegal immigrants.[151] Chinese in the United States continued to shoulder the burden of having to constantly prove their legal status in the United States.

The emergence of this consciousness was accompanied by the nationwide organization of American-born Chinese. As early as 1895, a small group of American-born Chinese met in San Francisco Chinatown and created an organization for themselves. Named the Native Sons of Golden State (NSGS), its expressed purpose was "to fully enjoy and defend our American citizenship; to cultivate the mind through the exchange of knowledge; to effect a higher character among the members; and to fully observe and practice the principles of Brotherly Love and mutual help."[152] This organization marked a conscious effort by the American-born Chinese to claim their American rights. Yet not until after 1910 did the organization develop and expand. In 1910, 20.9 percent of the total 71,531 American Chinese population was American-born, whereas in 1900 the proportion stood at 10 percent. With the ability to speak English and with American education, American-born Chinese served as bridges between American Chinese and the larger society.[153]

The search for a modern China energized American Chinatown politics and opened the way for the American-born and educated Chinese to express themselves. We have seen their participation in Chinatown activities in 1911. Their ability to invoke citizenship privileges to defend Chinese rights to immigrate and reside in the United States put them in the forefront of the Chinese struggle against discrimination. To more effectively resist anti-Chinese laws and practices and to participate more meaningfully in American politics, American-born Chinese in cities other than San Francisco also started to organize themselves. Branches of the NSGS were established in Los Angeles and Oakland in 1912 and Fresno and San Diego in 1914, making it a statewide organization.[154]

The significance of the organization was further highlighted when the NSGS won a victory in blocking an anti-Chinese bill in the California state legislature in 1913. The bill, introduced by state senator Anthony Caminetti, was to deprive American citizens of Chinese ancestry of the right to vote.[155]

As a collective effort to fight against discrimination in the United States, the NSGS, a statewide organization, became a national organization in 1915 as the Chinese American Citizens Alliance (CACA). Although it took a few more years for CACA branches to appear in Chinese communities outside California, the organization of the CACA was the natural result of a growing consciousness as an ethnic minority among Chinese in the United States. Whether American-born citizens or immigrants from China, they were claiming the United States as their home and fighting for the rights accorded them by American laws and the Constitution.

This emerging consciousness as a minority group in the United States was accompanied by a change of attitude toward the Chinese government as a potential protector. In 1912, the Chinese in the United States appealed to China's diplomatic envoy in Washington, D.C., to President Yuan, to the Beijing Parliament, and to the governor of Guangdong for help in blocking the anti-Chinese legislation. In 1914, a newly established CCBA in Fresno, California drafted a letter to President Yuan, asking him to issue a protest against the search for certificates among Chinese in the United States. The letter circulated to all Chinese communities for signatures before it would be sent to Beijing.[156] No response to it was reported.

This change of attitude marked the beginning of a rapid decline of trust in the Chinese government among Chinese in the United States. The republicanism in China that Chinese in the United States tried to defend started to disappear in 1914. After he suppressed the Second Revolution, President Yuan outlawed the GMD as the major opposition party and, soon after that, dissolved the parliament altogether. He then had a constitution passed, which concentrated all important powers in the hands of the president, whose term of office was ten years and who could serve as many terms as he wished. *Chung Sai Yat Po* deplored the fact that the president was in total control and that autocratic dictatorship was already a reality in China.[157]

Decline of trust in the Chinese government, a growing consciousness as an ethnic minority in the United States, and a new transnational cultural sensitivity paved the way for the development of a distinctive Chinese American identity. Events in 1915 in China and in America served as catalysts for the emergence and maturation of such an identity.

3   Constructing a Chinese American
Identity, 1915

In October 1915, Chinese in the United States celebrated the official establishment of the China Mail Steamship Company, a multi-million-dollar business venture, by holding a grand ceremony to raise the flag on the first steamship of the company. Swept by a wave of Chinese nationalism aroused by Japan's Twenty-one Demands, a list of humiliating proposals that, if accepted, would forfeit China's sovereignty, many Chinese in the United States enthusiastically bought stock in the company. Within less than two months, the company launched its first ship, *The China*. But the significance of the China Mail Steamship Company reached well beyond the spirit of Chinese patriotism that seemed to spur its growth. A couple of months earlier, the management of the company had refused to cooperate with the Chinese government in organizing a Chinese joint venture with Americans, so the establishment of this purely Chinese American business venture was a community event bearing the fruit of an intense search for a new identity.

The formation of the China Mail Steamship Company was shaped by a series of events that spurred actions and debates. The first of these was Japan's Twenty-one Demands. When, in response, Chinese in the United States organized an anti-Japanese boycott, they defied the Chinese government's order against such a boycott even as they demonstrated their strong Chinese nationalist sentiment. The implementation of the boycott, full of difficulties and compromises, was indicative of immediate concerns about life in the United States and of a conflict between traditional Chinese values and newly acquired ideas of democracy.

The second event revolved around the American Chinese responses toward two projects launched in China: national bonds issued by the Chinese government and the National Salvation Fund. In both cases, the attitudes of the Chinese in the United States demonstrated disillusionment with the political situation in China. In the process, American Chinese came up with their own proposals for China's salvation, proposals that signified a fundamental shift from their role as financial donors to China's nationalist causes to a more independent way of expressing Chinese patriotism.

The third event unfolded as American Chinese responded to the mainstream society's portrayal of an American Chinatown at the 1915 Panama Pacific International Exposition. Their efforts to close the Underground Chinatown Concession and their criticism of the Chinese traditional architecture further reinforced the emergent Chinese American cultural sensitivity.

Salvation of China and Survival in the United States

One of the reasons overseas Chinese have long been perceived as nationalistic, patriotic supporters of China was their clear commitment to maintaining China's national sovereignty and independence. In fact, in 1912 Chinese in the United States enthusiastically participated in a "Citizen Donation" so that China could avoid taking out a foreign loan that would threaten its financial independence; they also raised money for military preparedness when Russia made Outer Mongolia its protectorate. But how strong was this commitment? In the 1970s, Wang Gung-wu, an expert in southeast Asian Chinese studies, broke with tradition to suggest that at least among Chinese in southeast Asia, commitment to Chinese nationalism was limited.[1] He urged scholars in overseas Chinese studies to do more research to establish a more realistic understanding of overseas Chinese nationalism.[2]

What did the Chinese in the United States do when Japan made the Twenty-one Demands, which encroached on China's sovereignty and independence? They responded, but in ways limited by their community life and community politics. Their responses showed the direction in which their identity as Chinese was changing.

On January 18, 1915, Japan took advantage of the war in Europe, which made intervention in China by European powers and the United

States unlikely, to deliver the Twenty-one Demands on China. If accepted, the demands would have put China under Japan's control. Chinese in the United States reacted quickly and strongly to the news that came to them through Western media.[3] On February 20 and 21, the San Francisco Chinese Chamber of Commerce called two meetings. At these meetings, Chinese businessmen expressed indignation at the demands, proposing to boycott all Japanese goods in the United States and to send cables to all trading ports in China to boycott Japanese goods.[4] They suggested that a community-wide meeting be held at the Chinese Consolidated Benevolent Association (CCBA) to discuss details of a boycott.[5]

Several hundred people gathered at the San Francisco CCBA on February 22. The CCBA president read to the gathered crowd the rules and regulations prepared by the Chinese Chamber of Commerce. Approval was given by applause. A boycott of Japanese American services, including barber shops, bath houses, hotels, and ball-game clubs, was added at this meeting. Four people were chosen as temporary leaders of the boycott. One of the chosen leaders, Yu Ling, a self-declared wage earner, called on all Chinese workers to express their patriotism by boycotting Japanese services. Another leader, Liu Lin, the owner of a trading company that dealt with Japanese goods, declared that although he was born and raised in the United States, he still considered China his homeland and himself Chinese. He was willing to make financial sacrifices by cutting off business with Japanese. It was agreed at the meeting that cables should be sent to Japanese ports canceling all orders for Japanese goods and to all cities and towns across the United States where there were Chinese living to boycott Japanese goods and services.[6]

The idea of staging a boycott to help the Chinese government's negotiation with a foreign power was not new among Chinese in the United States. In early 1904, to support the Chinese government, the weak Qing imperial court at the time, in its effort to negotiate a more favorable treaty with the United States,[7] Chinese in the United States proposed an anti-American boycott. Chen Yikan, editor of *Sun Chung Kwock Bo*, a Hawaii Chinese-language newspaper, wrote that the best way to get rid of the Chinese Exclusion Act and to get better treatment of Chinese in the United States was to stage an anti-American boycott in China. He explained that a boycott meant that "merchants do not import American goods and consumers do not use American goods."[8] American Chinese appeals, in the form of more than twenty telegrams, were well received in China.[9] A boycott was carried out in China's port cities between July 1905 and May 1906 while Chinese in the United States sent money back to support the boycott. Although the boycott did not achieve the primary goal of getting rid of the exclusion law, treatment of Chinese in the United States was improved significantly.[10] More importantly, Chinese in the United States learned this new method of having their voices heard.

Chinese in the United States were not involved in organizing and implementing the 1905–6 boycott. The current proposed boycott against Japan's Twenty-one Demands thus was a challenge to its organizers and leaders. We now take a close look at the organization and implementation of the boycott. Unlike in a traditional Chinese society, where the elite provided leadership, the anti-Japanese boycott was first proposed by wage earners and small- and medium-sized businesses. They called the first two meetings, which attracted many Chinese and were held at the San Francisco CCBA. At the meetings they expressed indignation and proposed the boycott. Big businesses such as the Canton Bank, the Pacific Coast Cannery, and the Bayside Cannery were never mentioned. By the time the third meeting took place, there had been such a loud outcry among the local Chinese that the Chinatown elite found it impossible to avoid being drawn into the boycott movement.

The Chinatown elite's first reaction was to try to calm down the indignant Chinese and discourage them from taking radical actions such as a boycott, at least partly because they had not yet received any official word from the Yuan government. The Yuan government faced a dilemma of its own. On one hand, it had leaked the news of Japan's demands to the Chinese and foreign press to solicit support from the Chinese people and from foreign powers that had interests in China. On the other hand, the Chinese government feared that a radical response might give the Japanese government an excuse for further demands or even for military action. Therefore, the government discouraged actions such as boycotts. The government's initial discouragement soon became an official order to ban all activities advocating or supporting anti-Japanese boycotts.[11]

Although important Chinatown meetings usually were attended by Chinese consuls stationed locally, the consul general in San Francisco did not attend any of the three boycott meetings. *Chinese World* reported that the consul general in Vancouver, Canada attended the meeting held by the Chinese there. When he did, he told about 2,000 Chinese present at the meeting that they should have confidence in President Yuan's dealings with the Japanese; he cautioned them against taking radical action.[12] In New York, the Chinese consul told the Chinese who gathered at the New York CCBA, "What we know concerning Japan's demands was only from western news media." He advised all Chinese to wait for the Chinese ambassador to release the official word from Beijing and encouraged his Chinese compatriots to do nothing more than cable the Beijing government to express their patriotism.[13]

The second unusual thing about American Chinese reaction to the Twenty-one Demands was that they proposed an anti-Japanese boycott that was supposed to be implemented not only by all Chinese in the United States but also in all trading ports in China. Such a broad and bold response reflected their growing disappointment with the Yuan government, which had abolished the parliament and passed a constitution that concentrated all important powers in the hands of the president. Their disappointment soon was even more explicitly expressed when most Chinese in the United States refused to buy national bonds issued by the Yuan government.[14] By organizing a boycott, these Chinese were acting on their own to defend China's sovereignty and integrity.

Both the proposal for a boycott and the organization of an All American Chinese National Salvation Association (*Huaqiao quanti jiuguohui*) independent of the Chinatown elite, despite the objections of the Chinese government, were the first steps in the emergence of a Chinese American identity. The next step came in the ten-point proposal offered by the Salvation Association. Included in the proposal was a demand for the acquisition of a suitable place to hold public meetings. The association believed that there were about 10,000 Chinese in the San Francisco area[15] and argued that any important decision of the association should be made with at least half of all adult Chinese present. In addition, according to the proposal, a staff meeting place was needed because the association had been using the meeting hall of the San Francisco CCBA, which could hold only about 60 people, yet the total staff was 110 and a simple majority was required at each meeting to reach decisions. The association also proposed that term limits be placed on its offices. The last of the ten points in the proposal was to encourage all Chinese to be responsible citizens and make suggestions to the association.[16]

This ten-point proposal represented the growing resistance of certain groups of Chinese in the United States to the hierarchical control exercised by the established Chinatown organizations. Ironically, the persistence of Chinese exclusion and related discriminatory policies and practices of the mainstream society helped perpetuate the "despotic" control of the established Chinatown organizations.[17] Most Chinese in the United States at this time still relied on the CCBA and similar organizations for protection and support, and this dependence perpetuated their adherence to the Chinese tradition of following the elite and obeying authority.

Yet the discontent with Chinatown's established organizations soon spread to Chinese in Chicago, where a Chinese National Salvation Association (*Huaqiao jiuguohui*) was established. The declared goals of the Chicago association were to stop the Chinese government from "selling China out to Japan" and to lobby the United States to halt Japan's violation of America's open door policy.[18] In taking this stand, the Chicago organizers also broke away from the norms of following the elite and took upon themselves the responsibilities of citizens in a democratic republic by using their position as Chinese in the United States to defend China's interests in the world.

In New York Chinatown, resistance to established authorities emerged. The CCBA in New York Chinatown, just like other CCBAs, was a registered organization with the Chinese government. When news of the Twenty-one Demands came, the CCBA called meetings of local Chinese, sent cables to the Yuan government asking it to resist the demands, and promised to raise funds in case of a war. Such lukewarm responses apparently did not satisfy all local Chinese, especially GMD members such as Xie Yingbo, an editor of *Mun Hey* weekly, an anti-Yuan newspaper recently established in New York City. The dissatisfied Chinese gathered at the CCBA meeting hall and organized a New York All Overseas Chinese Collective National Salvation Association (NYAOCCNSA, *Lu nuyue quanti huaqiao hequn jiuguohui*). The association started to raise funds for the purpose of overthrowing the Yuan government, which the association said was selling China out to Japan.

Support for the NYAOCCNSA was short-lived. The antigovernment stance of the association caused fear and doubt among ordinary Chinese, and when the Chinatown traditional elite in New York woke up to the real purpose of this new association, they easily asserted their authority. Declaring the association an unlawful organization,[19] they replaced it with a New York CCBA Collective National Salvation Association (*Nuyue zhonghua hequn jiuguohui*). With the words "all overseas Chinese" erased and CCBA added, the association was put under the control of the CCBA, with the Chinese Consul in New York, Yang Yuying, as the supervisor.[20]

If the short life of the New York independent salvation association indicated a lack of support for an antigovernment stance, then the compromises the San Francisco association made with existing Chinatown organizations revealed tensions between practical concerns of everyday Chinese life in the United States and high-sounding slogans of Chinese nationalism and patriotism. Practical concerns about survival and business interests quickly rose above emotional indignation. Resistance from the Chinatown elite and from the more prominent businessmen caused boycott supporters to doubt whether they could exert any meaningful pressure on Japan. After the All American Chinese National Salvation Association had been formally established but before the boycott went into effect, a group of organizers asked Chinese businessmen in San Francisco to sign a declaration of support. They found that many businesses, including Liu Lin's trading company, made excuses, some delayed, and others refused to sign.[21]

Despite his verbal pledge, Liu Lin was reluctant to sign the declaration because his company sold many Japanese products, and a boycott would immediately hurt his business. By the beginning of the twentieth century, prejudice and discrimination had not only drastically reduced the Chinese population but also had driven the remaining Chinese into segregated ethnic businesses. Besides running restaurants and laundries, Chinese also managed grocery stores and curio shops that featured Asian products. A large percentage of Japanese in the United States lived in rural areas and engaged in farming,[22] and Chinese grocery stores and curio shops carried Japanese goods and catered to Japanese American needs.

After people such as Liu Lin, who had been one of the first and loudest voices against Japan's demands, expressed reluctance to join the boycott, other small Chinese businessmen in San Francisco followed suit. These businessmen said that they would give their signatures only if "so-and-so" signed the declaration.[23] Their responses reflected the complicated business relationships between the Chinese and Japanese and showed that traditional values of following the elite and maintaining a middle course still prevailed among Chinese.

In response, the association leaders gave up their earlier ambition of organizing an independent institution and assigned positions of real power and authority to presidents and merchant-directors of various established Chinatown organizations. The Department of Appraisal, which had the authority to judge what constituted a violation of the boycott and how a certain violating act should be dealt with, was staffed with merchant-directors from various established Chinatown organizations. The president of the association was elected from among the current presidents of the seven district associations. The remaining district association presidents served as secretaries who handled the day-to-day business of the association.[24]

Hoping to get the widest possible support, the organizers also tried to include other important Chinatown organizations. The Department of Public Speech, whose mission was to mobilize patriotic feelings among all Chinese, was headed by an eloquent Chinese Christian minister. The Liaison Department, aimed at winning support from the mainstream society, was staffed by Wu Panzhao and Lin Yaohua. Wu was recognized by the Chinese for his connections to the mainstream society, and Lin was at the time president of the Chinese American Citizens Alliance (CACA), whose members were voters in the United States political system.[25]

Although initial enthusiasm for the boycott came from working-class people and small- and medium-sized businesses, the final decision-making power of the association fell into the hands of the Chinatown elite. This compromise strengthened the association but did not guarantee success in implementing the boycott. The strict rules and regulations of the anti-Japanese boycott proved to be difficult for Chinese in the United States to carry out.[26] In Seattle, it was estimated that half the local Chinese disagreed with the boycott, believing that its provisions could not continue very long and that half-hearted implementation would only provide "outsiders with materials to laugh at us Chinese." In Seattle, there were complicated business relations between Japanese and Chinese, some of which made the boycott impractical. For instance, a Japanese was managing a hotel owned by a Chinese consul.[27] Another example was that many small Chinese fishing companies in Seattle employed Japanese workers at lower wages. The boycott would mean higher operating costs for Chinese businesses.[28]

Complicated business relations between Chinese and Japanese thus made the boycott impractical for many west coast Chinese communities. In Los Angeles, the Chinese Chamber of Commerce refused to impose a boycott on the businesses under its jurisdiction. The president of the chamber of commerce said that "in the business world, free trade is taken for granted. Boycott or not, it is up to individual businessmen." There, too, business interactions between Japanese and Chinese were so frequent that a boycott may have been impossible to maintain.[29] It was only after a few spontaneous gatherings at the Los Angeles CCBA that a Los Angeles Chinese National Salvation Association was organized; the organization ignored demands for a boycott and instead emphasized raising funds for military preparedness.[30]

Some smaller Chinese communities in California reported similar difficulties in carrying out the boycott or reported establishment of fund-raising activities without mentioning the boycott. In Fresno, although some Chinese moved out of a Japanese-owned apartment building in response, many expressed regret over conflicts and hatred caused by the call to boycott. In Bakersfield, there were about 700 Chinese and 300 Japanese living in mixed neighborhoods. Therefore, there was no organization in Bakersfield to implement the boycott. Chinese at Stanford University responded by donating money for military preparedness, without even mentioning the boycott. Chinese in San Diego either donated money for military preparedness or pledged donations once China was at war with Japan.[31]

Some shrewd Chinese businessmen turned the aroused Chinese nationalism into business opportunity in California. Chinese living in little towns surrounding Sacramento declared that they would boycott local Japanese-run barber shops and go to Sacramento on Sundays to give the business to Chinese barbers.[32] In San Francisco Chinatown, a new Chinese Bath and Barber Business was opened in April "to take back economic interest and protect national integrity." The business welcomed all Chinese "with a patriotic heart" to patronize.[33] The call to boycott Japanese services also prompted Korean barber shops to promote business among the Chinese. A Korean barber shop in San Francisco advertised its business in the Chinese-language papers.[34]

The anti-Japanese boycott was less of an issue for Chinese east of the Rocky Mountains. According to the U.S. census, only 5 to 6 percent of the total Japanese population in the continental United States lived east of the Rocky Mountains between 1910 and 1920.[35] Chinese communities in the East did not report difficulties in carrying out the boycott. Yet most of these communities ignored the San Francisco association's call to carry out a boycott locally and responded to Japan's demands in their own way. Chinese in Cincinnati, Ohio organized an Overseas Chinese Salvation Society and pledged to support a war with Japan with all they possessed. A letter from the Cincinnati Salvation Society, signed by thirty-seven local Chinese, called on all Chinese to put aside differences and stand behind the government. In a speech delivered at a meeting of the Cincinnati society, Chen Zhensheng, one of the thirty-seven who signed the letter, supported the boycott idea but believed that it was practical only in China, where a sustained nationwide boycott could hurt the Japanese economy.[36] A report from Boston said that Chinese in New England "enthusiastically pledged donations to military preparedness."[37] Chinese in New Orleans invited a Korean to speak at a rally. The Korean, Piao Dong Kuai, gave a personal account of the tragedy of having lost his national independence and urged the Chinese to fight, not to give in to the Japanese demands. An immediate resolution was reached at the rally to establish a national salvation society and to raise funds for a war against Japan.[38]

Lack of unanimous response to San Francisco association's call to boycott Japanese goods and services derived from the fact that American Chinese were no longer simply Chinese; they were Chinese living in their unique environment. They still identified with China as an entity from which they derived cultural pride and ancestral roots. Yet they ignored

Chinese government instructions not to carry out anti-Japanese activities[39] and neglected the San Francisco association's call to boycott. Further reflecting their diasporic environment, which was playing a significant role in transforming the Chinese American identity, Chinese in the United States distinguished Japan, the political entity, from Japanese in the United States. The prevailing racial prejudice in the United States made both Chinese and Japanese targets of discrimination, contributing to the lack of animosity between them. The Chinese-language newspapers used derogatory terms such as "the dwarf nation," "Japanese thieves," or "the eastern bandits" when they referred to Japan as a nation but referred to Japanese in the United States simply as "Japanese."

In this way, diasporic experience and environment became important factors shaping Chinese identity in the United States. They figured even more prominently among the Chinese in Hawaii, who lived so closely together with Japanese that they did not do anything during the first month after Japan's Twenty-one Demands. It was only after some Guomindang (GMD) members, through an organization named the Young China Public Speech Society, which was always looking for opportunities to attack the established Chinatown authorities, accused the Honolulu CCBA staff of being traitors to China that the Hawaii CCBA held a meeting. However, the meeting did not result in a boycott; instead, it resolved to send a cable of support to President Yuan.[40]

The boycott was half-heartedly enforced; in San Francisco and in Portland, Oregon it created more problems than results. In San Francisco, a Japanese entering a Japanese barber shop was mistaken for a Chinese and beaten up. Local Japanese reported the event to their consulate, asking their consul to settle the matter with the Chinese consul. The Japanese also appealed to the local police department for protection. As a result, there were more police patrols in the San Francisco Chinatown than usual, according to *Chung Sai Yat Po*.[41] Trivial violations were reported in Portland and Oakland: Two Chinese sailors were caught entering a Japanese-run shooting clubhouse, and other Chinese were spotted getting haircuts in a Japanese-run barber shop, staying at a Japanese-run hotel, and buying fruits and vegetables from a Japanese grocer.[42]

The boycott was never strictly enforced, even in the San Francisco area or in Portland, Oregon. *Young China* carried an advertisement for the Japanese steamship company in April 1915. The advertisement was paid for by a Chinese agent, Lei Guang.[43] Although both *Young China* and Lei Guang violated the boycott rules and regulations, they seemed not to be bothered by the association's investigators or their own consciences. The boycott forbade Chinese travel on Japanese-run steamships, yet both

Chinese World and *Young China* reported relatives of Chinese officials returning to China on Japanese steamships.[44] Relatives of Lei Guang, who continued to work for the Japanese steamship company, boarded a Japanese ship with no interference at all.[45]

The haphazard implementation of the boycott revealed the undemocratic nature of American Chinatown politics. Those who had the political, economic, and social power could stand above the rules and regulations of the boycott, whereas less powerful individuals and small businesses were subject to fines for trivial violations. By mid-August, disappointed small businesses asked to withdraw their signatures from the boycott agreement.[46]

These difficulties finally made the leaders of the San Francisco association admit the impracticality of the measure. They resolved to go back to the old method of collecting donations as a way of expressing Chinese patriotism; a Department of Fundraising was added to the association. This new department was staffed by nine people who represented various established Chinatown organizations such as the seven district associations. In the end, the boycott, which had started as a more independent way of expressing Chinese nationalism, was overshadowed by traditional expressions of patriotism in the form of each Chinese donating a few dollars and letting the authorities decide the fate of the Chinese nation. The fact that established Chinatown organizations collected and controlled the donations[47] made the San Francisco All American Chinese National Salvation Association a meaningless organization.

By proposing and then failing to implement the boycott, Chinese in the United States began to realize that their limited resources would not save China as a nation from external encroachment.[48] When it came to a choice between national salvation and their own livelihood in the United States, the latter commanded more support. In the meantime, more and more Chinese were becoming disappointed in the Chinese government. After the Yuan government succumbed to Japan's ultimatum and accepted the Twenty-one Demands in May 1915, a scheduled staff meeting of the San Francisco association had to be canceled because fewer than 20 out of 110 staff members showed up. Also canceled was an association-scheduled public speech because the speaker "was having a toothache."[49]

The Twenty-one Demands gave Chinese in the United States a chance to show their desire for democratic institutions, to challenge established Chinatown organizations, and to express their distrust in the Chinese government openly. However, the political clout in the hands of the Chinatown elite and the need of most ordinary Chinese in the

United States to stay out of trouble and mind their own affairs frustrated new ideas and daring challenges. Yet movement toward a Chinese American identity soon appeared in other arenas.

No More "Money Shaking Trees"

If the response of Chinese in the United States toward Japan's Twenty-one Demands revealed growing disappointment with the Chinese government, their refusal to buy national bonds and to participate in the National Salvation Fund showed that they were no longer content to serve as "money shaking trees" in the search for a modern China. It is true that American Chinese expressed support for the 1911 Revolution through financial contributions to the revolutionaries and to the newly established Republic of China. The tradition continued in 1912 in the form of a "Citizen Donation" and fundraising for military preparedness to protect Chinese territory in Mongolia. After the Twenty-one Demands, although the anti-Japanese boycott failed to get enthusiastic support from Chinese in the United States, raising funds for a Sino-Japanese war seemed a more acceptable way for American Chinese to express their patriotism.

Yet a close look at this financial support shows that it was becoming less and less popular among Chinese in the United States. Yuan Shikai's abolition of the parliament in early 1914 had disappointed many American Chinese, who saw the parliament as an important symbol of republicanism. These Chinese showed their disagreement with Yuan when they organized the anti-Japanese boycott despite Yuan's orders against it. There were open expressions of distrust in the Yuan government while Yuan negotiated with Japan over the Twenty-one Demands.

As their disappointment and distrust in the Chinese government deepened, the Chinese in the United States started to refuse to play their traditional role as "mountains of copper and mines of gold."[50] Key moments in this development occurred when Chinese in the United States rejected both the national bonds the Chinese government tried to sell and the National Salvation Fund launched in China in 1915. An examination of their reasoning can help us understand how these developments also contributed to the emergence of a Chinese American identity.

Before the outbreak of World War I, the Yuan government relied for its financial assistance on an international consortium of Western powers and Japan. After the war in Europe and the Twenty-one Demands made such assistance impossible, the Yuan government decided to raise money by issuing national bonds. Assuming that Chinese in the United States would continue to be an important source of financial support, the Chinese government sent a group of Finance Ministry officials headed by Li Xinling to the United States to sell the national bonds.

In early April 1915, Li and the group first landed in Honolulu. Apparently aware of tension between the Chinese in the United States and the Yuan government over how China should respond to Japan's Twenty-one Demands, Li shrewdly asked the Chinese consul in Honolulu to help arrange a meeting with local Chinese people. Because overseas Chinese held consuls in esteem, meetings called by a consul or attended by a consul generally were taken seriously. Also shrewdly, Li targeted businessmen, not only because businessmen were the wealthiest community members but also because businessmen might provide leadership and serve as examples to other Chinese.

At the first meeting with businessmen in Honolulu, Li explained the benefits of the bonds and pointed out that purchasing them was an act of patriotism. He was interrupted by some questions from the audience. Because there was no parliament in China to approve such bonds, who would be responsible for cashing them?[51] Li was not able to answer this question, and most Chinese present said that they would not buy the bonds without a satisfactory answer. Li's attempts to arrange other meetings with local Chinese at the Honolulu CCBA failed because there was too much resistance.[52]

In refusing Li's request, the Chinese in Honolulu demonstrated growing awareness of the workings of a democratic government and growing criticism of Yuan's abolition of the parliament. Chinese on the mainland went even further, demonstrating their commitment to establishing relationships between a republican government and a republican citizenry. In April, *Young China* reminded Chinese in the United States that when they had cabled the Yuan government for help in opposing the American government's discriminatory laws, the Chinese government did not give any response, nor had American Chinese received any reply when they cabled the Yuan government asking it to resist Japan's Twenty-one Demands.[53] In making these statements, Chinese in the United States showed that they had begun to assume that in a republic, the government was responsible for protecting its citizens and listening to their voices. Because the Yuan government had failed to meet either of these responsibilities, these Chinese no longer felt it was their duty to support it. This argument, first presented in *Young China*, paved the way for Chinese in the United States to distinguish the Yuan government from China as a nation and a country.

What the Chinese officials encountered on the American mainland showed the effect of *Young China*'s argument. The first meeting between the Chinese in San Francisco and the officials was held in the CCBA meeting hall. Li Xinling's explanation of his mission was constantly interrupted by questions. Li was asked how the government could ask American Chinese for money when it had been silent about the mistreatment of Chinese in the United States and had failed to stop bandits running wild in China. He was also asked whether he had been in Beijing when the Chinese government allowed Russia to make Mongolia its protectorate against the wishes of overseas Chinese. So many of those in attendance at the meeting asked questions and scolded the Chinese government officials that the meeting was dismissed without passing any resolution about purchasing the bonds.[54]

It is true that *Young China* had prepared the Chinese in San Francisco to react negatively to Li's arrival and that local GMD members enthusiastically attended the meeting and were partially responsible for the chaos that resulted, but such propaganda and instigation would not have produced real resistance if the general public had wanted to buy the bonds. The fact that Li did not succeed in selling many bonds in San Francisco revealed that American Chinese in general were no longer willing to support the Yuan government financially.

Although Li told a reporter from *San Francisco Examiner* that he was not afraid of being murdered,[55] no more public meetings were held for him in San Francisco. Instead, *Chinese World* carried a few articles promoting the sale of the bonds. One article explained the high interest rates and the security of bonds backed up by China's state treasury. It also explained that to make the bonds more credible to Chinese in the United States, an American bank was authorized to sell the bonds on behalf of the Chinese government.[56] The paper even gave a detailed explanation of how interest on the bonds would compound and argued that only when China's treasury had money could the government prepare for a military showdown with Japan. Therefore, the paper reasoned, buying the bonds was an act of Chinese patriotism.[57]

No matter how the bonds were promoted, there was no enthusiasm for purchasing them among San Francisco Chinese. When Yuan accepted the Twenty-one Demands, even *Chinese World*, the only paper that had supported the bond drive, stopped promoting it. Instead, the paper carried a letter proposing the establishment of a First Canton National Bank in the United States to handle the money that might otherwise have gone to the purchase of China's national bonds. The letter reasoned that if money were given to the Chinese government for bonds, it might be used for nonproductive purposes. The First Canton National Bank, on the other hand, would use the money to develop the Guangdong provincial economy and thus set an example for other provinces in China to follow. Such appeals would attract deposits so that there would be no need to send people around to ask for donations for development purposes, and financial resources would be used to develop China's rich natural resources instead of letting them be exploited by foreigners.[58] This letter not only reflected a lack of trust in the Chinese government among the American Chinese in general but also suggested that *Chinese World*, which usually represented the voice of the Chinatown elite, was trying to define a "patriotic" course other than supporting the Chinese government.

Li Xinling's trip to New York created even sharper conflicts among Chinese there. The CCBA held a meeting for Li to present information about the bonds. Attending the meeting were the Chinese consul in New York, GMD supporters and opponents, and representatives from various Chinatown organizations. GMD supporters bombarded Li with questions while its opponents counterattacked; the meeting turned into a physical fight when tong members were called in to take action. The fighting turned into a chase in the streets, which caught the attention of the local police. The police stayed in the area until midnight.[59]

Before the meeting, some Chinese in New York had pledged to buy the national bonds, hoping that their money would be used to resist Japan's demands. When the news of Yuan's acceptance of the demands came, however, most of them canceled their pledges. After such failures and frustrations, Li Xinling turned to China's ambassador in Washington, D.C., for help. The ambassador accordingly cabled CCBAs and Chinese chambers of commerce throughout the United States, calling on presidents and merchant-directors to buy the bonds and to help sell them.[60] It was the best he could do, and it was not enough. When Li Xinling left the United States for China around the end of July 1915,[61] there was no send-off party for him, as the San Francisco CCBA had given for Chinese government delegations and officials in the past, nor was there any final report on how successful Li's effort to sell bonds to the Chinese in the United States had been.

The failure of Chinese government bond sales signaled a significant decline in the credibility of the Chinese government among Chinese in the United States. The fact that China at the time did not have a parliament bothered American Chinese, who were living in a country governed by laws made by a representative body. Their acquired notions of citizenry and government, checks and balances in government, and rights and duties contrasted with the Yuan government's hierarchical structures. Much as they wanted to help "save" China, they had come to believe that supporting the Chinese government would no longer lead to the salvation of China.

The disappointment of American Chinese in the Chinese government soon translated to lack of interest in the National Salvation Fund, a project launched by Chinese businessmen in Shanghai in March 1915.[62] The proposal asked that each Chinese citizen contribute one-tenth of his or her property to establish a national fund. This fund would be used for the general purposes of building China's army and navy and developing China's domestic industry. Deposits would be handled by the Bank of China. The goal was to collect 50 million Chinese yuan (about U.S.$28,500,000) by the end of the year. From the first, the plan offered anxious investors something of an escape clause. If the 50-million-yuan goal was not reached, depositors could withdraw their money with interest for the time the money was in the bank. If the goal was achieved, then two-thirds of all depositors had to be present to decide specifically how the money would be used. The general headquarters for the fund was in Shanghai, and cities and towns in China and overseas Chinese communities were to have branches to publicize and promote it. Local branches of the Bank of China would be authorized to handle deposits. For places where there was no such branch, local credible businesses would be appointed as agencies for collecting deposits, which would finally be forwarded to the Bank of China.[63]

In response, the Chinese in the United States advanced a number of proposals, all of which showed their attempts to forge a form of patriotism that did not depend on existing institutions in China. Several suggested establishing their own independent institutions to collect and manage funds. One proposed that a national salvation bank be established in the United States to collect money that could be used for emergencies or long-term development. This proposal addressed the weakness of the old way of expressing patriotism, arguing that donations repeated too many times would naturally become unpopular. Instead, the national salvation bank would pay regular interest to depositors and invest deposits in China's industrial development during peace time, and in times of crisis in China, the bank's deposits could be used to support defense and relief efforts.[64]

Other proposals focused on building a modern Chinese defense system. One suggested that every ordinary Chinese in the United States donate $10 each year while businesses and rich people make higher donations. In five years, there would be enough money to buy a warship for

China. The plan rested on reasoning that overseas Chinese had been donating many millions of dollars to China in the past few years, yet that money had not helped China. It was better for "us overseas Chinese to watch over our own money."[65] This critique was echoed in other attempts to build a modern Chinese defense system. Another proposal suggested a two-part plan: Chinese in the United States would raise money for the purpose of purchasing several warships in the United States and establish a military school to prepare young Chinese in the United States to defend China. When the ships were ready, these trained sailors would operate them and pilot them to China, serving as models for a modernized Chinese navy.[66]

Yet another such idea was that if each Chinese put away at least a penny a day, an institution could be set up to collect the savings. Money from this institution could be used for China's development of military or industry, but, the proposal emphasized, measures should be taken so that depositors could check on how the money was used.[67]

All these proposals suggested that the Chinese in the United States were tired of being constantly asked to donate and suspicious of how their money would be used, either by China's national government or by different political parties. They wanted to have more control over their money. Chinese in the United States had accepted the modern capitalist idea of using banks to gather capital resources to develop an economy as well as Western democratic concepts such as checks and balances, citizen participation, and representation.

Chinese World, the voice of the Chinatown elite and prominent Chinese businessmen in the United States, served as the public forum for these suggestions. It supported the most conservative of the proposals, the National Salvation Fund, launched in China, telling its readers that the fund would allow Chinese people to defend and develop the Chinese nation independent of the Chinese government and that they would retain control over how their savings would be used. While people in China, because of natural disasters and a stagnant economy, were already having a hard time making a living, overseas Chinese were reminded of the value of a strong China in their everyday lives and encouraged to make more generous contributions to the fund. The paper also emphasized the benefits of putting money in the fund because it would produce dividends for depositors in normal times. The paper believed that there should be some organization in the United States to collect money for the fund.[68]

Chinese World was the only paper of the three that supported the National Salvation Fund. Yet even *Chinese World* distinguished the

Chinese government from China as a nation and country and emphasized the control people should have over savings in the fund. *Young China* dismissed the fund as some kind of a "vanity fair" by some rich people in China to curry favor of the Yuan government.[69] *Chung Sai Yat Po* kept silent on the matter.[70]

In some parts of the United States, there were sporadic responses to the calls from Beijing and Shanghai. In New York, about twenty Chinese individuals pledged one month's wages and deposited about $3,000 in a Chinese bank there.[71] In mid-July, *Chinese World* published the names of people who had made pledges to the fund. The list had only two names, one pledging $20 and the other pledging $10.[72]

Meanwhile, the general headquarters of the National Salvation Fund in Shanghai wrote to the San Francisco CCBA several times, urging it to organize an office in the United States and to send representatives to meetings in Shanghai. The Chinese embassy and consulates in the United States also received letters from the fund in China, calling for the establishment of branch organizations in American Chinatowns. The Chinese government also cabled, calling on Chinese in the United States for contributions.[73]

Despite all these efforts, no branch or any such organization was established in the United States. On December 8, *Chung Sai Yat Po* reported that the headquarters of the fund in Shanghai had announced that because it appeared that the goal of 50 million Chinese yuan could not be reached by the end of the year, depositors could withdraw their money with some dividends earned.[74] This announcement ended the National Salvation Fund.

Despite *Chinese World*'s insistence that the National Salvation Fund was not a government-controlled financial institution, Chinese in the United States refused to participate in it, thus signaling their growing distrust of the Chinese government and Chinese politics in general. This refusal to buy the national bonds and contribute to the fund stood in sharp contrast to actions they would take in 1915, when tens of thousands of dollars were collected and sent back to China for flood victims.[75] Such generous relief funds not only showed that most of these Chinese had the financial ability but also revealed that they were still compassionate Chinese; it suggested that their decisions not to buy Chinese national bonds or to contribute to the salvation fund were conscious ones. Their refusals marked the emergence of a Chinese American identity, one that still identified with the Chinese nation yet refused ties with the Chinese government.

Constructing a Modern Chinese Image in Diaspora

Just as the emergent Chinese American identity did, the construction of a modern Chinese image among Chinese in the United States also reflected their diasporic experience and environment. One factor that contributed to this experience and environment was the racial and cultural biases held by U.S. mainstream society. In American mainstream media, Chinese people were represented as morally depraved opium smokers and prostitutes, with sickly yellow skin, living in filthy, primitive conditions, and politically enslaved to tyrannical control.[76] These images contributed to the passage of discriminatory laws and ordinances against the Chinese in California in the nineteenth century and played an important role in the enactment of the 1882 Chinese Exclusion Act, which was extended permanently in 1904.

American Chinese had been combating racial and cultural biases for many years. American Chinatowns had been tourist attractions, and the Chinese welcomed visitors. Yet Chinese resented the depiction of Chinatowns as havens of opium smokers and gamblers. In July 1911, the CCBA in San Francisco instructed its lawyer to stop tourists from entering "improper places" in Chinatown. Carroll Cook, the CCBA lawyer, reported his successful negotiation with the chief of police of San Francisco. According to Cook, the chief agreed to give orders to all tour guides that "if they took any visitors into disreputable places, . . . their license would be revoked."[77] In late 1910 and early 1911, American Chinese successfully stopped a play in cities such as Seattle, Portland (Oregon), New York, Sacramento, San Diego, and Phoenix.[78] The play was based on the murder of a white woman allegedly committed by a Chinese man in New York City.[79] The Chinese argument was that the play would create anti-Chinese sentiment and add to racial prejudice.

Chinese in the United States were eager for American mainstream society to get to know the real Chinatown and the Chinese people, their long-established civilization and rich cultural heritage. In 1917, *Chung Sai Yat Po, Chinese World,* and the China Mail Steamship Company (established in 1915) welcomed the publication of *Chinatown: A Pictorial Souvenir and Guide* by Louis J. Stellman.[80] Wu Panhzao said in his letter, "I take great pleasure in indorsing [sic] your book, 'Chinatown Guide,' as the most reliable and faithful description of the condition, activity and tradition of the Chinese quarters of San Francisco, commonly called 'Chinatown.' . . . I hope this book will have a large circulation among the American public, so that a better understanding will be made lasting between the American people and the Chinese."[81] All three letters praised the *Guide* for its "reliable," "faithful," and "sympathetic" descriptions of San Francisco Chinatown. They all believed that prevailing biases were caused by lack of understanding or "erroneous impressions" of "Chinese customs and institutions."[82] Besides efforts to combat unfavorable depictions and to endorse "faithful" descriptions, American Chinese also watched for opportunities to present the real Chinatown and the rich Chinese cultural heritage to the larger society.

Such opportunity arose when the U.S. government decided to hold an international exposition in California in 1915 to celebrate the opening of the Panama Canal. To the delight of American Chinese, the new government in China, after delaying for more than a year because of domestic political unrest, positively responded to the invitation from the Panama Pacific International Exposition (PPIE) Corporation. *Chinese World* immediately printed the Chinese government document concerning the decision.[83]

As early as March 1912, *Chung Sai Yat Po* reported that local Chinese businessmen discussed a plan to raise funds to participate in the PPIE.[84] By July 1914, American Chinese businessmen had organized a Zhenhuang Company (Revitalize China Company), had registered and been approved by the Ministry of Industry and Commerce of the Chinese government, and had collected $200,000.[85]

Zhenhuang Company was authorized to act on its own, constructing a building for Chinese products at the "day-and-night fair" of the exposition in San Francisco.[86] Celebrating the opening of the Panama Canal were two fairs. In San Francisco there was the PPIE of 1915; in San Diego there was the Panama-California International Exposition of 1916. The PPIE was the main fair.[87] The "day-and-night fair" was the section where sponsors would exhibit and sell products, the managers of Zhenhuang Company believed. The Chinese building, which would take up 41,250 square feet, was to be constructed there to show and sell products from China. Profits made there would benefit participating Chinese businessmen.[88] The Chinese government, on the other hand, was responsible for an official exhibition hall at the main section of the San Francisco fair.

Chinese in the United States, in supporting Zhenhuang Company's goal of promoting trade and commerce for China, demonstrated their shrewd business-oriented insight. Discriminatory American laws and practices had driven Chinese in the United States out of most economically profitable niches, but potential trade and commercial relations between China and the West could provide new opportunities. To American Chinese represented by Zhenhuang Company, the opening of the Panama Canal marked the beginning of "a new era" in transpacific passage.[89] Being Chinese and standing on the American side of the Pacific Ocean, Chinese would contribute to and benefit from transpacific trade and commerce.

Behind such pragmatic business expectations were idealistic assumptions. Contrary to Zhenhuang Company's statement that the Chinese government had designated "a huge budget" for the participation at the PPIE, the Chinese government believed that the proposed budget of 1,902,740 Chinese yuan was very small compared with Japan's budget of 6,000,000 Chinese yuan. The government statement further cautioned that the proposed budget might be cut by the Ministry of Finance, for China at the time was relying on foreign loans for survival.[90] Chinese in the United States did not pay much attention to such statements. When Zhenhuang Company began to build the Chinese mall at the PPIE, a grand ceremony was held. Gentry-directors of the CCBA, leaders of the Chinese Chamber of Commerce, the Chinese Consul General and his assistants, managers of Zhenhuang Company, and representatives from various Chinatown organizations rode in fifty automobiles to the construction site, flying national flags of China and the United States and accompanied by live bands playing Chinese and Western music. The ceremony was also attended by representatives sent by San Francisco mayor James Rolph and California governor Hiram Johnson. The governor's representative said at the ceremony that "progressive" and "republican" China's presence at the PPIE would "add glory" to California.[91] Chinese in the United States expected the new Chinese republic to present a positive image at the exposition.

American Chinese expectations were quickly frustrated by reality. When in early July 1914 a group of about thirty Chinese construction workers came to San Francisco to put together Chinese government exhibition halls,[92] the workers' appearance upset San Francisco Chinese. *Chung Sai Yat Po* carried an editorial complaining about the clothing the workers were wearing. It said,

> When abroad, one at least should be clothed in a popular and generally acceptable style. Workers should appear clean and tidy in order to show that ours is a civilized nation and thus deserves respect. But what we have seen is that the Chinese workers at the construction site provided a scene for others to laugh at us. These workers wore blue cotton tops with red and green trimmings, with colorful underwear exposed at the waist, and ropes hanging down from the waist. They wore cloth shoes and cloth socks, with strings tying together the pants at the ankles. Their clothes were usually very greasy and soiled. Such an ugly scene was an oddity even in Chinatown. It would definitely increase hatred against Chinese

among the mainstream society, which usually associate dirty clothing with lack of morality.

The editorial then went on to suggest that Western overalls, which were only a dollar a pair, were tidier, more practical, and less expensive than Chinese clothes with trimmings.

This editorial moved on to describe the conditions of the workers' living quarters. "The living quarters are just stacks of untreated planks of wood clumsily put together. There are cracks in the roofs and walls and they are not at all rain or wind proof. The workers sleep on beds that are just propped up on the beach sand, with no floors at all. Bed sheets are also very soiled, with all kinds of things lying around with no arrangement or order. Then there is the administrative office of the construction team. Right beside the desk in the office is a bed with mosquito net over it. The kitchen is even less rain and wind proof, with greasy utensils and cleaning rags strewn all over, millions of flies humming around, and ashes from the stove covering the kitchen floor." All these, the editorial said, were so damaging to the Chinese image that measures had to be taken to remedy the situation.[93]

Chung Sai Yat Po was not the only newspaper voicing such criticism. According to *Young China*, the Chinese construction workers were wearing those "long gowns with mandarin jackets, which were no longer seen even on hoodlums," and their "unwashed faces and uncombed hairs could be a challenge to the imagination of ghosts." Chinese in San Francisco could hardly hold their bitter laughter at the sight of those workers, the paper observed.[94] In addition to these editorials, several Chinese individuals also wrote to the Chinese officials in charge of the construction team, asking them to improve the workers' living quarters, clothing, and habits, which, according to the letters, "were bringing insult to China's image."[95]

These criticisms revealed that some Chinese in the United States had come to accept Western standards of housekeeping, clothing style, and public appearance. Chinese in San Francisco had been subject to discriminations such as the San Francisco "cubic air" ordinance, which was passed in 1870 and soon became a law of the state, and the "queue" ordinance, which was passed in San Francisco in 1876. Both directly targeted the Chinese; the "cubic air" ordinance required a house to provide at least 500 cubic feet of clear space for each adult person living in it, and the "queue" ordinance required all male prisoners to have their hair cut to "a uniform length of one inch from the scalp."[96] These laws criminalized the personal and private conduct of Chinese people, reflecting the aversion of mainstream society toward them. Like other discriminatory ordinances, they were based on the assumption that the Chinese were dirty and diseased.

In such a context, harsh criticisms of the clothing and living conditions of the Chinese workers revealed a gap between the idealized conceptions of Chinese culture and civilization held by Chinese in the United States and actual cultural practices that existed in 1915 China. The clothing and the living conditions described in the newspapers were common among ordinary Chinese living in China at the time. Yet to the Chinese in the United States, they had become unclean, untidy, ugly, almost inhuman, and, most of all, damaging to the Chinese image. Such idealized expectations conflicted with the real China, where people were still living in poverty. Yet when the officials heading the construction team tried to explain the reality in China and said that the budget to manage China's presence at the exposition was very small,[97] the Chinese in the United States responded that unless the nation's presence at the exposition could help enhance China's prestige in the world, it had "better stay home and hide its clumsiness."[98]

The Chinese officials' effort to explain contemporary life in China to the Chinese in the United States opened the door to further attacks on the Chinese government. *Chung Sai Yat Po* complained about the lack of a democratic tradition among Chinese, in China and in diaspora, and about corrupt Chinese politics. It said that one of the problems in China and in Chinese communities abroad was that there were too many irresponsible officials who would not listen to people's voices. China was not a rich country, the paper admitted, yet China maintained a large and expensive bureaucracy whose government officials enjoyed high salaries and lived comfortable lives.[99] *Young China* agreed, concluding that it was the impotence and corruption of the present Chinese government and its officials that had brought such insult to China and to the Chinese people. A capable Chinese government, the paper declared, would have provided its workers with proper clothes and built better living quarters.[100]

Building on their idealized notions of Chinese culture and civilization while longing for a government of the people and for the people, Chinese in the United States criticized the two "traditional style" Chinese buildings representing China at the exposition. To the Chinese in the United States, the buildings were small and the architectural style "moribund." Compared with other governments' grand exposition buildings, the Chinese buildings were like "children's game houses"; their walkways looked like "horse stables." Such old-fashioned buildings could only harm China's prestige. In making these criticisms, *Young China* was joined by *Chinese World*, the paper ordinarily known for its defense of Chinese culture and tradition. Claiming to represent all overseas Chinese, both papers demanded that the eaves of the walkways be raised three feet so that they would not block visitors' views.[101] In making this demand, Chinese in the United States revealed their acquired appreciation of Western architecture and their longing for big and spacious buildings that stood in contrast to their "ghettoed" Chinatown living conditions. Their diasporic experiences and conditions led them to adopt new aesthetic criteria.

The American Chinese criticism of the government halls contrasted sharply with what the mainstream society wanted to see. The *San Francisco Chronicle* introduced the Chinese government halls by printing a whole-page picture of the Chinese-style complex in its Sunday magazine. In its effort to attract visitors, the *Chronicle* said, "The Forbidden City, that long mysterious imperial quarter of Peking for centuries no outsiders ever set foot, is reproduced in part on the grounds of the exposition."[102] It was exactly that "mysterious" feeling, which attracted non-Chinese visitors, that bothered Chinese in the United States. It reinforced the stereotypes about American Chinatowns that American Chinese had been working to correct. The contradiction between the *Chronicle*'s depiction and American Chinese desires indicated a long and tough road that American Chinese had to travel before their cultural heritage would be appreciated accurately.

The desire of Chinese in the United States for a splendid exhibition of a modern China and Chinese products was further frustrated when they found that the tea houses were serving foreign pastry and using Japanese table ware and Japanese-style decoration, and servers were wearing "high hats and strange looking suits."[103] The exposition coincided with Japan's Twenty-one Demands, which had heightened nationalism among the Chinese in the United States, so observers were sensitive on this point. The frustrated Chinese in San Francisco gathered at the CCBA, demanding that the tea houses be removed and the space turned into resting places for visitors.[104] When Chen Qi, head of the Chinese delegation to the exposition, told the San Francisco CCBA that the tea houses were intended to introduce Chinese tea to the world and that no Japanese products were used in them, *Chinese World* replied that "although the chief of the delegation suffers some disability in the leg, we Chinese compatriots do not have any problems with our eyes."[105] Such an angry reply from *Chinese World*, a paper that had long been a conservative supporter of the Chinese government, revealed the extent to which the Chinese government had lost credibility among the Chinese in the United States.

Despite their disappointments and frustrations, however, American Chinese showed their continued attachment to China by offering to help

remedy the clear lack of management displayed by the Chinese delegation to the exposition. Three days before the Chinese government exhibition halls were to open, the exhibits were still in boxes, waiting to be
displayed. The San Francisco CCBA held a meeting and organized a group
of Chinese businessmen and secretaries from various Chinese associations to help display the exhibits.[106] When it became known that some
porcelain from Guangdong would not be displayed for lack of space in the
exhibition halls, the San Francisco National Salvation Association held
a public meeting at which all patriotic Chinese were encouraged to contribute ideas about how to display the porcelain.[107] It was finally resolved
that the presidents of various district associations, representing all Chinese in the United States, would talk to Chen Qi directly and propose
that the tea house business be removed so that the space could be used
to display the Guangdong porcelain.[108] Although the Chinese representatives failed to get Chen Qi to remove the tea houses, the idea and actual effort showed how badly Chinese in the United States wanted to
present China's best side to the world.

If the American Chinese reactions to China's presence at the PPIE
demonstrated diasporic dimensions of their Chinese identity, then their
concerted effort to stop the exposition's "Underground Chinatown Concession" revealed both their ethnic and cultural pride and their growing
determination to integrate themselves into U.S. mainstream society.

This concession was part of the Joy Zone at the PPIE, a section of the
fair that provided visitors with joy and amusement. The joy and amusement came from "village concessions" where the nonwhite world was
portrayed as "barbaric and childlike." The Joy Zone, dotted with many
village concessions depicting Mexicans, Samoans, Africans, Japanese,
Chinese, and other nonwhite peoples, was designed to give ethnological
and scientific sanctions to America's discriminatory immigration policy at home and imperialist policy abroad.[109]

To the great indignation of Chinese in the United States, the Chinese
building constructed by Zhenhuang Company in the Joy Zone housed an
Underground Chinatown Concession. A Caucasian theater executive, Sid
Grauman, was operating a "chamber of horrors," which featured actors
and actresses who portrayed Chinese addicts inducing and teaching white
people to smoke opium and to gamble.[110] Despite Chinese expectations
for and efforts to present a positive, modern Chinese image, to the exposition directors the Chinese were barbaric people with ugly and sinister
habits. Together with other nonwhite peoples, Chinese were inferior and
were not among those selected for "the world of tomorrow."[111]

The underground scenes aroused immediate attention among Chinese in the United States. An editorial in *Chinese World* suggested that Zhenhuang Company cancel the contract and order the operator, Sid Grauman, to close the concession. The editorial further suggested that Chen Qi ask Charles C. Moore, president of the exposition, to condemn the concession, arguing that it was contrary to the main purpose of the exposition, which was to promote good feelings among peoples. It also suggested that all Chinese in San Francisco gather at the CCBA to write a letter to the Chinese consul general, asking him to use governmental and diplomatic channels to stop the operation.[112]

The editorial thus suggested an all-around effort to close the Underground Chinatown Concession. Chinese in the United States needed no more urging; they took concrete measures immediately. The San Francisco Chinatown elite held a dinner meeting in a Chinese restaurant and invited the official Chinese delegation to the exposition to discuss the matter. Because the president of Zhenhuang Company at the time, a Chinese businessman, was in China on a business trip, his wife attended the dinner meeting and explained that Zhenhuang Company did not know how Sid Grauman would use the space. She said that efforts were being made to cancel the contract and then asked everybody present to help find ways to stop the concession in order to save China's prestige from being hurt too much.[113] Her presence and words evidently calmed Chinese in the United States, who associated the concession with the company and blamed it for making money at the expense of China's prestige and the future of all Chinese in the United States. *Chung Sai Yat Po* had already published a letter that raised the question of whether Zhenhuang Company should be allowed to profit by leasing the space to someone for such an anti-Chinese operation.[114]

It was not only the Chinatown elite who responded immediately; American Chinese religious leaders, schoolteachers, and other educated professionals collectively wrote a letter to the exposition president, explaining why the Chinatown Underground Concession should be shut down. The letter stated that, first, American Chinatowns never had such an underground place. Therefore, the concession was put up just to take advantage of exposition visitors to make money; second, the concession distorted the Chinese image and was insulting to all Chinese; third, it demeaned Christianity because it depicted an opium smoker who pretended to be a Salvation Army worker when police came; and, fourth, most Chinese people in Chinatowns had always been honest and law-abiding, had been promoting progress in Chinatowns, and had been paying particular attention to public and civic concerns. The letter finally said that the operation was harming the "magnificent and splendid Exposition."[115]

The letter's reasoning indicates a conscientious effort on the part of educated Chinese to present themselves as a part of the United States by arguing that the concession was a distortion of historical facts and of the Chinese image and also an insult to Christianity that harmed the exposition. Getting rid of the offending concession was necessary not only for the sake of saving the Chinese image but also for restoring truth and morality and protecting the magnificence of the exposition itself.

The Chinese Language Press Association in San Francisco, which included *Chung Sai Yat Po, Young China,* and *Chinese World,* wrote a collective letter to President Charles C. Moore of the exposition, protesting against the Underground Chinatown Concession. Insisting that it was clear that some greedy people had put up a degrading show to make money from exposition visitors, the letter stated that the San Francisco Chinatown had never had an underground opium den, even before the big San Francisco earthquake. The earthquake's destruction, the letter pointed out, had so exposed Chinatown that it proved there was no such opium den. As the papers saw it, white people had conjured up such Chinatown hells. Before the earthquake, the letter continued, some white people ran tourist attractions in San Francisco where they presented ugly scenes of Chinese gambling and smoking opium. Those Westerners used their wild imagination and made up all kinds of stories and scenes to make money. They were ordered to close down by the San Francisco police because it was tarnishing the city's reputation. The present operation, the letter concluded, would certainly tarnish the image of the exposition if it were not stopped immediately.[116]

The Underground Chinatown Concession was nothing new to American Chinese. Just as the Chinese Language Press Association pointed out, Caucasian businessmen ran "opium dens and gambling joints" to attract tourists before the San Francisco earthquake. As recently as October 1914, "western tour guides" took tourists to New York Chinatown, showed them "Chinese smoking halls" where tourists shot pictures, and introduced the halls with "words intolerable to the ear."[117] A month later, in November 1914 in San Francisco, some photographers, dressed as Chinese and pretending to be carrying out an official mission, went into private residences in Chinatown and took photos. The Chinese Consul General, Xu Shanqing, wrote a letter to the police chief, asking him to stop the concocted mission. To the disappointment of American Chinese, the photographers continued their project.[118]

This resentment toward the depiction of Chinese as opium smokers and gamblers and of a dark, filthy underground network of opium dens and gambling joints was echoed by a San Francisco Chinatown old-timer in the early 1970s. Gim Chang, a retired rice merchant, said angrily, "You read about underground tunnels in old Chinatown? I know nothing about them. I'm quite sure they didn't exist at all. When I was a boy, you know, I used to follow the older boys everywhere and I knew all the dirty, secret places. When white people come to Chinatown looking for curiosities I used to tag along behind the Chinese they took as guides, but I never saw an underground tunnel. Just mahjong rooms in the basements."[119] Gim Chang also remembered that on Jackson Street in San Francisco Chinatown, there was an old man (presumably Chinese, although Chang did not make it clear) who "lived in a dirty house with sand and mud floors and never took a bath in all his life." He kept himself dirty to make money from tourists, Chang added. Some tour guides even took their customers to see Chinese ladies with bound feet as a way of making money, according to Chang.[120] The capitalist ideology of making money took advantage of and further promoted the racially oriented prejudice and stereotypes.

These voices of protest from Chinatown organizations were joined by the CACA, an organization representing Chinese born in the United States. To demonstrate their resentment of and aversion to the ugly, dark Underground Chinatown Concession, the CACA announced that all Chinese, especially parents of young children, should stay away from the concession to keep their minds free of contamination. The CACA also issued English-language flyers advising non-Chinese parents not to take their children into the concession. It also suggested that the concession be declared "the dirty spot" of the exposition. Finally, the CACA said that it wanted to let the world know that "we Chinese know the importance of education."[121]

This concerted effort was capped by a letter jointly written by the Chinese consul general, the Chinese Chamber of Commerce, the CCBA, and Chen Qi to the president of the exposition, asking him to close down the concession immediately.[122] On March 26 President Moore visited the place in question; he ordered it to close down.[123] According to *San Francisco Chronicle*, "The drastic action is said to have been prompted by objections filed against the exhibit by the Chinese of this community, backed by the Chinese Consul-general, the Chinese Six Companies, and, in particular, the exposition commissioners from China, upon the grounds that the depictions therein were low and conveyed false and biased impressions of the habits of their people, with the further objection that the customs represented, together, with the furnishings of the dens and the assumed decrepitude of the performers, showed celestials of the old re-gime and not those of the modernized republic."[124]

When the president of Zhenhuang Company returned from his trip to China, he made a public announcement in *Chinese World*. First, the statement said that the so-called contract with Sid Grauman was not valid because neither the president nor his associates had ever signed it. Nevertheless, the president would still formally cancel the so-called contract to make sure that the operation could never return.[125]

Chinese in the United States scored only a very limited victory. In place of the Underground Chinatown Concession, there appeared an Underground Slumming, which lasted until the close of the PPIE in December 1915. This time, no Chinese entertainers were used. However, it still portrayed a ghettoed Chinatown where illegal and immoral activities prevailed.[126] When the Panama-California International Exposition opened in January 1916, in San Diego, it featured an Isthmus, its equivalent of the Joy Zone at the San Francisco fair. Demonstrating "stages of mankind, the Isthmus portrayed Chinese again as inferior and dirty people inhabiting underground Chinatowns."[127]

It is not the degree of success in changing the views of mainstream society but the ways by which the Chinese expressed, reasoned, and struggled against representations of China and Chinatown life that are significant in the study of an identity transformation. This new Chinese American identity incorporated a cultural sensitivity that idealized Chinese cultural heritage, processed and internalized racial and cultural prejudices prevailing in the United States, and adopted Western aesthetic standards, customs, and norms. The new identity also included a disappointment in and departure from the government and politics in China. Having never questioned their Chinese heritage and identity and determined to claim the United States their home, American Chinese were emerging with a transnational identity and a transcultural sensitivity.

Maturation of a Chinese American Identity

On top of all the disappointments that American Chinese felt in the Chinese government, now came word that China might go back to the monarchical system. In mid-June 1915, a Chinese official visiting a Sacramento Chinese school said that "China could not become a rich and strong country unless its system changes to a constitutional monarchy."[128] By September, all three papers, including *Chinese World*, carried editorials insisting that China could not and should not change from the republican system to the monarchical system.[129] In mid-September, the

San Francisco CCBA wrote, on behalf of all Chinese in the United States, to American president Woodrow Wilson, asking him to stop Yuan Shi-kai from restoring the monarchy in China.[130]

As patriotic Chinese recognizing their special position in the United States, American Chinese had been taking actions to protect China from losing too much pride and economic interests in the world. Then in June 1915 came the news that the only U.S. steamship company providing transpacific services from San Francisco would be out of the Pacific business within a few months.[131] This meant that a Japanese steamship company would be the sole provider of transpacific services from San Francisco, the main port of entry for Chinese passengers and goods. At the time, the anti-Japanese boycott was still in force.

It was the La Follette Seamen's Act, passed by the U.S. Congress under the pressure of labor unions in general and the International Seamen's Union in particular, that had made it impossible for the Pacific Mail Steamship Company to operate the transpacific business profitably.[132] A clause of the Seamen's Act, passed in March 1915, provided that at least 75 percent of the crew on American ships had to understand the language of the ship's officers to increase the safety and security of the passengers in case of an emergency.[133] Because officers on American ships were mostly white Americans speaking only the English language, that meant crew members had to understand English. Until that time, the Pacific Mail Steamship Company had been using Asians, especially Chinese, as sailors. Asian sailors were cheap labor. Using Americans would have increased wages, drastically raising the company's costs. The company thus declared it would discontinue its business in the Pacific in November, when the Seamen's Act took effect. In August, the Pacific Mail Steamship Company sold its transpacific liners to an American shipping company providing service across the Atlantic Ocean. On September 29, the *New York Times* said that "the Pacific [was] swept clean of American ships by the law of Andrew Furuseth and the Seamen's Union."[134]

After the demise of the Pacific Mail Steamship Company, the Japanese steamship company monopolized transpacific business from the San Francisco port, although the Northern Steamship Company, a small American company providing services between Seattle and the Far East, was still in business. This situation caused urgent problems for the Chinese in the United States. The San Francisco National Salvation Association, which came into being as a response to Japan's Twenty-one Demands, convened a staff meeting to find ways to deal with the situation. Some participants favored changing the boycott rules and regulations so that Chinese could travel on Japanese ships under certain conditions.

However, there was strong opposition to this suggestion, so the meeting finally resolved that those who needed to cross the Pacific immediately would go to Seattle for non-Japanese service. The boycott would not be compromised.[135]

Yet when it became clear that because of time limits on their visas, some Chinese could not afford to wait any longer, the association granted individual exceptions to the boycott rules. The association later had to make compromises in response to the urgent need of some Chinese to return to China for various other reasons. The compromise was that a Chinese could take a Japanese ship after he or she had paid a $20 fine.[136]

The La Follette Seamen's Act and Japan's Twenty-one Demands thus were the occasion for Chinese in the United States to demonstrate the maturation of the Chinese American identity by establishing the China Mail Steamship Company, a multi-million dollar Chinese American business. Even before Pacific Mail announced its decision to stop its transpacific business, *Chung Sai Yat Po*, which had been emphasizing China's domestic industrial development as the most positive route to China's salvation, analyzed the possible result of the Seamen's Act. It perceptively pointed out that under the new legislation, Pacific Mail would inevitably discontinue its business, for it would not be able to compete with the Japanese company subsidized by the Japanese government. The paper hoped that Chinese businessmen in the United States would take advantage of the opportunity and that all Chinese would support such an effort.[137]

The San Francisco Chinese Chamber of Commerce promptly responded to the official announcement that Pacific Mail would discontinue its transpacific service. The chamber called a meeting of businessmen to discuss the possibility of establishing a steamship company. Those present expressed great enthusiasm for the idea and proposed to make it a communitywide effort. It was suggested that the matter be discussed in the CCBA, the organization not only for businessmen but for all Chinese in the United States.[138]

Yet by the end of August, the San Francisco CCBA had failed to call a meeting, and Chinese businessmen concluded that they had to take the initiative. Another meeting was then called by the Chinese Chamber of Commerce. All present at the meeting supported the proposal of establishing a Chinese steamship company. In the long run, it was agreed, a Chinese steamship company would be a means for American Chinese to fight for China's economic rights in the international arena. Businessmen would take the lead in launching the venture, but it was emphasized at the meeting that the company would have to involve all Chinese in the United States. People were appointed to be temporary managers, secretaries, and clerks, and it was resolved that further meetings would be held, and bylaws for the new company would be drafted and discussed.[139]

The China Mail Steamship Company was launched by Chinese businessmen to win back China's economic rights and protect Chinese integrity. Although the initial expenses were paid by businessmen, the company was a stock-sharing venture that encouraged Chinese businessmen and wage earners, Chinese men and women, to buy shares. The company's capital was set at 5 million Hong Kong dollars (about U.S.$2,136,000), and each share was only 50 Hong Kong dollars, or about U.S.$21. The company would have a board of fifteen directors elected from those who owned a minimum of 1,000 dollars of stock and by all who owned shares in the company. The board of directors would then appoint a president, vice presidents, and other officials and reserve the right to change appointments whenever it deemed necessary. Bylaws could be changed and adjusted as long as a majority of shareholders gave approval.[140]

Efforts were made to make the steamship company a community business. One of the first initiators of the company was Lu Runqing (Look Tin Eli), who at the time was president of the Canton Bank and secretary of the San Francisco Chinese Chamber of Commerce. Around this time, the Canton Bank was looking for opportunities to expand its business.[141] Yet despite the pressing need posed by the anti-Japanese boycott, the bank did not invest large amounts of money in the steamship company. There were two reasons. One was that establishing a Chinese steamship company to compete with the subsidized Japanese one was at best a shaky business venture. The other, related reason was that nationalist feelings ran very high among Chinese in the United States; therefore, it was a good time to organize a community business. Because each share cost only U.S.$21, almost all Chinese could participate in the business. When most Chinese had stock in the company, they would naturally use the company's services and refuse to sail on Japanese ships or other ships managed by potential competitors.

Among the initiators, many of whom became the company's temporary officials, were the president of the Chinese Chamber of Commerce,[142] the president of the San Francisco CCBA,[143] Yu Ling, chief investigator of the National Salvation Association, and Chen Sushi from *Chung Sai Yat Po*. Lu Runqing, president of the Canton Bank, became its temporary president. During the first few days, all stock shares were bought by businessmen. When the CCBA finally held a meeting on September 9, 1915 to encourage all Chinese to participate and bought 10,000 Hong Kong dollars' worth of stock, it became a community event, and many Chinatown businesses became places where shares could be purchased.[144]

American Chinatown leaders were determined to take advantage of this tide of patriotism to start a solely Chinese American community business. When the Chinese government, via different channels, invited these leaders to join a Sino-American steamship company, which was allegedly already established, they flatly refused.[145] *Chung Sai Yat Po* ran an editorial exposing what it believed was behind the so-called Sino-American company. It claimed that the company would be controlled by American businessmen who, by jointly running the company with Chinese, could avoid federal laws regarding employment of cheap labor. The editorial appealed to Chinese in the United States to be steadfast in their determination to run an independent Chinese American business and not to waver in the face of the Sino-American company's propaganda.[146]

Chinese World was very supportive of the China Mail business venture and encouraged all Chinese to buy its shares. The paper predicted that the steamship company would be profitable and stated that it would help China claim its navigation rights on the Pacific Ocean. Buying shares in the company was thus a good business investment as well as a contribution to the defense of China's rights in the competitive world.[147]

Young China did not voice enthusiastic support for establishing the company at first; it even published one editorial cautioning those who initiated the company not to harbor selfish ambitions but to establish a solid business enterprise with clearly written bylaws.[148] This paper at this time was devoted to attacks on Yuan's effort to restore the monarchical system in China, which was perceived by the GMD as an opportunity to step up its anti-Yuan campaign. Yet it did not carry negative editorials or comments concerning the establishment of the company. Like the other papers, it printed detailed news of its founding and the progress of stock purchases. During this period, big businessmen in the American Chinese communities either considered themselves above partisan politics or tilted to the Chinese government side. Therefore, it was not surprising that *Young China* would be suspicious of their motives. Before long, however, the clearly written bylaws, the democratic process of electing a board of directors, and the effort to make it a community business cleared away suspicions. By October, *Young China* had begun to encourage all American Chinese to contribute to the effort of establishing the company. By mid-November, it complained that Chinese in the United States had not done enough to support it.[149]

The company sent many representatives to various Chinese communities in the United States to sell shares. These representatives were well received. There was no controversy around the effort. Chinese of different occupations expressed enthusiasm and purchased company stocks according to their abilities.[150]

Most Chinese in the United States at this time were not rich, and most purchases were of a few shares. Yet the anti-Japanese boycott prevented Chinese from taking Japanese steamships or transporting goods to and from China. It was this pressure that made company leaders decide to solicit support from Chinese businessmen in Hong Kong, who enthusiastically purchased the company's stock.[151] That the Chinese American businessmen refused to cooperate with the Beijing government or white businessmen yet were willing to ask for support from businessmen in Hong Kong was indicative of the nature of their new identity. Chinese in Hong Kong were part of the global Chinese diaspora.

The company bought its first steamship, *The China*, in mid-October. The ship, originally one of the Pacific Mail Steamship Company's fleet, was purchased from the Atlantic Transport Company.[152] This 5,000-ton ship, built in 1889, was considered old.[153] The same officers and crew, who had operated *The China* under the management of the Pacific Mail Steamship Company, were now employed by the China Mail to operate the same ocean liner. With the purchase of its first ship, the China Mail Steamship Company was registered with the state of California on October 14. The company's capital stock at the time was $2,100,000, with 100,000 shares at $21 each. According to President Lu Runqing, "All this money is American capital subscribed by Chinese throughout this country." All fifteen directors of the company were American Chinese.[154]

A grand ceremony was held to raise the company flag on the ship. Invited to the ceremony were 1,000 American Chinese and 1,000 non-Chinese Americans. A prayer was offered by a Chinese Presbyterian minister. *The China* set out on its maiden voyage for Asia under the new flag on October 30, 1915.[155]

The China Mail Steamship Company not only drew its capital mostly from Chinese communities in the United States but also depended on their patronage for its business. In its first seven months the company reaped a profit of more than $300,000.[156] Most of its passengers were Chinese, and most of the goods it carried were from Chinese importers and exporters or from Americans engaged in importing and exporting between the United States and Asia. A network of Chinese forwarding agents, ship insurance brokers, and freight contractors was established in the Americas, especially in New York and San Francisco.[157]

The company's attempt at expansion and American Chinese refusal to have Westerners serving on the company's board of directors led to financial difficulties. In April 1917, the company decided to buy the *S.S. Congress* as its second ship to meet the needs of increasing business. After the purchase, the ship was renamed the *Nanjing*. The newly purchased ship needed some repair, for its top had been damaged in a fire. The purchase price of $900,000 and the final repairing cost of more than $2 million went beyond the company's budget. After a failed attempt to increase the company's capital under the existing bylaws, the board of directors decided to organize a new company with the property of the old one as security. The new company would then sell bonds to raise money. The fact that the new company's board of directors consisted of three Westerners and two Chinese[158] caused loud protests from Chinese in San Francisco. Several hundred Chinese gathered at the CCBA to question the motive of the new company and to demand a detailed account of the high repair cost for the *Nanjing*.[159]

Although no evidence of embezzlement or ill management of funds was found in the purchase and repair of the *Nanjing*, Chinese suspicion of Westerners taking over the business killed the new company. It had been Chinese nationalism that gave birth to the China Mail; it was now their determination to keep it a purely Chinese American business that temporarily stopped the original company from an immediate demise. The leaders of the company managed to pay off the debt incurred by the purchase and repair of the *Nanjing*.[160]

The effort to sustain this Chinese American business was finally crushed by the reality of the capitalist world. In the wake of World War I, the transpacific business witnessed a rapid increase in competition. Such fierce competition threatened the already struggling China Mail. In 1922, Chen Duanpu, president of the company at the time, journeyed to Beijing to petition the Chinese government for financial aid. The Beijing government at the time had its hands full dealing with regional warlords and the challenge from the GMD in the south. Chen then stopped in Hong Kong, hoping to get support there. Shrewd Chinese businessmen in Hong Kong said that they had to investigate before making any commitment. Resisting Caucasian involvement while asking for aid from the Chinese government or Hong Kong businessmen attested again to the Chinese American identity that helped establish and sustain the company. With no extra help, the company struggled to keep itself floating by calling on all Chinese in the United States to use its services. "Take the ships of the China Mail or use the ships to transport goods," its stock holders cried out, "in order to maintain Chinese integrity and guard the right to profit" in the transpacific business.[161] In 1923, the company's debt of more than $1,740,000 finally led to its bankruptcy.[162]

The establishment of the China Mail Steamship Company was a direct outcome of Chinese nationalism, brought to a height by Japanese imperialism, and of racial discrimination against Asians in the United States. Yet its greatest significance was that it proved the maturation of a Chinese American identity. This new sense of Chineseness identified with an idealized Chinese culture yet criticized Chinese realities; it maintained Chinese ethnicity yet showed a willingness to be an integral part of American society and demonstrated a determination to help defend and modernize China from across the ocean.

4 An Ideological Foundation of the Chinese American Identity, 1916–24

In late December 1915, Yuan Shikai declared that January 1, 1916 would be the first day of his Hong Xian Empire. Yuan Shikai's attempt to restore a monarchical system in China met with strong resistance from Chinese in the United States. An angry editorial carried in *Chinese World* called for a concerted effort to fight a life-and-death struggle against Yuan's restoration of the monarchical system. Having supported and defended Yuan's government against Sun Yat-sen's challenge, *Chinese World* stated that the Chinese people had supported Yuan because he had saved China from national division and had vowed not to restore the monarchical system.[1] The other two major newspapers, *Chung Sai Yat Po* and *Young China*, also expressed strong opposition to the restoration of a monarchy.[2] After this unanimous condemnation in the press, the All American Overseas Chinese Military Fundraising Bureau for the National Protection Army in China was founded.[3]

This overwhelming rejection of the monarchical system in China served as an element of an ideological foundation for the new Chinese American identity. Before 1916, in debating the meaning of a modern China and a modern sense of Chineseness, Chinese in the United States demonstrated their own visions and revealed their transcultural values. Between 1916 and 1924, major events in China further widened the gap between China's reality and American Chinese visions of a modern

China. An examination of this widening gap demonstrates the emergence of a comprehensive ideology that supported and guided the new Chinese American identity.

Underlying this comprehensive ideology were four elements that crystallized as the Chinese in the United States responded to events in China. The first element was faith in republicanism as a suitable political system for a modern China. This conviction solidified as Chinese in the United States opposed Yuan's monarchical restoration and supported the National Protection Army in China. The second element was a strong belief that Confucianism and traditional Chinese cultural values should be preserved as the core of a modern sense of Chineseness. Chinese in the United States made this belief very clear as they opposed the New Culture Movement in China, which condemned Confucius's principles and traditional Chinese cultural values as obstacles to progress. The third element was the inclusion of selected Christian values in envisioning a modern China and constructing a Chinese American identity. This acceptance of Christian values was demonstrated not only through disagreement with the anti-Christian movement in China but more significantly through the ways in which second-generation Chinese Americans were raised and the focus on establishing permanent Chinese American communities. The fourth element was the strong belief that capitalism was the best economic system for a modern and prosperous China. This view conflicted with the political platform of the Guomindang (GMD) in China. In 1923, the GMD planned to ally with the Soviet Union and cooperate with the newly established Chinese Communist Party (CCP).

Republicanism versus Monarchical Restoration

The possibility of a monarchical restoration in China appalled Chinese in the United States. To an increasing number of them, republicanism seemed the world's most modern form of government, and keeping it in China would help improve their status in the United States. Not all nations could enjoy a republican form of government. In the eyes of Chinese in the United States, the establishment of the Republic of China had demonstrated to the world that China was a great Asian nation, comparable to the United States on the American continent and France in Europe.[4] Republicanism would thus help to correct the Western image of China as a "backward and uncivilized" nation. Restoring the monarchical system in China, on the other hand, would only reinforce the negative view of Chinese people as too backward to appreciate the best form of government. If Chinese could not maintain a republican govern-

ment in China, as the argument went, they might logically not be entitled to enjoy equal rights in the United States. American Chinese feared
that political change in China might be used to justify further and more
severe prejudice and discrimination against them in the United States.[5]

Republicanism was an inclusive concept used by all three major
Chinese-language newspapers under investigation. For *Young China*, only
a republican form of government could realize the three principles of the
people: nationalism, democracy, and people's livelihood. For *Chung Sai
Yat Po*, only republicanism would guarantee liberty or freedom, equality, and universal love. For *Chinese World*, constitutionalism was the
essence of a modern China.

However, the movement for monarchical restoration picked up its
momentum in China right after China's humiliating acceptance of Japan's
Twenty-one Demands. Conservative forces pushed for the change of the
political system in the name of saving the nation from domestic turmoil
such as the Second Revolution and foreign encroachment such as Japan's
demands. The restoration movement was helped by Frank J. Goodnow,
an American constitutional scholar and soon-to-be president of the Johns
Hopkins University. Acting as Yuan's constitutional advisor, Goodnow
in August 1915 prepared a memorandum, at Yuan's request, comparing
merits of the republican and monarchical forms of government, with
special reference to China's conditions. According to Goodnow, "If the
present [Chinese] government could be turned over to a monarchy without disorder, if a scheme of succession could work out, and if the monarchy established should be a constitutional monarchy, then I believe that
China would make faster and longer strides than as a republic."[6] Such
an argument, made by a prominent constitutional scholar from the United States, a model of the republican form of government, gave the necessary support to the conservative forces in China. In late 1915, a Peace
Planning Society was organized for the sole purpose of helping Yuan restore a monarchy in China. The society argued specifically that monarchism was better than despotism under the name of a republic. It also
argued that military generals would be more faithful to an emperor in
hopes of securing their wealth and positions for their offspring and that
a devoted army would, in turn, deter rebellions.[7]

The monarchical movement triggered strong reactions from all three
newspapers, representing the full spectrum of opinion in the Chinese
American community. First of all, Yuan's monarchical restoration proved
that *Young China*, the newspaper of the GMD in the United States, had
been right to accuse Yuan of harboring the ambition of becoming emperor
and to condemn Yuan as an enemy of the new republic in China. As Yuan

was contemplating his restoration, the paper theorized on the essence of republicanism and the meaning of patriotism. In a republic, which was made up of land, people, and sovereignty, the government existed to carry out policies made according to the will of the people, the paper stated, whereas in a monarchy people had to follow the will of the monarch. Now that China was a republic, it was the duty of the Chinese people, including those in the United States, to stop the government from destroying it.[8]

The paper called Yuan "the thief,"[9] accusing him of cheating all Chinese, stealing the presidential power, and trying to destroy the republic to satisfy his own selfish ambition. The only way to stop Yuan from destroying the republic, *Young China* argued, was for all Chinese to rise up against him. Now that Yuan had revealed his real ambition, the Chinese people would have to show their worth as republican citizens by checking his betrayal. The paper feared that China would die not only because of a bad government and corrupt bureaucracy but also because of "subservient people."[10]

When Yuan declared his empire, the paper suggested that all Chinese should act as responsible citizens and refuse to recognize the Year of Hong Xian, the title of the empire. It explained that the National Protection Army that opposed Yuan was "not a revolutionary army" and that its aim was not to take revenge against Yuan. Instead, the army was fighting to preserve the republic and to rid China of the seeds of turmoil. It reasoned that only republicanism could bring "humanitarianism and justice" to all Chinese. For all these reasons, it called upon Chinese everywhere to support and donate money for the army's military effort.[11]

For the first time since Yuan had become president of the Republic of China in early 1912, *Young China* finally had a chance to promote a nonrevolutionary cause. By reasoning that the National Protection Army was "not a revolutionary army" and that republicanism meant "humanitarianism and justice," its managers and editorial writers showed they were aware that most Chinese in the United States preferred peace and order to rebellions or revolutions.[12] At the same time, this argument implied that China, as a nation in the international community, had not been treated with humanitarianism and justice for several decades and that Chinese in the United States were still fighting for humanitarian and just treatment for themselves. By focusing on such characteristics of republicanism, the paper was finally speaking a language familiar to the majority of Chinese in the United States.

To *Chung Sai Yat Po*, China's road to modernization could not be anything other than republican. According to the paper, republicanism was the only political system that could guarantee freedom for and equality among all people and bring about the gradual realization of a middle-class society essential for the practice of democracy.[13] The paper had articulated its strong conviction that China had a superior cultural heritage to draw upon in its search for modernization. However, it admitted that China had become a backward and weak country compared with the fast-developing West. To catch up and restore its status in the world, China had to reform and progress. The establishment of the republic had brought China out of "a moribund feudal system" into a modern and progressive state, a definite step forward. Yuan's restoration of the monarchical system was seen as a retrogressive act, instigated by "a conservative party" in China.[14]

When the republic was supplanted by Yuan's monarchical restoration, *Chung Sai Yat Po* immediately called on all Chinese to put aside their differences to oppose Yuan and his conservative party.[15] The paper celebrated the independence of Yunnan, the first province to secede from the central government and the province in which the National Protection Army raised its flag, and hoped that Guangdong, the province from which most Chinese in the United States had come, would soon follow Yunnan's example.[16] *Chung Sai Yat Po* called Yuan "the thief," one who had stolen the presidential power of the Chinese republic and turned China into a monarchy.

When Yuan, under pressure from military leaders and foreign countries, abandoned his monarchical attempt on March 22, 1916,[17] *Chung Sai Yat Po* editorialized on the meaning of patriotism in a republic. Now that the short-lived monarchy was gone, China needed a concerted effort among different factions to unify the country, organize a new republican government, and elect a president, all based on the collective interest of the Chinese nation.[18] Patriotism in a republic, the paper argued, required noble character, a sense of responsibility, and devotion to working for the happiness of all Chinese people.[19]

Chung Sai Yat Po thus stated clearly its moral prescription for China. Rebellion or revolution against Yuan could be rationalized when it was the only way to save the republic, but once Yuan gave up his monarchy, rebellion or factionalism no longer had any legitimacy. All patriots should be selfless people working for the preservation and development of republicanism, which was the only way for China to restore its greatness in the world and provide for the happiness of all Chinese people.

For *Chinese World*, Yuan's restoration of a monarchy was an autocratic challenge to the primacy of a constitution in China. Although the paper had favored constitutional reforms and supported a constitutional monarchy before the 1911 Revolution, it had also welcomed the actual result of the 1911 Revolution, which was the establishment of the Republic of China, and had been supporting republicanism ever since. For this paper, the most essential element for a strong, modern China was government according to a constitution. Having amassed all political powers in his own hands by dissolving the National Assembly and proclaiming the restoration of monarchism, Yuan had virtually declared the death of constitutional principles in China. Yuan's action thus betrayed all Chinese people, so rebellion against such a national traitor was "perfectly justified." The paper referred to the National Protection Army in China as "the Republican Army," for its purpose was to save the Chinese republic.[20]

Chinese World also argued that Yuan's monarchical restoration was bringing disaster to China. When the paper advocated constitutional reforms and argued against revolution in China before the overthrow of the Qing dynasty, it reasoned that China could not afford to have a radical revolution, for that would provide opportunities for foreign powers to divide and engulf it. When the 1911 Revolution ended with no physical division of China and the establishment of a republic, the paper celebrated that result; it had been an advocate for protection and maintenance of the republic. Then Yuan's monarchical attempt pushed China to the verge of national extinction, according to *Chinese World.* The paper reasoned that China could no longer afford such drastic changes. First of all, stated the paper, China was beset with domestic poverty, natural disasters, and especially rebellious forces. A change in its political system would only deepen the problem of poverty and open the way for more rebellions. Second, the world had finally recognized the Republic of China, and a change of the form of government while China was still very weak would cause China to lose legitimacy in the world.[21]

When Yuan abandoned the monarchical attempt, the paper carried a series of editorials proclaiming constitutionalism as the only road to China's salvation. According to this paper, the most important element of a modern nation-state was its people, who had the natural right to make decisions for the future of their country. The paper detailed the workings of a constitutional government: a legislative body, composed of representatives democratically elected by the people; an executive body, composed of a president elected by the people and a cabinet carrying out laws and policies; and a judicial body, making judgments and decisions independent of the other two government branches.[22] Although *Chinese World* called such a system "constitutionalism," it was modeled exactly after the U.S. system. The success of such a constitutional system, the paper pointed out, depended on a people equipped with a sense of responsibility as masters of the country and a government determined to adhere to constitutional principles.[23]

The expressed ideological preference for republicanism as opposed to monarchism reached beyond the three newspapers. As early as September 1915, the Chinese Consolidated Benevolent Association (CCBA), on behalf of all Chinese in the United States, wrote a letter to President Wilson, asking him to advise Yuan not to restore monarchism in China. The letter said that monarchical restoration was against the wishes of most Chinese people. Such an attempt would inevitably plunge China into chaos, which would not benefit American interests in China.[24] This public expression of opposition against the monarchical restoration attempt by the most important American Chinatown organization opened the gate for such expressions. The CCBAs in Boston and New York made their public announcements against the attempt in October 1915.[25] Chinese in Chicago, Detroit, Canada, Cuba, Portland (Oregon), and Mexico started to raise funds in preparation for military actions in China.[26] In San Francisco, a Chinese theater advertised performances to raise funds for the defense of republicanism.[27]

On January 1, 1916, Chinese in central California gathered in Fresno to celebrate the fifth anniversary of the Republic of China. According to a report in *San Francisco Chronicle*, the gathering was "the most remarkable and epochal mass meeting ever held by the Chinese in Central California." Chinese sang the new Chinese national anthem, which, according to the *Chronicle* reporter, was to the tune of the Star-Spangled Banner. Participants at the meeting expressed enthusiastic support of the idea of raising funds for the anti-Yuan movement in China.[28]

Support of fundraising for the revolt against Yuan's monarchical restoration was expressed throughout Chinese communities in the United States. Although there was a report that nearly $1 million had been raised for the revolt against Yuan's monarchical restoration by early 1916,[29] a formal organization did not appear until after the CCBA in San Francisco received "official authorization" (*weiren*) from Tang Jiyao, the governor of Yunnan, to raise funds for the National Protection Army in April. An All American Overseas Chinese Military Fundraising Bureau for the National Protection Army was organized in the middle of May 1916, under the leadership of the CCBA.[30] This fundraising effort was supported by various American Chinatown organizations, including the seven district associations, the GMD, the Chinese American Citizens Alliance (CACA), the Zhigongtang, the Constitutionalist Party, the Chinese Christian Church Alliance, *Young China, Chinese World, Chung Sai Yat Po,* and *Ta Tung Yat Po.*[31]

Yuan's monarchical restoration served as an impetus for all Chinese in the United States to unite. The fundraising bureau thus represented a rare historical moment in which American Chinese were united in their response to politics in China.[32] However, the organization of the fundraising effort came too late. Yuan died in June 1916 and with him the attempt for monarchical restoration. Therefore, no result of the fundraising effort was reported in any of the three Chinese-language newspapers under investigation.

Besides fundraising activities, Chinese in the United States organized their own volunteer corps to participate in the anti-Yuan military campaigns in China. In these Overseas Chinese Corps of Volunteers (*Huaqiao yiyong tuan*), more than 500 young Chinese men from the United States and Canada "took upon themselves the responsibility for national salvation" and vowed to wipe out national traitors and restore the republic. The volunteers were sent to Japan for concentrated military training and then arrived in Qingdao, China in May 1916. Because the Corps was equipped with three planes, it distributed leaflets from the air to people in China, which helped create strong feelings among citizens against Yuan's restoration attempt. After Yuan Shikai died on June 6, 1916, the Overseas Chinese Corps of Volunteers dissolved, and its members all returned to North America, for none of them was "seeking personal fame or gain" in volunteering for the mission.[33] Considering that the "dare-to-die" teams, organized by the Tongmenghui in early 1912 for a proposed northern expedition to militarily unify China, were discouraged by Sun Yat-sen and thus never left the United States, the Volunteer Corps was an extraordinary effort organized by Chinese in North America. It was a clear expression by American Chinese for republicanism against monarchism. They were ready to sacrifice their lives to defend the republican form of government in China.

Preserving Confucianism and Chinese Traditional Culture

In mid-September 1916, Chinese in the United States cabled the Chinese government, protesting its proposal to abolish Confucianism in China. One of these cables said, "Chinese civilization is rooted in Confucianism. To abolish Confucianism is to commit national suicide, for such an act cuts off the fountainhead for Chinese civilization. Education should make Confucianism its principal content. We hereby beg you [the government] to keep it."[34]

Chinese World pointed out in a series of editorials that there was no conflict between republicanism and Confucianism.[35] In fact, the paper argued that Confucianism was of utmost importance if China wanted to end its current political, social, and economic problems. According to the paper, China had stood in the world as a great civilization for thousands of years and had survived wars and natural disasters mainly because of "the four pillars of the nation." The paper concluded that if the four pillars were not observed, China was doomed.[36]

The "four pillars of the nation" were *li,* decorum or rites; *yi,* righteousness or duty; *lian,* integrity or honesty; and *chi,* sense of shame. These four pillars were the essence of Confucian world order. If all under the heavens conformed to accepted standards of conduct, carried out their proper duties, maintained integrity, and subdued selfish desires, whose expression was shameful, the world would be perfect, according to Confucius and his disciples. Besides such standards for moral and social conduct, Confucianists also prescribed a hierarchical society in which the refined and educated ruled and set the standards for moral and social conduct, and the inferior or common people obeyed and followed. Also in such a Confucian hierarchical society, men were superior to women, and the old controlled the young. Rebellion or disobedience from the ruled, the inferior, and the controlled constituted disconformity to prescribed rules of conduct, negligence of one's duties, and expression of a lack of integrity and were thus shameful and punishable behaviors.

Both the cable and editorial argument highlighted the centrality of Confucianism and Chinese traditional culture in Chinese American life and identity at the time. Racial prejudice and cultural discrimination notwithstanding, American Chinese believed that their native culture provided the most appropriate framework for a rich and harmonious life and that nothing was superior to it. Alice Fong, who was born in California, took pride in her Chinese cultural heritage. When she became a Christian, she did not see any conflict between what she had learned from her parents about Confucian virtues and Christian morals. In fact, she realized that Confucius' teachings "contained all the virtues of Christian teachings, that only those who were unfamiliar with the heritage of China's wisdom failed to see that."[37] To the immigrant generation, Confucian virtues and Chinese values were superior. In *Fifth Chinese Daughter,* a novel by Jade Snow Wong about her experience of growing up in San Francisco Chinatown, the author's father firmly stated that nothing could replace "the practical experience of the Chinese, who for thousands of years have preserved a most superior family pattern."[38]

The centrality of Confucianism in Chinese American identity was also enhanced by a possibility of being driven out of the United States and back to China. Despite the growing number of families established in the United States, American Chinese were under the constant threat of having to go back to China. The 1912 congressional attempt to deport wives and children of deceased merchants, the fact that some came into the country on purchased papers and therefore lived in precarious legal status, and other legislative or administrative proposals further regulating Chinese immigration and residence served as sources of fear. Thomas Chinn's parents decided to move the family from Oregon, where there was no Chinese school, to San Francisco in 1919, to send their children to a Chinese school. Thomas Chinn recollected that his parents wanted him and his siblings to learn the Chinese language and culture because they "always felt . . . that they may be forced to go back to China, not by choice but because they were kicked out." But Thomas was not learning much from his Chinese school in San Francisco, partly because his earlier years were spent in Oregon, where he played with white children and spoke English even with his siblings. In 1924, his father decided to send Thomas back to China to learn the Chinese language and culture.[39] Thomas's parents' decisions to move to San Francisco, which was financially a disadvantage to the family, and to then send their eldest son to China at the expense of their limited financial resources were based on their concerns for their children. They apparently were afraid that their children would not be able to handle life in China without the language and an understanding of Chinese culture if they were forced to leave the United States for China.

The centrality of Confucianism in Chinese American identity was also supported by Chinese men for control over women and by the Chinatown elite for protecting their own privileged positions. Confucian social order was reached when everyone in society behaved according to the prescribed rules of conduct and their respective social positions. The Confucian hierarchy delegated power to the educated, positioned men in control of women, and regarded seniority as equivalent to wisdom. CCBAs in American Chinatowns therefore were strong supporters of Chinese schools. Chinese schools opened and concluded school semesters with ceremonies worshipping Confucius.[40] Chinatown CCBAs organized celebrations of Confucius's birthday.[41] *Chinese World*, representing the American Chinatown elite, repeatedly argued against equality and freedom for women. Chinese men preferred to marry China-born girls because American-born girls had too much freedom and no longer knew their subordinate position in the Confucian hierarchy. According to Chin Cheung, an American-born Chinese man in Seattle, American-born girls were "too independent. [They] go out in the evening, dance, spend money, don't like stay home much. . . . Girls this country don't make so good wives as girls in China. Girls in China have more respect I think for husband. They look after husband better; look after children better; have more children." Chin Cheung thus wanted his children to receive a Chinese education first, because "If they don't have this old country education they no good."[42]

This desire to keep women subordinate to men and to have children behave according to Confucius's teachings stemmed from another reality of life in American Chinatowns. Some Chinese men still kept their families in China. To ensure that such transpacific families would stay together, observation of female chastity, filial piety, and female devotion to husbands and subordination to in-laws were essential.

Whereas Chinese in the United States regarded Confucian precepts as essential elements in their search for a modern Chinese identity, intellectuals in China sought more radical ways to solve their country's problems. Led by Chen Duxiu, dean of humanities at Beijing University, and Hu Shi, who studied with pragmatist philosopher John Dewey at Columbia University and was then a professor of philosophy at Beijing University, Chinese intellectuals came to believe that the country's political problems were rooted in Chinese traditional culture in general and in Confucianism in particular. The *New Youth*, a magazine edited by Chen, Hu, and some other Chinese intellectuals, compared the health of Chinese society to a human body. According to the *New Youth*, Chinese society was full of "old and rotten cells" that had accumulated for thousands of years. If the society were to flourish again, these cells had to be replaced by new and vital cells.[43] By "new and vital cells," they meant China's youth as well as "Mr. Democracy" and "Mr. Science." According to Chen, for "Mr. Democracy" to be introduced to China, "we are obliged to oppose Confucianism, the codes of rituals, chastity of women, traditional ethics, and old fashioned politics." To make way for "Mr. Science," Chen continued, "we have to oppose traditional arts and traditional religion."[44]

With such a theoretical foundation, China's intellectuals started campaigns aimed at eradicating the roots of China's problems. A New Culture Movement was launched, with Chen attacking Chinese traditions and calling for an ideological awakening among China's youth under the slogan "Down with Confucius and Sons." Hu concentrated on a literary reform, de-emphasizing literary Chinese in favor of writing in the Chinese vernacular and advocating literature of contemporary spirit, not of imitations of ancient works.[45]

Such attacks on Confucianism and Chinese traditional culture ran counter to the needs and desires of many Chinese in the United States.

They not only regarded Confucian precepts as guidance in their life but also believed that neither traditional culture nor Confucianism hindered China's development and modernization. *Chinese World* answered the accusations of New Culture Movement intellectuals one by one. The paper argued that China did not have to borrow from the West because Confucianism not only prescribed moral standards but also advocated civilian participation in politics, emphasized economic development, and promoted humanitarianism. In fact, the paper said, so-called Western democracy had been practiced in China for thousands of years. An emperor's right to rule was based on civilian support, without which the emperor, together with the dynasty, would fall. One of the principal tasks of the governing body under Confucianism was to take care of the welfare of the people. In the modern world, that meant developing the national economy to make China fit for survival. Confucianism was humanitarian in nature, for it was against wars and ill treatment of prisoners of war.[46]

To counter the attack on China's traditional arts and religion and the effort to introduce "science" into China, *Chinese World* argued that Confucius was a great scientist who advocated reason against superstitious fallacy. Confucius, on his own, had concluded that the earth could not be square, for its corners would not be covered by the sky, which was believed to be round.[47]

Chinese World worried that intellectuals in China had taken the wrong road and that their New Culture Movement was plunging China more and more deeply into trouble. People hated Confucianism because it prescribed more duties than rights, the paper pointed out. The attack on Confucianism played into the hands of corrupt politicians and despotic militarists. The movement would prolong the turmoil in China, eventually leading to the downfall of China as a nation.[48]

The literary reform was a "laughable movement" that would kill the Chinese language, *Chinese World* maintained. As Chinese intellectuals saw it, such reform aimed to make education and literature more accessible to ordinary Chinese, but *Chinese World* argued that the written language had been an important means of unifying all China, a vast country with numerous spoken dialects. Replacing the standard written language with the spoken vernacular, consisting of different dialects, would render people in China unable to communicate with each other, thus leading to the country's disintegration. The paper also believed that written Chinese was concise and precise, whereas the vernacular Chinese was lengthy and tedious, adding difficulty to the learning process. Furthermore, literary Chinese embodied the accumulated wisdom and intelligence of the Chinese nation and was a symbol of the great Chinese civilization. For both practical and symbolic reasons, the paper concluded, literary reform was a mistake.[49]

However, such fundamental differences did not suggest any lessening of patriotic or nationalist feelings for China among the American Chinese. When in May 1919 news came that the Paris Peace Conference had agreed to transfer Germany's rights in China's Shandong Province to Japan,[50] Chinese in the United States responded rapidly and strongly. The San Francisco CCBA, Chinese Chamber of Commerce, Chinese Church Alliance, Chinese Language Newspapers Association, CACA, Confucian Society, and Constitutionalist Party cabled the Peace Conference and the Chinese delegation in Paris, rejecting the decision. Some of these organizations also cabled the president of the United States and the U.S. Congress, asking them to maintain justice and to refuse to recognize the decision concerning Shandong.[51] Patriotic organizations were established, and fundraising activities followed. The San Francisco CCBA initiated the National Salvation Association (*Jiuguo hui*), which raised funds for the northern government to resist Japan's demands on Shandong.

The nationalism aroused over the Shandong territory once again gathered support beyond political factions. The GMD in the United States, which supported the southern government in China and argued that it was the northern government that had sold out Shandong to Japan, organized the Chinese National Welfare Society in America (*Qiaomei zhongguo guomin waijiao hui*) and started to raise funds for the patriotic cause.[52] While *Chinese World* publicized the organization of the society, *Chung Sai Yat Po* carried an editorial endorsing the society and encouraging American Chinese to make generous contributions to it.[53] In a letter to Joseph Rowan and D. J. O'Connell, members of the U.S. House of Representatives, H. C. King, president of the society, claimed that the Chinese National Welfare Society represented "nearly all Chinese residents in America." The letter further said that "on behalf of our country," the society "appeals to you . . . and begs of you to do your utmost to see that justice is done to our country."[54]

The response to "the Shandong decision" in China demonstrated a national awakening that the New Culture Movement intellectuals had been trying to arouse. On May 4, 1919, together with angry mass protests against the government betrayal of Chinese sovereign rights, college students in Beijing marched to the house of Cao Rulin, minister of communications, and demanded to see Zhang Zongxiang, China's minister to Japan, who was having a meeting with Chao in the house at the time. When Zhang refused to come out, students set fire to the house.[55] The arrest of more than thirty students by the police on the spot triggered large-scale demonstrations in Beijing and other major Chinese cities. The incident, which happened on May 4, gave a new name and brought new meaning to the New Culture Movement. Known as the May Fourth Movement, it focused on anti-imperialism and antifeudalism. Whereas the former aroused nationalistic feelings among the Chinese people, the latter examined traditional culture and Confucianism as a way to find fundamental solutions to China's political, economic, and social problems.

The scope and significance of the May Fourth Movement are beyond this study, but the fact that it further questioned the precepts of Confucianism widened the gap between the ideological foundation of Chinese American identity and politics in China. As student demonstrations in China turned into campus strikes and violence against authorities, *Chinese World* editorialized that there was a difference between the May Fourth demonstrations and the widespread student agitation throughout China. The former, the paper said, derived from students' patriotism, whereas the latter was nothing but anarchism among young people that threatened China's educational system. The paper believed that the young students were being used by anarchists in China to destroy Chinese culture and civilization.[56] The May Fourth demonstrations were expressions of patriotism. However, campus strikes and students' actions against authorities upset the established order and thus were a violation of propriety.

Also against Confucian propriety was the liberation of women. *Chinese World* argued that woman's position at home was as important as man's responsibilities outside the home. At home, women with good education and high moral standards would bring up children with useful talents for the country. If women successfully fulfilled such an important role in the society, their contribution could never be ranked as inferior to that of men. Yet the women's liberation movement was sending women into tea houses and salons, where they talked about politics with men. These women, with very little education and knowledge about the real world, were only making fools of themselves, the paper pointed out.[57] Women's appearance in tea houses and salons, strictly male social territory, and participation in politics were gross violations of Confucian propriety and a threat to male domination.

Chinese World's opinion of women's participation in politics reflected the conservative mindset not only of Chinese men but also of American men. It was only in 1920 that the nineteenth amendment to the U.S. Constitution was passed to give women the right to vote. Chinese American women themselves had been struggling for freedoms, not political rights. As Sucheng Chan pointed out, whereas Chinese American men "fought for their rights—the right to be in the United States, the right to vote, and the right to own property," "Chinese American women fought for freedoms—the freedom to not behave according to Chinese customs, to choose their own mates, to work, and to be recognized for their individual achievements."[58] Even the reform-minded Wu Panzhao told a newspaper reporter, "As for equality between men and women, and between their relative positions in the world, that need not enter into the discussion. There is no equality in nature. Everywhere, in physique, in intellect, in all her affairs, we find inequality. So the status of the woman is the home, and there is no excuse for her not being there and rearing a family. It is her province to raise the family, and that should settle the question."[59]

Chinese World's response seemed to represent the prevailing mentality among Chinese in the United States. There was no opposition to or even controversy over the arguments expressed by the paper. *Young China* had no substantial editorial on the New Culture Movement or the Literary Reform in China until after the May Fourth demonstrations. In late June 1919, *Young China* carried an editorial titled "On the Conflict between the New and Old Schools of Thought in Beijing." The editorial linked the old school with "dark forces in Beijing" and the new school with young democratic forces in China. It called on Chinese students in the United States to write to the paper, supporting the Chen-Hu group in China.[60] Yet the paper published no such supportive letters or articles. In August of the same year, the paper's editorial staff wrote another article praising the students' antigovernment activities and hoping that their next step would be to get rid of Xu Shichang and Duan Qirui, the president and the prime minister of the northern government.[61] However, this editorial also emphasized the importance of education, which was being neglected in China because of strikes, demonstrations, and assaults on professors. It reasoned that the best road for China's national salvation was to develop its national industry and that education was the only way to prepare for industrial development.[62] The editorial was thus an expression of hope that reinforced some of the objections *Chinese World* expressed about the New Culture or May Fourth Movement.

Chung Sai Yat Po did not carry any comment on the New Culture and May Fourth Movement in China. It supported the students' demonstrations on May 4, 1919 and accused the northern government of being corrupt and impotent. It even argued that China would not have peace unless it got rid of the northern government.[63] However, the paper used the term "anarchism" to describe the student demonstrations and other activities of late 1919, pointing out that patriotism and anarchism were incompatible.[64]

Chinese American responses to events in China between 1916 and 1920 indicated a point of departure in the ideologies supporting the construction of a modern Chinese identity. Intellectuals inside China saw conflicts between democracy and Confucianism. Living in diaspora created different needs and desires and allowed distance and space from China's political reality. When the Chinese in diaspora disagreed with the theories and practices of the May Fourth Movement and continued to revere Confucianism and Chinese traditional culture, the result was that the Chinese identity constructed in the United States was more "in sympathetic resonance with Chinese culture."[65] This departure thus signified the appearance of "a cultural China,"[66] an imagined community outside China's geographic boundaries, not affected by Chinese politics or controlled by the Chinese government. Within this "cultural China," people identify themselves as Chinese, observe Chinese traditional festivals, take pride in being sons and daughters of the Yellow Emperor, and use Confucian precepts and traditional Chinese values in living their lives and in handling human relationships.

Christianity in the Construction of the Chinese American Identity

For most Chinese in the United States, revering Confucius and preserving Chinese traditional culture did not preclude adopting Christian values. According to *Chung Sai Yat Po*, China's national character (*guomin renge*) was in a state of bankruptcy in the early 1920s. The paper explained that since the establishment of the republic, China had witnessed contention for political power between different factions, two attempts at monarchical restoration,[67] military fighting between regional warlords, the New Culture Movement's blind allegiance to foreign ideologies such as socialism and communism, and popular inertia or ignorance of citizenship rights and duties. All this showed not only that traditional Chinese values were neglected but also that those values were no longer adequate for the construction of a modern democratic republic. Constructing a modern republic entailed restoring the essentials of Chinese traditional values, adding new elements, and finally perfecting the blend.[68]

To address the internal and external problems encountered by China in the 1910s and early 1920s, *Chung Sai Yat Po* believed that Christianity could offer and had already offered help in the following ways. The core of Christian beliefs was universal love. Sharing universal love would make people charitable for public causes, bring up filial children in the family, foster responsible citizens for the country, and create public servants for the society.[69] Not only would Christian values help solve China's problems, but Christian teachings also emphasized world peace and respect for each nation's own sovereignty and independence, which China badly needed at the time. After World War I started, President Wilson called on all Christians, including American Christian missions in China, to pray for world peace. The paper praised this call and believed that it was a true demonstration of Christianity's broad love and pointed out that Christian teachings went beyond political entities and emphasized interdependence between human beings, making Christianity an agent for world peace.[70]

Besides *Chung Sai Yat Po*'s advocacy of Christian values, diasporic life in the United States made the Christian church an inevitable part of the emergent Chinese American identity. Although there were only about 4,000 Christians among the Chinese in the United States in the early twentieth century, the Christian church played a significant role in the everyday life of many American Chinese. Whereas for women and youth, the hierarchical society prescribed by Confucianists was oppressive, Christianity was liberating for them. While Chinese intellectuals in China launched radical campaigns against Confucianism as a means of building a modern and democratic China where everyone enjoyed freedom and equality, American Chinese women and youth used modern American concepts such as individual rights and gender equality to negotiate for escape from the Confucian constraints and turned to Christian churches and facilities for spiritual solace and intellectual and physical growth.

It was the presence of women and the appearance of the second generation that characterized Chinese American community development of the 1910s and 1920s. The important role of women in this development was facilitated by Christian churches, and the coming of age of the second generation paralleled the growth of the Young Men's and Women's Christian Associations (YMCAs and YWCAs) and other church-sponsored programs. The San Francisco Chinatown YMCA was established in 1912 and served as an example for Chinatown YMCAs in New York City (established in 1916), in Oakland (established in 1921), and in Seattle (established in 1923).[71] Chinatown YMCAs were designed to provide programs and facilities that included physical training, which would help raise a generation of healthy and strong Chinese and correct the image of "the sick men"; practical or vocational training, which would bring education to ordinary Chinese to prepare them for modern life; and moral and ethical training, which would teach Christian love for all and a sense of duty as citizens of a republic.[72]

More specifically, YMCAs played the following roles. The YMCA in San Francisco's Chinatown sponsored lectures that taught Western ways of housekeeping. For example, in November 1912 the YMCA held a lecture on the hygiene of milk. Because dairy products were not part of a traditional Chinese diet, such knowledge was important. At the lecture, pictures and drawings were shown to demonstrate how cow's milk was taken and what harm it would do if it went bad.[73] According to *Chung Sai Yat Po*, part of the reason that Chinese were discriminated against was that Chinese neglected physical exercises and personal hygiene as well as "human compassion for each other" (*renlei huxiang qinai zhi jingsheng*).[74] In an effort to address such issues, the YMCA put on plays that encouraged martial qualities, disseminated ideas of civic responsibility, and promoted patriotism.[75]

The San Francisco Chinatown YMCA also sponsored talks on various subjects to educate and broaden the horizons of the Chinese community. In May 1913, it invited a secretary of the International YMCA, who had just finished a tour of the world, to share his travel experiences.[76] In June 1914, it sponsored a talk on California, its land, and its people. The speaker, a white clerk working for the California YMCA, showed more than sixty colored photos at the talk. In the same month, the YMCA sponsored another talk on morality. The speaker was a Chinese college student in California who had been studying religion for many years. Both these talks were advertised in *Chung Sai Yat Po* and welcomed all Chinese, men and women, to attend.[77] Another talk on morality, to be held at the YMCA, was scheduled for July 26, 1914.[78]

The Chinatown YMCA also played a significant role in transforming old Chinese customs and habits. Whereas *Chung Sai Yat Po* carried articles condemning Chinese traditions of encouraging early marriage, regarding women as property, allowing only arranged marriages, and taking concubines, the YMCA put on plays that advocated reforms of the overall Chinese customs and habits. As a result of such publicity, Chinese in San Francisco established a Customs Reform Society (*Gailiang fengsu hui*). *Chung Sai Yat Po*, the YMCA, and the society were advocating the same thing. They promoted marriages based on the free will of two mature adults, attacked wasteful Chinese wedding banquets, exposed superstitious beliefs about death, and introduced Western ways of conducting weddings and funerals.[79]

In the first few years after the establishment of the Chinatown YMCA in San Francisco, there were changes in the way of conducting weddings among American Chinese. *Chung Sai Yat Po* reported a Chinatown wedding that was carried out by a Christian minister in a Christian church as early as September 1912. The paper said that the wedding was between a Li and a Kuang, a prayer was offered, no relatives or friends were invited, no presents were accepted, and the newly wed couple were scheduled to return to China to help develop their native country.[80] King Yoak Won Wu was married to Reverend Daniel Wu at Grace Cathedral outside San Francisco's Chinatown in 1913. Mrs. Wu, who rightfully claimed to be among the first American Chinese women to have a Western wedding, said that she met her future husband without a matchmaker, and they decided not to go through the Chinese ceremony, where there would be "loud crying or colorful layers of clothes." Instead, she made her "own wedding dress and veil" and had a Christian wedding.[81]

Chinatown YMCAs also served as meeting places for the growing second generation. For Thomas Chinn, whose family moved to San Francisco from Oregon in 1919, when he was a teenager, the YMCA was the place where he met and made friends with contemporaries he otherwise would not have been able to meet. The YMCA had a library and a lounge where people could "sit and converse." Young Thomas, who had found himself a stranger in San Francisco, visited the Chinese YMCA daily. There he found Chinese people of his age who "spoke decent English."[82]

Because of its important role in Chinatown life, the YMCA in San Francisco Chinatown had been expanded several times since its establishment. In 1915, the Chinese YMCA headquarters moved to a much larger place to accommodate increasing demands for social, intellectual, religious, and vocational training. By mid-1922, $170,000 of a needed total of $200,000 had been collected from Chinese in the United States to build an entirely new YMCA building.[83]

Besides YMCAs, there were also Chinese YWCAs in American Chinatowns. These YWCAs provided programs and services similar to those of the YMCAs, mainly to teach Chinese women Christian values and prepare them for a life in the modern world. At the YWCA in San Francisco's Chinatown, which was established in 1916, Chinese immigrant women studied English, learned American ways of housekeeping and baby care, and obtained help when they had problems at home or received unfair treatment at work.[84] Just like Chinese YMCAs, Chinese YWCAs were aimed at helping to improve the public image of the Chinese people and to build the bridge, for immigrant women as well as for the American-born Chinese, between Chinatown and American mainstream society. The Chinese YWCA in San Francisco was well supported, and its programs were enthusiastically joined by local residents. Within four years of its establishment, the Chinese YWCA had a membership of 500 in 1920.[85]

Christian churches provided the earliest opportunities for American Chinese women to step outside the home and to learn English. In the early 1900s, when Chinese traditions dictated that women be homebound, Foo Tai, "a Christianized Chinese woman" in San Francisco, attended church meetings as president of the Chinese Women's Society of the Baptist Mission." Chan Fuk Tai, an educated Chinese woman in San Francisco, mingled with other women by teaching "Bible study, Chinese language, and embroidery to Chinese girls at the Baptist church." Other Chinese women stepped outside their homes to "have lunch or socialize" as members of the "(Congregational) Mothers and Daughters Society, (Presbyterian) Circle of the King's Daughters, and (Methodist) Missionary Society."[86] It was through church activities, as Judy Yung pointed out, that Chinese women developed social and leadership skills and were "among the earliest women leaders in the community to organize events on behalf of women, the church, and national salvation."[87]

Christian churches also offered English classes for Chinese immigrants, and Christians even delivered English lessons and tutoring to American Chinese homes. In the early 1920s, when Law Shee Low, an immigrant woman in the San Francisco Chinatown, "had no time to take advantage of English classes offered by the churches," her husband "asked a 'Jesus woman' to come teach her English" at her home.[88]

As these examples suggest, by the early 1920s, many connections had developed between Christian churches and American Chinese communities, and Christian values had become an integral part of American Chinese identity. Most Chinese in the United States at that time would have rejected arguments that Christian churches served only as agents of Western imperialism. Yet in China, in the wake of the Paris Peace Conference's resolution regarding the Shandong question, students and intellectuals at the forefront of the May Fourth Movement raised the banner of an anti-Christian movement. In early 1922, leaders of the World Student Christian Federation decided to hold a conference in China, hoping to present their side of the story about Christianity. Contrary to what the leaders wanted, the news of the conference only accelerated the rising tide of anti-Christian sentiment, resulting in the appearance of the Great Confederation of Antireligionists and the Anti-Christian Student Alliance in March 1922.

The main theoretical argument of the Antireligious (also called Anti-Christian) Movement was that religious teachings cultivated passivity and dogmatism and were obstacles to free and objective thinking and the development of society.[89] The more practical argument of the movement centered around Chinese history of the preceding seventy years, which was full of humiliating experiences caused by Western aggression. The Manifesto of the Anti-Christian Student Alliance declared that Christianity had been the instrument of imperialism. It concluded that Christianity was harmful to the development of a modern and independent China.[90]

Chung Sai Yat Po responded with a series of editorials that not only exposed and attacked the anti-Christian movement but also challenged the New Culture Movement. The paper argued that the anti-Christian argument prevailing in China was based on the remnants of antireligious movements throughout history. It had been commonly acknowledged by philosophers throughout the world that "all human beings were religious animals" and to deny such a fact was just an act of ignorance and ridicule.[91] The paper argued that if intellectuals embraced science at the expense of religion, they would develop the material part of a modern China without developing its spiritual part. The paper added that development of science depended on human intelligence and inspiration, both of which were available only when the spiritual part of human life was nurtured and given full play.[92]

The paper then launched a comprehensive attack on the New Culture Movement, arguing that it had gone too far. The paper agreed with the movement's attacks on the warlords' dominance of China's political arena because it believed that the survival of democracy depended on civilian control of the government apparatus and the political participation of all citizens. The paper even accepted literary reform because it supported making education accessible to all Chinese, which in turn would help create civic awareness among republican citizens. Yet instead of trying to achieve their original goals, the paper charged, the leaders of the movement had decided to attack Christianity and to advocate communism,[93] which, the paper argued, was just like "neglecting one's own field while weeding in someone else's." The paper compounded its criticism of the movement by holding its leaders responsible for the social turmoil and political anarchism in China.[94]

Chung Sai Yat Po's opposition to the anti-Christian movement in China also represented the dominant opinion of Chinese in the United States. Neither *Chinese World* nor *Young China* argued against it, and *Ta Tung Yat Po*[95] reinforced it. Representing working-class Chinese in the United States and run by the Zhigongtang, *Ta Tung Yat Po* agreed with *Chung Sai Yat Po* that religion was an undeniable part of human life. It hoped that there would be calm discussion about different religions and that freedom to believe in a religion would be protected in China.[96]

Regarding the issue of foreign control and Christianity, Chinese in the United States agreed with their compatriots in China. According to a Chinese Protestant, "China must have Christianity, but it must be its own Christianity, not what some one else thinks."[97] *Ta Tung Yat Po* emphasized that Christian churches in China should develop into independent churches controlled by Chinese, not by ministers from Europe or the United States.[98] *Chung Sai Yat Po* quite aptly pointed out that some independence and autonomy in managing Christian churches had already taken place in China.[99] For example, the China Christian Independent Church Association (*Zhongguo Yesujiao Zilihui*) in 1920 had more than 100 member churches, ran its own newspaper, *The Chinese Christian* (*Zhongguo Jidutubao*), organized its own annual national meeting and had its own bylaws. There were smaller but similar confederations of independent Christian churches in China. These churches were self-supporting, self-governing, and independent from foreign missionary control.[100]

Whereas foreign missionary control in China conflicted with the rise of Chinese nationalism, Christian churches and programs helped facilitate Chinese entry into American mainstream society. Although Chinese Christians in the United States also tried to gain independence from white missionary control, their urge for independence was not as acute. In New York City, Trust of God Mission, a Chinese self-supporting and self-governing church, was established in 1899. Chinese Christians in the San Francisco Bay Area founded the Chinese Independent Baptist Church 1906.[101] There was no obvious attempt at self-government between 1910 and 1930. For American Chinese, it was more important to defend their overall rights as residents or citizens of the United States.

Capitalism in the Construction of the Chinese American Identity

Besides republicanism and the blend of traditional Chinese and Christian values, the emerging Chinese American identity was supported by another ideology, the ideology of capitalism. Most Chinese immigrants came to the United States to seek a better life. Those who succeeded in getting rich would return to China with pride, but many who did not would not return. Those who did not get rich would say in Chinese that they did not "have the face to see their elders on the other side of the river" because they were failures. By 1920, 28 percent (12,559) of all Chinese on the mainland were in the laundry business and another 30 percent were in the restaurant business.[102] A common characteristic of American Chinese businesses was that many who worked in them owned shares.[103]

Their goal of accumulating wealth determined that they would not willingly support socialism or communism, and the political atmosphere

in North America in the late 1910s discouraged radical ideas. In October
1918, a GMD meeting held in Toronto, Canada was interrupted and several dozen Chinese were arrested and accused of conspiring against the
Allies in World War I. The GMD Canadian branch was ordered to dissolve
and, despite a lack of evidence, three GMD leaders were sentenced to one
year in prison.[104] Such fear of conspiracy and radicalism was a response to
the Bolshevik success in Russia. In the United States, the antialien and
antiradical Espionage Act of 1917 and the Sedition Act of 1918, together
with the deportations of and raids on aliens and radicals of the 1918–20
period, sent strong messages against socialist or communist sympathies.[105]

The combination of their own mentality and their environment determined that American Chinese would resent both socialism and communism. According to a study published in 1993, Chinese in the Soviet
Union enthusiastically supported the GMD's alliance with Soviet Union
and cooperation with the CCP. In fact, from 1918 to 1921, Chinese in the
Soviet Union used their geographic location to "deepen the understanding" and "broaden the contacting channel" between the Soviet government and the Third International on one hand and Sun Yat-sen on the
other.[106] In the United States, *Chinese World* depicted communism as an
evil force in the world. It said that Lenin and his like in Russia were re-
actionaries trying to take away individual rights and destroy the world
civilization in which constitutions and laws protected the ownership of
property and provided incentives for work and punishment for laziness.
In place of the civilized system in Russia, Lenin and his like had confiscated what others owned and created a dictatorship more cruel and tyrannical than any the world had ever witnessed.[107] The paper then warned
that such an evil force was coming to China. Years of disorder and lack
of industrial and commercial development had made China weak. This
weakness paved the way for radicals in China to sell the argument that
only socialism and communism could bring peace and dignity to Chinese
people. The editorial asked all Chinese patriots to help stop the spread
of this evil force.[108]

Chung Sai Yat Po believed that China did not have the material base
for socialism or communism. It pointed out that China's capitalist development was in such an infant stage that there was little existing capital
or means of production to be nationalized. The paper argued that advocating socialism and communism could only lead people to despise material
development, which China badly needed, and prevent capitalists from
investing for fear of having their capital nationalized.[109] Even *Young China*, which had been the most radical paper in the Chinese communities
in the United States, did not print editorials supporting socialism and com-

munism. The paper made reference to Lenin and his party in Russia as the "radical" party, whose influence was spreading like "a plague."[110]

Opposition to socialist and communist ideology was solidified by the fact that many Chinese in the United States had been sending money back to families in China. In the early 1920s, families living in *qiaoxiang* or "overseas Chinese villages" in Guangdong lived in "western houses" and owned land. According to one study, between 1914 and 1937, the overseas Chinese remittance to China totaled 15.7 percent of China's international revenue.[111] Most of this money was used to build "western houses" and to buy land.[112] These high-profile houses became targets of local bandits and poverty-stricken thieves. To protect their property and families, Chinese in the United States collected money to build walls around their villages or had their houses built like military strongholds with gun holes. Such fortified structures were a distinctive feature of "overseas Chinese villages" in the early 1920s.[113]

Besides building and defending their own homes and villages, Chinese in the United States had been investing in China. Some owned real estate, hotels, retail, entertainment, and financial businesses in Guangzhou in the early 1920s. Others owned shares in the steamship company that provided services between Guangdong and Hong Kong, the trolley company that provided services in Guangzhou, and the transportation business that built roads and ran buses in the districts from which most Chinese in the United States had come. The biggest investment for Chinese in the United States was the Ningyang Railroad, the first non-government-subsidized railroad built in China.[114]

Not every Chinese in the United States had surplus money to invest in China, but most Guangdong families with members in the United States belonged to the well-to-do class in China at the time. This fact conditioned them to oppose socialism or communism in China and to resist the idea of using Guangdong as a base for a further revolution aimed at national unification. What they wanted to see in China was capitalist development, in which they could participate, along with peace and stability for their families and their investments.

What happened in China proved to be just the opposite. Sun Yat-sen, frustrated by his failure to get moral and financial support from the West and the United States, became receptive to both the ideas expounded by New Culture Movement leaders and the help offered by the Soviet Union. Believing that China had to do away with its regional militarists, whom the New Culture Movement leaders accused of being remnants of the old culture and instruments of imperialism, Sun insisted on a further nationalist revolution to unify China under his leadership.

However, militarist-controlled provinces strongly supported the movement for federalism in China and the decentralization of power. The advocates of federalism hoped that once the system was in operation, provincial representatives would gather to make a new constitution, so that the war between the North and South would end.[115] In Guangdong, the chief military man, Chen Jiongming, was a strong supporter of the federalist system and an advocate of building an efficient provincial government in Guangdong and then joining with other self-governing provinces in a confederation. Chen also promoted the idea of "protecting the borders of Guangdong province and turning soldiers into civilians."[116]

Chen's idea apparently was more in tune with what Chinese in the United States wanted to see. To their dismay, however, Sun prevailed, and an "Extraordinary Parliament" was organized, which elected Sun "Extraordinary President." With the government headquarters based in Guangdong, this extraordinary government planned to restore true republicanism in China and appointed many advocates of the New Culture Movement, such as Chen Duxiu, to important government positions.

Such a situation in China gave Chinese in the United States reasons to reveal concern for their home province and opposition to the radical ideologies of communism and socialism. *Chinese World* argued that it was Sun who was bringing misery to the people of Guangdong and prolonging divisions in China. Running the government in Guangdong were people such as Chen Duxiu, who would destroy the values, moral standards, and family system by advocating anti-Confucian and antitraditional ideas and by promoting communism, the paper warned, which included collectivization of wives and property. The paper then reported that Sun's government program to unify China put heavy burdens on local people by issuing new currency, denying payment of bonds issued by the previous government, confiscating private property, and forcing businesses to contribute to its military funding.[117]

According to *Chinese World*, Sun's government in Guangdong was an evil force. Chinese traditional values concerning family were of utmost importance to most American Chinese, many of whom had wives and children in China. The chastity of women and the obedience and respectfulness of children, all of which were prescribed by Confucius's teachings, were the most important elements in maintaining their transpacific families. The ownership of private property had become sacred to most Chinese, who sacrificed their normal family life in the hope of accumulating wealth for themselves and their families. Ideological beliefs combined with practical business concerns and worries about the safety of their immediate families in Guangdong determined that American Chinese would oppose Sun's political aims and his plan to use Guangdong as his revolutionary base.

Chinese World was not the only paper to oppose Sun's plans. *Ta Tung Yat Po* accused the Sun government of selling a piece of land in Guangdong to Japanese interests who planned to build a race course. Such an action showed that Sun was "a national traitor" bought by Japanese business interests and that Sun had abused his power by confiscating private land and selling it to foreign businesses, the paper pointed out. The potential race course would turn Guangdong into a land of gamblers, the paper further argued.[118] This accusation was challenged by *Young China*, which denied such a deal between the Sun government and the Japanese business, resulting in "an editorial war" between the two papers that lasted ten days and had to be mediated by a third party.[119]

Ta Tung Yat Po further reflected the mentality of Chinese in the United States by supporting Chen Jiongming's rebellion against Sun's idea of a northern military expedition to unify China. The paper said that Chen favored reducing troops and military provisions, which would lessen the burden on the people of Guangdong. Chen, acting on behalf of the people of Guangdong, proposed to give the army and the people a rest, which, the paper argued, was indeed a "super tonic" for building peace and order in Guangdong.[120]

Chinese World editorialized that the fact that Chen, who was one of Sun's staunch supporters, had rebelled against Sun showed that Sun had exhausted all support. The paper pointed out that besides the "crimes" Sun was committing in China[121] and the miseries he was bringing to the people in Guangdong, he had also revealed his true nature as an absolute dictator. His catchwords were "obey my order," and he required all his followers to give fingerprints and pledge allegiance to him.[122] The paper even accused Sun of murdering people who voiced dissenting opinions.[123]

The split between Sun and Chen apparently worked against Sun. Before the split, Sun's supporters and GMD members carried out small-scale fundraising activities for the planned northern expedition; *Young China* reported, rather sporadically, individual donations. But right after the split, reports on fundraising activities or on individual donations suddenly vanished. *Young China* never said how the previously raised funds were used.

Sun's efforts to reorganize the GMD directly conflicted with the interests and mentality of many Chinese in the United States. Chen's rebellion frustrated Sun and made him willing to cooperate with almost anybody to achieve his goals. With secret cooperation from some militarists he used to hate, Sun was able to make a comeback in January 1923 by driving Chen and his troops out of Guangdong and into the neighboring province.[124] He then announced a joint declaration with Adolf Joffe, a Soviet communist agent, which started the formal alliance between Sun's GMD and the Soviet Union in 1923. Determined to unite all progressive forces in China, Sun initiated reorganization of his party to include *sanda zhengce*, or three major policies. These three policies were "to ally with the Soviet Union, to cooperate with the Chinese Communist Party, and to help the workers and peasants." The ultimate goal of these policies was to achieve the three principles of the people, namely nationalism, democracy, and people's livelihood in China. Delegates representing Chinese in the United States at the reorganization conference in Guangzhou in 1924 spoke against the three policies, particularly the alliance and cooperation with communism. But their opinion was ignored.[125]

The conflict between the new political platform of the GMD and the interests and ideology of many American Chinese was further revealed in the Chinese-language press. *Chinese World* pointed out that Sun had allied with Soviet Russia because he could not get diplomatic recognition for his so-called government from other countries. Soviet Russia had been isolated in the world because of its radical communist ideology. It was looking for opportunities to spread its ideology to stir up revolutions throughout the world and upset the world order. This radical, destructive communist ideology complemented Sun's ambition of becoming China's president by overthrowing the existing government. The paper concluded that Sun's alliance with Soviet Russia was a conspiracy.[126]

Measures adopted by the reorganized GMD, whose base was confined to Guangdong Province, further upset many Chinese in the United States. To protect its position in Guangdong against attacks from local militarists and military forces working for the northern government, Sun's regime increased taxes, confiscated properties that belonged to churches and other charitable organizations, and demanded contributions or loans from various businesses. According to *Chinese World*, Sun's government made the Guangdong Province a miserable and dangerous place to live.[127] To recruit soldiers, troops went among civilians, impressing young and able-bodied men. Such impressment put family businesses in jeopardy. Taking the work force away from the fields led to the starvation of hundreds and thousands. Worse still, the military situation destroyed families when husbands, fathers, and sons were killed.[128]

Chinese World also reported that public land in Guangzhou was being sold, piece by piece, to foreign businesses by Sun and his son, Sun Ke, who was made mayor of the city after Sun returned to Guangdong. It would not be long, the paper warned, before all Guangzhou's land was owned

by foreigners,[129] and this was only one of many methods Sun had adopted to increase revenues and maintain his government. Whereas impressment made life miserable and business stagnant in Guangdong, the Sun
government's sale of opium was a disgrace. The paper reminded its readers that the image of all Chinese as sick men derived from opium smoking, and that China had been fighting against this practice for many decades. But the Sun government, in the name of controlling the opium
trade, monopolized the crop and promoted its sale in order to collect more
revenues, the paper claimed.[130]

One other way to collect revenues the Sun government considered
was to use the customs revenues from the port of Guangzhou. Ever since
China's defeat in the Opium Wars of the 1840s and 1850s, the Chinese
customs service had been controlled by foreign governments. Customs
revenues went directly to foreign governments, which subtracted the
yearly payments of China's debts and indemnities before returning the
surplus to China's national government. After foreign governments refused Sun's request for the surplus of customs revenues from the port of
Guangzhou, he protested against Western imperialism and threatened to
use military force to seize control of the customs office.[131] Yet *Chinese
World* argued that Sun's threat was intended not to end but to encourage foreign intervention, which Sun hoped would help create chaos in
China so that he could topple the central government. Sun's threat was
thus another of his dirty conspiracies to achieve his selfish ambitions at
the expense of China's peace and unification.[132] The paper further editorialized that it was the internal competition for power that blocked the
abolition of China's extra territoriality,[133] not imperialism, as Sun and the
GMD had claimed.

All the complaints carried in *Chinese World* were echoed in *Chung
Sai Yat Po*. The latter referred to Soviet Russia's foreign policy as "socialist
imperialism" aimed at instigating social unrest in other countries for the
purpose of taking control. The paper reminded all Chinese that Soviet
Russia had stationed troops outside China's Manchuria, refused to recognize Mongolia as Chinese territory, and insisted on maintaining control over a railroad in China's northeast. The paper warned all Chinese
not to be carried away by Soviet Russia's radical propaganda, which, the
paper said, was only a shield for its imperialist ambitions in China.[134]

Chung Sai Yat Po carried a series of editorials describing a Guangdong beset with evil curses related to the existence of Sun's military government and his insistence on unifying the country by another revolution. The list included gambling, opium smoking, banditry, war, and
despotic and abusive government. The paper editorialized on each of these

curses, explaining how the current authorities, referring to Sun's government, were plundering Guangdong's resources, blocking development of its industry and commerce, destroying its moral fabric, and bringing misery to its people.[135]

Young China tried to defend Sun by arguing that the GMD's political platform differed from that of Soviet communism.[136] Yet the political situation in China was developing in the opposite direction from the common values embraced by the Chinese in the United States. The political discourse carried in the Chinese-language newspapers represented the interests of its readers and guided public opinion in Chinese American communities. The anti-Sun arguments carried in *Chinese World* and *Chung Sai Yat Po* were reinforced by correspondence readers had with families and relatives living in Guangdong. Because many of them owned businesses and property in that province, Sun's heavy taxes and demands for financial contributions directly affected the interests of many Chinese in the United States.

The crisis over Ningyang Railroad is just one example. The Ningyang Railroad Company (known as the Sunning Railroad Company before 1916) was established in 1905 by Chen Yixi, a Chinese who had made a fortune in the United States as a laborer and then a foreman for the Central Pacific Railroad.[137] Having acquired some experience in capitalist management and knowledge of railroad engineering, Chen decided to return to China and help develop China's railroad system. One of China's first railroads managed by Chinese, the Ningyang Railroad was financed by money collected mostly from Chinese in the United States. According to *Chung Sai Yat Po*, the company was worth more than 8 million Hong Kong dollars (about U.S.$6 million) in 1918. When Sun returned to Guangdong in early 1923, he asked the company to support him financially, and it contributed about 100,000 Chinese dollars (roughly U.S.$75,000). When Sun asked for another 300,000 (about U.S.$225,000), the president, Chen Yixi, refused, replying that it was beyond the company's financial ability.[138] Sun sent troops to take over the railroad; Chen fled to Hong Kong. From Hong Kong, Chen cabled to stockholders in the United States, asking them to protect the company.[139]

This event touched many Chinese in the United States, a large number of whom were from Ningyang, a region in Guangdong province. Ningyang people, whether stockholders or not, were affected because the railroad had been very beneficial to the economic life of their home region, where most of their families still lived. Stockholders, whether they were from Ningyang or not, were shocked by Sun's action and worked hard to protect their immediate interests. Sun finally withdrew the troops from the railroad when Chen Yixi agreed to lend some more money to the government.

Chung Sai Yat Po took this opportunity to ridicule Sun's slogan of "protecting the constitution" and his three principles of the people. The paper printed pictures of old Republic of China bonds and claimed that many Chinese in the United States were still holding those bonds, which Sun had promised to redeem after the republic was established, using them as evidence that Sun cheated these Chinese.[140] The paper then called on all Chinese, especially stockholders of the Ningyang Railroad Company, to unite in an effort to drive the Sun government out of Guangdong.[141]

Although *Chung Sai Yat Po* had the reputation among Chinese in the United States of being nonpartisan, the paper was very harsh in its attacks on the Sun government. In the wake of the Ningyang Railroad incident, it directly blamed the government for all the troubles and misery in Guangdong. It accused the government of selling Guangdong province and all China to foreigners and of allying with regional militarists such as Zhang Zuolin to block the unification of China.[142] The paper said that Sun had done everything to harm China and humiliate the Chinese people except opening ancestral graves for valuables to support his military effort, selling Chinese women overseas to increase his revenues, and eating human flesh and sucking human blood.[143]

Such severe attacks triggered a two-month editorial fight between *Chung Sai Yat Po* and *Young China*. Despite its effort, *Young China* could not find any reasonable arguments to defend Sun and the government in Guangdong. Sun's newly announced political platform was too radical and his measures were mostly against the interests and ideology of Chinese in the United States. The paper thus carried on the fight with personal attacks on the editorial writers of *Chung Sai Yat Po*, accusing them of speaking for traitors (namely, Chen Jiongming), wronging good people (namely, Sun and his colleagues in the government), betraying Chinese religion (by believing in Christianity), and manufacturing rumors. *Young China's* editorial attacks were largely groundless; they sounded confused and unconvincing. This fight revealed the confusing state of the GMD American branch and the waning of political conviction of party editorialists in the period after the GMD in China announced its new orientation in early 1923. In early 1924, *Young China* admitted that the new GMD was not getting support from Chinese in the United States.[144]

Beginning in early 1924, *Young China* took a new stand. It tried to distinguish the GMD from communism. The paper argued that whereas communism abolished private ownership of property, the GMD allowed it; whereas communism advocated working-class control over the means of production and the distribution of wealth, the GMD advocated the government's equal distribution of land and control over capital; whereas communism advocated social revolution, the GMD emphasized reforms of politics and improvements in people's livelihoods.[145] According to *Young China*, these were essential differences, visible in the GMD's new political platform. The charge that the GMD had turned communist was nothing but a rumor, and a new alliance with Soviet Russia was only an expedient way to rejuvenate China.[146]

Such arguments indicated that *Young China* was a product of the Chinese American mentality. Managed and supported by American Chinese who wanted to help build a strong and democratic republic in China, like the other papers it had come to represent the newly arisen petit bourgeois class. Its understanding of equality and democracy derived from prevailing ideologies in the United States. Communism was beyond what it could embrace or support.

Chinese American interests and ideology were further revealed in the three papers' coverage of the Guangzhou Merchants' Association Incident in 1924. The Sun government and the Guangzhou municipal government had been imposing all kinds of taxes, especially on businesses, to collect more revenue. At the same time, however, the GMD's advocacy of working-class interests against exploitation by capital owners had encouraged an increase in strikes by employees against employers.[147] Furthermore, militarists and corrupt bureaucrats in Guangdong had been looting stores and demanding all sorts of donations and contributions from businessmen. In response to this situation, business owners and capitalists organized themselves into a merchants' association to protect their interests.[148]

In May 1924, the Guangzhou Merchants' Association directly confronted the Guangzhou municipal government when the latter imposed a special tax on all businesses in Guangzhou to rebuild streets in the city. The association called for a general strike in protest against the tax and put together a private army to prevent government pressure. The government then repealed the special tax law, and the general strike was called off. The private army continued its existence.

Both *Chinese World* and *Chung Sai Yat Po* congratulated the merchants on their success against the government and supported the organization of the private army.[149] *Chinese World* editorialized that because government military forces no longer protected the lives and interests of the people, people in China had to organize their own military forces.[150] The success of the Guangzhou Merchants' Military Corps revealed that only with military forces as a backup could business interests stand up against the government. The paper also said that the government was no longer representative of ordinary people in Guangdong because its pro-communist programs and its reliance on militarists to sustain its power had brought only misery and turmoil to Guangdong. The Merchants' Association, on the other hand, represented the interests of most people in Guangdong, *Chinese World* stated.[151] *Chung Sai Yat Po* agreed, adding that the association's private army not only had to be maintained but also should be strengthened.[152]

The Guangzhou Merchants' Association did try to strengthen its private army. In August 1924, the association's president, Chen Lianbo, who worked for the Hong Kong and Shanghai Banking Corporation in Hong Kong, applied for a license from the Sun government to import weapons for the association. Four days after Chen got the license from the government, more than 9,000 guns arrived in Guangzhou on a Danish ship. The number of guns was much greater than that allowed in the license, and the four-day period in which the purchasing, loading, and shipping were accomplished was unexpectedly short. The Sun government associated this surplus and the quick arrival with the fact that Chen Lianbo supported Chen Jiongming against Sun and with the fact that Britain, which controlled Hong Kong, was also against the Sun government because of its pro-Soviet policy. The Sun government declared that the weapons had been smuggled into Guangzhou and so detained them.

Both *Chinese World* and *Chung Sai Yat Po* attacked the government's detention as a "despotic action" trampling the Guangzhou Merchants' Association.[153] They informed Chinese in the United States that the association's private army was protecting the people in Guangdong from the Sun government forces and other bandits and looters. The weapons were legally purchased to strengthen the self-defensive forces organized by the association. Yet self-defense was being suppressed by the Sun government.[154]

Young China did not voice any direct opinion until two weeks after the government detention of the weapons. When it did, though, the paper claimed that it stood together with the merchants in Guangdong but questioned the action of the president of the Guangzhou Merchants' Association. The paper believed that the merchants' private army should be used to help the local government and local police force maintain public security in Guangdong. The president of the merchants' association was "an unscrupulous merchant" working for the militarists in North China, the paper accused. The paper then reported that most merchants in Guangdong, especially in the provincial capital, Guangzhou, wanted to end the dispute over the arms' detention and return to normal business life. The paper further pointed out that the business strike declared by the merchants' association only hurt various businesses. The paper also hypothesized that if the local government were overthrown, anarchism would prevail, and there would be no safety or security for business. Once there was a political vacuum in Guangdong, the northern militarists would move in to take control. Would people in Guangdong welcome such an alternative?[155]

Young China's arguments revolved around the question of what benefited businesses and avoided any mention of the Sun government's new plan of allying with the Soviet Union and cooperating with the Chinese Communist Party. The paper was also evasive about the nature of the Sun government, which was a military government leading a nationalist revolution against the existing government. Most Chinese in the United States hoped to see peace, order, and business development in their home province. Most did not like the militarists, especially those in the North, and by this point they had lost almost all confidence in the Beijing government. *Young China*'s response to the Guangzhou merchants' incident thus reflected the prevailing ideology and interests of Chinese in the United States. Anticommunism, business development, and desire for peace were important elements of the emerging Chinese American identity.

Their interest in business development, their resentment of radical ideologies, and their desire for peace and stability in Guangdong determined that Chinese in the United States would not support a military showdown between Sun's government and the Guangzhou Merchants' Association, which, it quickly became clear, was supported by the British in Hong Kong.[156] The San Francisco Chinese Chamber of Commerce, claiming to speak for all Chinese in the United States, cabled the association in Guangzhou, asking it to protect merchants and work for the good of the people, to seek a peaceful resolution of the conflict, and not to resort to military force.[157] The Guangzhou Merchants' Association asked the Chinese Chamber of Commerce in San Francisco for financial support to prepare for a military showdown, but no fundraising activities were organized, and there was no report of the chamber ever sending any money back to Guangzhou. Chinese in the United States resented the Sun government because of its radical ideologies and its insistence on another revolution for national power. For the same reasons, they would not sacrifice their home province to a bloody battle between the Sun government and the British interests in Hong Kong.

In September 1924, Sun decided to launch a northern expedition to leave Guangdong, where he had exhausted his support, and "to open a new field" for his nationalist revolution.[158] The departure of the GMD from Guangdong brought an end to the string of episodes in which Chinese in the United States revealed elements in the ideological foundation of their identity. They had come to believe that only a combination of republicanism and capitalism could make China a strong and modern nation in the world; they did not see Confucianism and Chinese traditional culture as barriers to the development of a modern Chinese identity; and they accepted Christianity as a supplement in the process of adapting and reforming China to make it fit the modern world and in selecting their route to becoming an integrated part of American society.

By 1924, contention between various militarists for control of the Beijing government had gotten to the point where the president was widely known to have bribed his way into his position. The GMD's alliance and cooperation with communists and its insistence on having another nationalist revolution had alienated most Chinese in the United States. In the next few years, from 1924 to 1927, a combination of disappointments in the government and politics of their home country and their emerging independent Chinese identity would push American Chinese to make more concerted efforts to build self-sufficient and self-protective communities in the United States. These efforts would entail challenging the American mainstream society's stubborn discrimination.

5 Building Permanent Chinese American Communities and Displaying American Chinatown Culture, 1920–27

In 1922, Chew Fong Low, a widowed American-born Chinese mother of seven, sold the family businesses in Nevada, Missouri, and Arkansas and moved the family to San Francisco, planning to make a trip to China. She soon found that China was beset with troubles, including floods, droughts, and widespread famines. Worst of all, political rivalry between the northern and southern governments and military skirmishes between regional warlords filled everyday life with terror and death. Chew Fong Low canceled the trip to China and settled her family in San Francisco. In 1926, she invested $250,000 in the first modern apartment building to relieve "the congested living conditions" of the local Chinese.[1]

Chew Fong Low's story reveals that to an increasing number of Chinese in the United States, China was no longer an attractive place. Neither the northern government in Beijing nor the southern government in Guangdong could bring about peace or stability. The attacks on Chinese traditional culture and on Christianity in China did not make any sense to American Chinese. The GMD's alliance with the Soviet Union and cooperation with the Chinese Communist Party (CCP) served as the final breaking point between the prevailing ideology among Chinese in the United States and the politics in China.

More importantly, Chew Fong Low's story is indicative of the effort made by Chinese in the United States to make their residence more permanent. Besides Chew Fong Low's modern apartment building, in 1926 the first Chinese hospital was completed and opened in San Francisco, the Chinatown YMCA building was completed, and a three-story building was completed as the headquarters of the Chinese Chamber of Commerce. With the coming of age of an American-born generation and the increasing desire to live as Chinese in the United States, the 1920s witnessed community development at an unprecedented pace.

But there were obstacles to living in the United States as Chinese. The Immigration Act of 1924 prevented Chinese from bringing their families to the United States, and the California bill to control Chinese herbal medicine showed continued hostility to Chinese customs and practices. Chinese reactions toward the act and bill proved not only their resourcefulness but also their tenacity in fighting for their right to live in the United States as Chinese.

Their willingness to accommodate to norms of American mainstream society peaked in this period. American Chinatowns sponsored beauty contests. Chinese women's role in the public arena became increasingly more prominent through organizations such as the YWCA and the Square and Circle Club, a Chinese American women's service organization. The 1920s also witnessed the organization of the Yoke Choy Club, a Chinese young men's club to "promote Christianity, music, and athletics."[2] However, these accommodations were not made at the expense of Chinese traditional values. As Judy Yung observed in her book on the social history of Chinese women in San Francisco in the 1920s, Chinese women, both China-born and American-born, were "pragmatic, . . . taking what was useful to them from western religion and seeing no contradiction in practicing both cultures at the same time."[3] The same was true of Chinese men, both China-born and American-born.

In contrast to earlier depictions of American Chinatown life in this period as "silent years" marked by a China-oriented mentality,[4] this chapter shows that, in the last part of the 1920s, Chinese in the United States revealed their determination to stay and be an integral part of American society, perfected their own communities as permanent bases, and demonstrated the extent of their transculturation.

Fighting for Their Right to Stay and Have Families in the United States

The early 1920s witnessed a big increase in the numbers of wives of Chinese merchants and of American citizens of Chinese ancestry joining their husbands in the United States. Immigration statistics show that in the four-year period between 1901 and 1904, 241 Chinese women and girls entered the United States. In the four-year period between 1921 and 1924, 3,329 Chinese women and girls did so.[5] Of the 3,329, approximately 2,800 entered as wives.[6] The coming of such wives brought normal family life and vitality to the Chinese American communities. The increase in the number of married women in the American Chinese population demonstrated the American Chinese intention to make the United States their permanent home.

This trend was dealt a serious blow by the Immigration Act of 1924. Section 13(c) of the act said that "no alien ineligible to citizenship shall be admitted to the United States."[7] Aliens ineligible to citizenship included Chinese. Chinese immigrants were deprived the right of naturalization first in the 1878 case *In re Ah Yup*. The Circuit Court for California ruled that Chinese, who belonged to the Mongolian race, were not white and therefore could not become naturalized citizens.[8] This ruling was affirmed in the 1882 Chinese Exclusion Act.

The 1924 act made several exceptions. Chinese merchants belonged to the category of aliens "entitled to enter the United States solely to carry on trade under and in pursuance of the provisions of a present existing treaty of commerce and navigation." Also exempt by the act were an alien "who seeks to enter the United States solely for the purpose of carrying on the vocation of ministry of any religious denomination, or professor of a college, academy, seminary, or university; his wife, and his unmarried children under 18 years of age."[9] The act did not say anything about the right of entry to wives of Chinese merchants and of American citizens of Chinese ancestry.

The serious effect of the Immigration Act of 1924 on Chinese immigration went beyond what American Chinese community leaders anticipated. While the bill was being deliberated in the U.S. Congress, Chinese-language newspapers reported how the bill would affect Japanese immigration into the United States and how the Japanese government threatened action as a response to the bill. They also commented on how this anti-Asian bill would adversely affect American trade and commerce in Asia and how the bill reflected an increasing anti-Asian trend in the

United States.[10] Chinese in the United States did not anticipate any impact the bill would have on the already limited right of entry given to Chinese. Even after the bill had been passed by both houses of Congress, John McNab, an immigration attorney hired by the Chinese Consolidated Benevolent Association (CCBA), pointed out that the omission of alien wives of Chinese merchants in the 1924 Immigration Act should not cause concern because the right of entry for such wives was not given in any previous congressional legislation; instead, this right was established by a Supreme Court decision.[11]

The right of entry for wives of Chinese merchants domiciled in the United States was decided in 1900 by a Supreme Court decision in Mrs. Gue Lim's case. Mrs. Gue Lim was the lawful wife of Fook Kee, a Chinese merchant in Seattle. She was allowed to enter at the port of Tacoma in May 1897. In October of that same year, she was arrested on the charge of being a laborer who had failed to produce a certificate of registration as a laborer.[12] The District Court for the District of Washington discharged her from custody because the court decided that she was the wife of a Chinese merchant and was not excluded by the laws of the United States. But the U.S. district attorney appealed the court's decision, and in 1900 the case appeared in the U.S. Supreme Court. Justice Rufus W. Peckham, representing the Supreme Court, argued that Mrs. Gue Lim was "the wife of a merchant [and] it is not possible to presume that the treaty [of 1880], in omitting to name the wives of those who by the second article were entitled to admission, meant that they should be excluded." Nor did the 1884 act exclude such wives, Justice Peckham stated.[13] Wives of Chinese merchants lawfully domiciled in the United States were given the right of entry.

Nor did American Chinese predict that the 1924 act would prevent alien wives of American citizens of Chinese descent from immigrating to the United States. The right of entry for such wives was established in the Tsoi Sim case in 1902. Tsoi Sim was born in 1879 in China and entered the United States when she was three years old, before the passage of the Exclusion Act of 1882. In 1900, Tsoi Sim was lawfully married in California to Yee Yuk Lum, who was born in the United States and therefore an American citizen of Chinese descent. Tsoi Sim was arrested in 1901 on the charge that she was a Chinese manual laborer and ordered to be deported. The deportation judgment was affirmed by the district court. The defendant then appealed, and the case was brought to the Circuit Court of Appeals for the Ninth Circuit in 1902. Judge Thomas P. Hawley overturned the district court's decision and granted Tsoi Sim the right to remain in the United States. Judge Hawley said,

When appellant came to the United States there was no restriction or exclusion act which prohibited her coming. . . . Her marriage was not fraudulent, but lawful. . . . By this act [marrying], her status was changed from that of a Chinese laborer to that of a wife of a native-born American. . . . The native born . . . is entitled to greater rights and privileges than the alien merchant. The wife has the right to live with her husband; enjoy his society; receive his support and maintenance and all the comforts and privileges of the marriage relations. These are her, as well as his, natural rights. By virtue of her marriage, her husband's domicile became her domicile, and thereafter she was entitled to live with her husband, and remain in this country.[14]

The fact that American Chinese community leaders did not realize the serious effect of the 1924 act on Chinese immigration is reflected in the blame it put on the Chinese diplomatic authorities in the United States and the complaint made by the Chinese ambassador in Washington, D.C. After immigration officers put aside the court precedent and used the 1924 act to prevent Chinese from entering the United States, a letter printed in *Chinese World* said that Chinese diplomatic authorities in the United States ignored the well-being of their people. The Chinese ambassador in Washington, D.C., on the other hand, complained to George A. McGowan, an attorney hired by American Chinese, that it was a grave mistake for American Chinese not to take action while the bill was being deliberated or not to let his office know their opinions toward the bill.[15]

American Chinese organizations were very alert in 1924 and took some actions while the bill was being deliberated. According to *Chinese World*, in January 1924, Lin Yaohua, representing Chinese American Citizens Alliance (CACA), went to Washington, D.C., to obtain more information on the immigration bill being deliberated in Congress to strategize against any provisions concerning Chinese American rights. According to the paper, the CACA had heard that U.S. citizenship would be limited to Asians only if both their parents were American citizens.[16] In April, *Chung Sai Yat Po* reported that the CCBA in San Francisco sent its representative to lobby against perceived provisions of the bill under deliberation that would forbid wives of Chinese students from entering and that would reduce the admissible age of merchants' children from twenty-one to sixteen and demand a literacy test of such children.[17] This newspaper report did not indicate CCBA's worries over the right of entry for wives of Chinese merchants or of American citizens of Chinese descent.

The Immigration Act of 1924 seriously affected Chinese immigration into the United States. After the act became effective on July 1, 1924, the right of entry for wives and children of Chinese merchants and wives of

American citizens of Chinese ancestry was put to the test. In Seattle, Boston, and San Francisco, Chinese wives and children were detained as immigration authorities regarded them as "aliens ineligible to citizenship."

American Chinese reactions to the detentions were strong and prompt. Local Chinese organizations hired immigration lawyers and declared that they were going to court to test the applicability of the new act to Chinese immigration. If necessary, stated *Young China* and *Chinese World*, American Chinese would fight all the way to the U.S. Supreme Court to defend their right to enter the country.[18] *Chung Sai Yat Po* argued specifically that the 1880 treaty between the United States and China[19] protected the right of Chinese merchants and their families to enter the United States just as it protected the right of American merchants and their families to enter China. Angered by the detention of the Chinese wives and children, the paper suggested that the Chinese parliament pass an act to prohibit foreigners from entering China to counter anti-Chinese laws and practices all over the world.[20]

As specific measures, Chinese all over the United States made the following suggestions. The CCBA in Boston said that the CCBA, the Chinese Chamber of Commerce, and the CACA should gather together and organize a committee to coordinate efforts. The CCBA in Seattle suggested a mandatory donation of $50 from all American Chinese to fight the new law. Suggestions were also made to organize demonstrations and publicity campaigns to arouse sympathy from American mainstream media and attention from mainstream American people. It was also suggested that efforts should be made to encourage people in China to carry out boycotts to pressure the American government.[21]

As a response, the CCBA in San Francisco organized a special Bureau Resisting the New Immigration Act (*Kangliju*) and asked existing Chinese American organizations to set up local branch offices to coordinate efforts in early August 1924.[22] By mid-September, branch offices of the bureau had been established in Chicago, Los Angeles, Boston, Seattle, and New York City.[23]

The CACA set up its own Committee for Protecting Citizenship Rights (*Weichi jichuan weiyuanhui*).[24] The mission of this committee was to study the American legal system and laws, to raise funds, to publish a newsletter in both Chinese and English, and to campaign for support from the mainstream society.[25] It called on all American-born Chinese to unite in the effort to defend their citizenship rights and to fight for legal entry for Chinese wives into the United States.[26] In early 1925, the committee sent its representatives to Washington, D.C. in an attempt to petition Congress to change the 1924 act. But Congress did not take the petition very seriously, and no action was taken.[27]

The Committee for Protecting Citizenship Rights sharply pointed out that the Immigration Act of 1924 could only hinder the Americanization program, which the U.S. federal government had been carrying out since 1910.[28] One of the arguments used to discriminate and exclude Chinese immigration was that Chinese did not intend to make the United States their home. But if wives of Chinese men residing in the United States were barred from coming to join their husbands, then Chinese were actually deprived of their right to make the United States home. As it was pointed out at the beginning of this section, immigration statistics showed a distinctive trend that by the early 1920s, many Chinese were establishing families and making the United States their home. By barring Chinese wives from entering, the new immigration act disrupted family formation among American Chinese, thus undermining the goal of the Americanization program.

The Chinese wives and children detained by immigration authorities received different court decisions. The District Court for the District of Massachusetts ruled in mid-October 1924 that Chiu Shee, as wife of an American citizen of Chinese descent, was not excluded by the Immigration Act of 1924. District Judge James Arnold Lowell said, "The result desired by the passage of the act would not be furthered by prohibiting a wife from joining her husband, who is a citizen of the United States." In fact, Judge Lowell believed,

> The omission of subdivision (a) of section 4 from the provisions of section 13 arose, not from a settled purpose of Congress to exclude such a wife, but from the fact that in considering section 13 Congress had only aliens in mind, and did not realize that the section as passed diminished the rights of American citizens, already carefully safeguarded by section 4 (a). The reason why this inconsistency was overlooked was that the report of the House Committee stated specifically that wives of American citizens were exempted, and the chairman of that committee, . . . in the debate in the House, emphasized this feature of the bill. . . . The discrepancy between section 4 (a) and section 13 (c) is thus reconciled by construing the latter provision as applying only to aliens who are not related to American citizens.

Judge Lowell thus ordered Chiu Shee be discharged.[29]

The District Court for the Northern District of California made two separate decisions in late October 1924, one involving Cheung Sum Shee et al. seeking admission as wives and children of domiciled Chinese merchants and the other involving Chan Shee et al. as alien Chinese wives of American citizens. Judge Frank H. Kerrigan ruled against the wives and children of Chinese merchants. He said that "the treaty of 1880, while permitting 'teachers, students [and] merchants together with their body and household servants' to enter, does not in terms permit their wives and children to do so, and their entry has been so far sanctioned by virtue of their relationship to a member of one of those classes. The present act designates such merchants as nonimmigrants, and the provision alluded to, to the effect that an alien who is not particularly specified in the act as a nonimmigrant shall not be admitted as such by reason of relationship to any individual who is so specified, seems to me to be directly pointed at persons in the situation of these petitioners."[30]

For wives of American citizens, Judge Kerrigan ruled in their favor, for he "cannot believe that it was the intention of Congress to exclude such persons. . . . To admit an alien teacher or minister of religion ineligible to citizenship, and their wives and minor children, also ineligible, and to exclude the wife of an American citizen solely by reason of a like ineligibility, is so inconsistent and unreasonable that it is impossible to believe that Congress intended it."[31] However, Judge Kerrigan did not allow Chan Shee et al. to enter, for they were not able to produce the immigration visas required by section 9 of the 1924 act.[32]

Chinese in the United States refused to accept Judge Kerrigan's decisions. They decided to appeal to the Supreme Court of the United States and raised funds to hire special immigration attorneys. In Seattle, the branch office of the Bureau Resisting the New Immigration Act argued that the Immigration Act of 1924 was unreasonable and inhumane and conflicted with the existing treaty between the United States and China. The Seattle organization believed that the act did not reflect the majority opinion of the American people. Instead, it was the result of a small group of anti-Asian fanatics. All Chinese were called on to support bringing the case to the Supreme Court, where justice was expected to prevail. The Seattle Chinese organization further declared that this effort affected long-term interests of all Chinese in the United States as well as rights and privileges of "our sons and grandsons."[33] The branch office in Boston organized fundraising theatrical performances.[34] The Los Angeles branch office appealed to the tongs on the East Coast to stop fighting among themselves and to unite behind the Chinese effort in the Supreme Court.[35]

The Supreme Court handed down two separate decisions on May 25, 1925 concerning the applicability of the 1924 Immigration Act to Chinese wives and children. In the decision concerning wives and children of Chinese merchants, *Cheung Sum Shee et al. v. Nagle*, the court ruled favorably to the Chinese appellants by stating, "The wives and minor children of resident Chinese merchants were guaranteed the right of entry by the treaty of 1880. . . . That Act [of 1924] must be construed with the view to preserve treaty rights unless clearly annulled. . . . Mrs. Gue Lim . . . was . . . allowed to enter, upon the theory that a treaty provision admitting merchants by necessary implication extended to their wives and minor children. This rule was not unknown to Congress when considering the Act now before us."[36]

But in the decision concerning wives of American citizens of Chinese descent, *Chang Chan, Wong Hung Kay, Yee Sin Jung et al. v. Nagle,* the Supreme Court ruled against the Chinese petitioners by reversing the interpretations of judges Lowell and Kerrigan. Justice James C. McReynolds said that the court could not approve "the suggestion that the provisions contained in Subdivision (a) of Section 4 were omitted from the exceptions in Section 13 (c) because of some obvious oversight and should be treated as if incorporated therein. . . . The applicants should be refused admission if found to be Chinese wives of American citizens. It is unnecessary now to consider the requirements of the Act in respect of visas."[37]

American citizens of Chinese ancestry refused to accept the Supreme Court decision. Their organization, the CACA, continued the fight. CACA members used their citizenship privileges and lobbied in their home districts and in Washington, D.C. In February 1926, when the House Committee on Immigration and Naturalization debated a proposal to amend the 1924 act to make wives of American citizens admissible, CACA representatives, together with Caucasian attorneys they hired, presented their argument to the committee.[38] However, the proposal failed to get the majority support in the committee.

The CACA representatives persisted in their petition to amend the 1924 act. In February 1928, Congress proposed another bill titled "Admission as Nonquota Immigrants of Certain Alien Wives and Children of United States Citizens." Testifying before the Subcommittee of the Senate Committee on Immigration was the eloquent speaker Y. C. Hong, who was born in San Francisco in 1899, had worked for the Immigration Service from 1918 to 1928, had received a law degree from the University of Southern California in 1925, and was at the time president of the Los Angeles Chapter of the CACA.[39]

Y. C. Hong pointed out that the "right of a man to have his wife with him . . . is a fundamental right recognized, not only in civilized society, but even among the savages. . . . But this right is denied to us who are American citizens. I really do not believe it is the intent of Congress to bring about that hardship." Y. C. Hong then argued that the causes of the hardship lay beyond the control of Chinese American citizens. The first cause was that many states in the United States prohibited Chinese from interracial marriages. Second, there existed a sex ratio imbalance among the American-born Chinese population. According to the 1920 census, there were approximately 18,000 unmarried American-born Chinese in the United States, only about 5,000 of them female (a ratio of more than two males to one female). Many Chinese American men thus had no choice but to find a wife in China. To marry a woman and to leave her behind in China is "something inhuman, cruel, and harsh. . . . If we cannot marry, we will have to live a life of celibacy. That is not natural. To expect a great number of us to do that is too harsh for any words to express," Y. C. Hong said, appealing to human sympathy.[40]

In his presentation to the Senate Subcommittee, Y. C. Hong argued that to give the right of entry to Chinese wives of American citizens would also benefit the United States as a whole. Such right of entry would first "discourage interracial marriage," against which many states had passed laws. Second, it "would elevate morality. It is not good for a great body of men to remain single." Third, "it is in harmony with our present immigration policy, namely, to humanize the law and bring about family life." Finally, it would "quicken the process of assimilation" because instead of having Chinese mothers raise American citizens in China, Chinese children would be born and brought up in the United States.[41]

CACA also solicited support from American mainstream society. Letters that detailed the hardship in which American citizens of Chinese descent found themselves as a result of the Immigration Act of 1924 were sent out to "representative Americans, prominent in the educational and the religious life of the nation." Responses to the solicitation of support were many in number and positive in attitude. Nicholas M. Butler, president of Columbia University, wrote, "I have no question as to the righteousness of the proposal made in your letter. . . . Cases have come to my own notice where the existing legislation brings not only hardship but downright cruelty to families." Walter D. Scott, president of Northwestern University, said in his response "I sympathize with you . . . in the situation which you find yourselves. Sincerely, I hope this matter will be brought to the attention of Congress and that some measure will be passed by which your wives may gain the right of admission to this country." Joseph H. Johnson and W. Bertrand Stevens, bishops of the Episcopal Church in the Diocese of Los Angeles, gave their whole-hearted support by writing that "the refusal to admit alien wives of American citizens of the Chinese race works a serious hardship and is inconsistent with the spirit of American institutions. We shall be glad to add our voice to any appeal to have the barrier . . . abolished. We shall be glad to be quoted as being opposed to the restriction and as advocating its removal." Dozens of such responses were selected and presented to the Subcommittee of the Senate Committee on Immigration.[42]

The CACA's effort in 1928 to change the Immigration Act of 1924 was very comprehensive. Its representatives also made appearances before the House Committee on Immigration and Naturalization. In addition to their appearances, the representatives prepared a pamphlet titled "A Plea for Relief," in which they detailed the hardship imposed on American citizens of Chinese descent by the 1924 act, and submitted it to relevant committees of the House and Senate. With the pamphlet were also notarized affidavits from individual Chinese American citizens whose lives were directly affected by the 1924 act.

One of these citizens was Tom Wong Hoe Sing. A citizen of the United States and a resident of San Francisco, Tom Wong Hoe Sing was twenty-three years old and a waiter by occupation. He married Quan Shee, a Chinese woman, in China in January 1924. While "applying at the steamship office in Hong Kong for passage to the United States for himself and his wife" on July 12, 1924, he was informed by "steamship-company officials" there that under the Immigration Act of 1924, his wife was not admissible to the United States. Compelled by his financial situation, which required him to return to work in San Francisco immediately, he departed for the United States alone, leaving his wife behind in China. As a waiter, Tom Wong Hoe Sing could not afford frequent visits to China. As of January 19, 1928, when the affidavit was taken, he had not seen his wife since his return in 1924. He was "deprived of that home life which is essential to the well-being of every man." His "living expenses are increased by reason of the fact that he must not only provide for himself here, but maintain a home for his wife in China." Tom Wong Hoe Sing "prays that the immigration act of 1924 be so amended as to remove the hardship from which he suffers in his separation from his wife."[43]

The CACA's effort to fight for the right of entry for Chinese wives of its members finally bore limited fruit. A bill was passed in 1930 to amend the Immigration Act of 1924, allowing the Chinese wives of American citizens who got married before May 26, 1924, the date the act was passed, to enter the United States. Tom Wong Hoe Sing's wife could join him in the United States. Yet the amendment did not provide relief for marriages that had taken place after May 26, 1924. The amendment apparently discouraged American citizens of Chinese descent from marrying women in China.

Fighting for Their Right to Preserve Chinese Cultural Practices

The fight for the entry rights of Chinese wives paralleled a struggle against a California bill to subject all herbs to the control of the State Board of Health. Whereas the fight for entry rights demonstrated Chinese determination to live and have families permanently in the United States, the struggle against the herb bill revealed their intention to preserve their cultural heritage and to live in the United States as Chinese.

Chinese herbal medicine had accompanied the Chinese since their arrival in the United States. According to Haiming Lui's study of "Chinese herbalists in the American medical profession," a pioneer Chinese named Fung Jong Yee opened an herb shop in Fiddletown of Amador County, California in 1851. In 1869, an article in the *Overland Monthly*, a San Francisco–based journal, commented, "Judging from the number of their apothecary stores, one would suppose that the Chinese were large consumers of medicines."[44]

Use of herbal medicine was made necessary by racial discrimination. Between 1852 and 1870, Chinese "were excluded from the city hospital in San Francisco and the only ones to which they were ever freely admitted were the insane asylums and the pest-house."[45] In 1881, the *San Francisco Chronicle* carried an article titled "No Room for Chinese: They Are Denied Admission to the County Hospital." The Chinese Consul in San Francisco had petitioned the county hospital to admit a Chinese man, who was "suffering from phthisis, and was poor and had no friends." Although the sick and poor Chinese man was allowed to stay in the hospital temporarily, the Board of Health held a meeting and decided to continue adhering to its own resolution passed several years earlier, which said, "Chinamen were not allowed in the hospital as a patient." One board member reasoned at the meeting, "If they [the hospital] once opened the gates to the chronic and incurable diseases existing in Chinatown, they would soon have the place full." The board thus resolved that "in consequence of the crowded condition of the City and County Hospital, the Superintendent be and is hereby instructed to admit no person suffering from chronic diseases of an incurable character." The board at the same meeting appointed an inspector to examine the "filthy conditions of Chinatown."[46] As a result, Chinese in the United States relied largely on Chinese herbs and herbal doctors for medical care in the nineteenth and early twentieth century.

Chinese herbs and herbal doctors not only took care of Chinese immigrants but also benefited European-American frontier pioneers. Chuck

Ah-Fong, a Chinese herbal doctor, rendered his medical services to his fellow Chinese and to non-Chinese in the gold fields of Idaho and later in Boise, Idaho between 1870 and 1910. He became a respected figure among the Chinese and acted as a bridge between local Chinese and European-Americans. Doctor Ah-Fong became the only Chinese member of the Boise Businessmen's Association and was the only Chinese herbal doctor fully licensed as a physician and surgeon in Idaho during that period.[47]

The famous, almost legendary China Doctor in John Day, Oregon, offers another such story about how Chinese traditional medicine benefited Chinese and non-Chinese pioneers in the American West. His Chinese name was Ing Hay, and he worked out of a Chinese business establishment called Kam Wah Chung and Co. From the turn of the century through the first few decades of the twentieth century, Ing Hay treated numerous patients, most of whom were non-Chinese. Because he was able to diagnose by reading descriptive letters from patients and to mail out prescribed Chinese medicine, he treated patients in a wide area covering the present Washington, Oregon, and Idaho states. Among the most famous cases he successfully treated was one in which he cured a boy dying of blood poisoning caused by a wound suffered on his father's frontier ranch. He saved the lives of all his patients in the 1915 and 1919 flu epidemics in eastern Oregon. He was also famous for providing cures for meningitis. Known as China Doctor, he took in patients when other doctors had given up and "practiced the healing arts among a strange . . . people," his non-Chinese biographers said.[48]

By the 1920s, that the use of traditional Chinese medicine and Chinese herbs was widespread in American Chinatowns was obvious from advertisements in Chinese-language newspapers. All three Chinese-language newspapers under investigation here filled more than one-third of their pages with advertisements for Chinese herbal medicine, and I have randomly selected the April 7, 1924 issue of *Chung Sai Yat Po* for a close look. Approximately 68 percent of this eighteen-by-twenty-two-inch, eight-page daily newspaper was devoted to advertisements. Of this 68 percent space, 64 percent was occupied by advertisements for Chinese herbal medicine. In other words, 44 percent of the entire newspaper was filled with advertisements from Chinese herbal doctors or dealers.[49]

The medical advertisements in this issue of *Chung Sai Yat Po* show us the scope of health problems that Chinese traditional medicine claimed to cure or relieve in the early 1920s for Chinese in the United States. The health problems mentioned in these advertisements ranged from men's impotence to women's menstrual cramps, from sexually transmitted disease to skin irritation, from hemorrhoids to arthritis, from athlete's foot to contusions, and from itches to coughs. Besides providing cure and relief, the advertised Chinese medicine also included various tonics that would enrich blood, build health, bring back youthfulness, prolong life, and add sexual vitality. Many of these advertised medicines and tonics were ready-made pills and balls or were in packages and bottles ready to be purchased without prescriptions.

Many of these medical advertisements were testimonies from patients. These testimonies all provided names. Some identified where they lived at the time, and others gave names of their native villages in China. These testimonies came from patients who were residing as far away as Canada, Mexico, New York, Philadelphia, New Jersey, and Idaho and as near as Oakland and San Francisco. They attested to the effectiveness of a Chinese herbal doctor's prescribed treatment or to the curing and healing power of certain ready-made Chinese herbal medicines.

The practice of Chinese herbal medicine encountered legal barriers in the United States. The 1880s and 1890s witnessed state legislation requiring licenses to practice medicine.[50] Chuck Ah-Fong defended his medical practice in courts, and finally the state supreme court ruled in his favor, by making him a licensed doctor in 1901.[51] Ing Hay in Oregon was charged with practicing medicine illegally, but "no jury would convict him" in 1905.[52]

In 1887, the California state legislature passed the Medical Practice Restriction Act, which required licenses to practice medicine in the state.[53] Chinese herbal doctors usually developed skills without formal education. Even if they received formal education, they did it in China. Knowledge and skills involved in the practice of Chinese herbal medicine were based on very different theories and assumptions from those involved in the practice of Western medicine. As a result, Chinese herbal doctors at the time usually practiced medicine without licenses, so they suffered all kinds of harassment. Tom Leong, an herbal doctor in Los Angeles, was arrested more than 100 times for practicing medicine without a license.[54] According to a study published in 1899, many Chinese herbal doctors had been arrested and fined in California.[55] Because of such harassment, many Chinese herbal doctors worked out of herbal stores, seeing patients while selling herbal medicine. Famous Chinese herbal doctors in San Francisco and Oakland worked mostly out of "herb companies."

Despite their handicap in practicing medicine without medical licenses, Chinese herbal doctors in California reached out to the American mainstream society, and they presented testimonies from their non-Chinese patients to advertise their businesses. The *San Francisco Chron-*

icle repeatedly carried ads from Fong Wan Herb Co. and Dr. Wong Him Herb Co. of Oakland, and Chan and Chan, Chan and Kong, Leung Wing Herb Co., Hing Wan Herb Co., Lau Yit-Cho Chinese Herb Co., and Chew and Chew Herb Co. of San Francisco. These ads usually offered free consultation, guaranteed best results, and pointed out that "experiments [were] not needed."[56] "Unsolicited testimonials" from non-Chinese patients also were used. John P. Rodge wrote the following testimonial for Oakland's Fong Wan Herb Co.: "My son, Harold, has been troubled with bloody urine for several years. He tried a number of physicians but none seemed able to do him any good. . . . One of our friends who had been cured by the Fong Wan Herbalist suggested that we try him. He supplied my son with herbs to cook at home. After having drunk the tea for a little more than two months, Harold is now in the finest condition."[57] The writer dated the testimonial and gave his home address. Louis Faurie wrote for San Francisco's Chan and Kong, "I will add my testimony to the lot you showed me of people you have relieved. I had rheumatism awfully bad. . . . Sometimes it almost made me cry with the twinges it gave me and when I was told that you had made some wonderful cures with giving Herbs and no drugs at all to ease the pain I thought it would be best to give you a chance with me. You would better believe I was glad that I did, because in five weeks the whole trouble was wiped out. If I hear anyone I know having rheumatism or any other trouble, you, doctor, I shall send them to." The writer signed and gave his home address.[58]

Another method used to attract customers was to get permission from former patients to list their names and professions. For example, one of the ads of San Francisco's Chan and Chan listed A. D. Keef, U.S. naval escort to the late President Harding, while touring in Alaska; Frank M. Bell and A. Winter, former U.S. sergeants in World War I; John Tuohy, manufacturer; J. K. Kaar and M. R. Haims, realtors; and Mrs. Ann Gustufson, nurse. At the end of the list, it said, "Some of their addresses can be found in the phone directory. Others can be had at the Chan and Chan offices."[59]

By providing alternative medicine to mainstream society, Chinese herbal doctors took away business from non-Chinese doctors. To protect white doctors' business opportunities, Edward J. Smith, a representative in the California State Assembly, proposed a bill "to regulate the manufacture, sale and use of herbs, roots or other nature products used in the administering of sickness or treating diseases of a human being and providing a penalty for the violation thereof." The bill said, "No person, firm, corporation, copartnership or individual shall manufacture or offer for sale, when the inducement for same is the curing of ailments and diseases of the human body, any herbs, roots or other products of nature unless same shall have first been submitted to the state board of health and their approval . . . has been given in writing. . . . No person, firm, corporation, copartnership or individual shall set themselves up as one who prescribes herbs, roots or other products of nature for the curing of mental or physical sickness or disease unless they shall first have been licensed by a state board of medical examiners of the State of California."[60]

The American Chinese response to the bill was immediate and strong. A letter written by a Chinese in Los Angeles sharply pointed out that the bill would hurt not only Chinese herbal doctors but also many businesses that sold herbal medicine. Worse still, the letter stated, the bill would make the import of Chinese herbs so difficult that American Chinese would no longer be able to buy their tonic or supplemental herbs.[61] Chinese medicine was used not only according to doctors' prescriptions to cure all kinds of illness and disease but also in nonprescription forms for nutritional and preventive purposes. Without consulting a medical doctor, Chinese mothers brewed herbs at the beginning of the fall season to "clear the body of excessive heat" or at the beginning of summer to "prepare the body for excessive heat." A survey conducted in 1979 in the San Francisco Chinatown revealed that "seven out of ten respondents said that they used Chinese home remedies of ointments and herb teas" and "nine out of ten . . . drank Chinese herb soups."[62] Herbs would be used also in cooking for people who had recently given birth or who were recovering from an illness, again with no advice from medical experts.

To combat the proposed antiherb bill, an Herb Dealers' Protective Association of California was established. All Chinese businesses, either herbal doctors or stores selling herbs, became members of the association. They pooled money and hired lawyers.[63] On February 21, *Chinese World* reported that Chinese in San Francisco had held a banquet for state legislators. On February 25, the paper reported that fresh flowers were delivered to state legislators.[64] At the same time, the Herb Dealers' Protective Association reached out to the mainstream society for support. The association compiled a pamphlet in English on the benefits of Chinese herbal medicine and on the reasons for its existence, distributing copies of the pamphlet to all hospitals and clinics of Western medicine throughout California and to individuals for signatures of support.[65] The pamphlet said, "The American Public has always been in favor of the herbs; persons who have been freed from pain and have felt their strength return have not been backward in expressing appreciation of the harmless herbs so wisely provided by Mother Nature. . . . The Chinese Herb Dealers . . . are in a very difficult situation and undergo the greatest hardships at the hands of the Medical Examiners. All that the Herb Dealers ask for is fair play and backing of all persons interested in herbs."[66]

Leaders of the association did not neglect the leverage an increasing number of American-born Chinese possessed. They asked assistance from the CACA, which mobilized all its members with citizenship rights to sign a letter to the state legislature defending Chinese medicine. Furthermore, the association asked Chinese people with fluent English, good reputations, and close contacts in mainstream society to present the Chinese argument to the legislative committee, where the bill was deliberated.[67] Wu Panzhao, the Chinese Presbyterian minister and owner of *Chung Sai Yat Po;* Lin Yaohua, president of the CACA; and Deng Xianshi, a secretary of the Chinese Chamber of Commerce were among representatives sent by the association to Sacramento.[68]

The association's effort to defeat the bill was supported by American Chinese organizations and non-Chinese friends and sympathizers. The San Francisco CCBA, the Chinese Chamber of Commerce, the CACA, major Chinese-language newspapers, and Chinese churches in California all joined the campaign. More than ten white men and women traveled to Sacramento from various places in California and testified how their illnesses, which Western medicine had failed to cure, were cured by Chinese herbal medicine, arguing that the pending bill could only do harm to the general public.[69] Leaders of the association also asked non-Chinese organizations and white friends and sympathizers to write letters, arguing against the pending bill.[70]

These strategies proved effective. The bill was withdrawn from the California legislative agenda in mid-March 1925, after it failed to get enough votes in the Committee on Medical and Dental Laws, to which the bill had been referred.[71] The Chinese in the United States had again shown both pride in their cultural heritage and knowledge of how to get things done in the American political system.

The Herb Dealers' Protective Association of California also worked out a long-term plan to legitimize the practice of Chinese medicine and carry it down to future generations in the United States. This plan suggested that the present practitioners of Chinese herbal medicine get licensed and that young Chinese be sent to American medical schools to acquire diplomas in Western medicine before they were trained in Chinese medicine. Future doctors of both Western and Chinese medicine would then enjoy the full rights and privileges granted to Western doctors while promoting the treasures of Chinese medicine.[72] This long-term plan confirmed American Chinese pride in their cultural heritage and their determination to stay in the United States permanently.

The successful strategies of the association made Chinese in the United States realize the importance of being organized. Right after the bill was withdrawn from the California State legislative agenda, *Chung Sai Yat Po* editorialized on the lessons learned from the effort, including prompt reaction to the proposal of a bill, a concerted effort by Chinese organizations, and determination to stop it. The paper then pointed out that, considering the rampant discrimination Asians had been encountering in the United States, all Chinese trades, businesses, and professions should get organized. The paper believed that traditional family and clan associations, district associations, and Chinese church organizations had not been able to provide enough protection. The CCBAs and Chinese Chambers of Commerce were too general to take special care of any particular groups. The paper therefore suggested organizing according to trades, businesses, and professions. Such organizations would pay special attention to upcoming laws and regulations pertaining to their particular interests, so that prompt and appropriate actions could be taken. Because the paper believed that organizational voices and actions usually carried more weight than individual voices and actions, it admonished its Chinese readers to be united, quoting a famous Chinese proverb: "It is easy to break a single arrow, but it is difficult to break a bundle of ten arrows."[73]

By the 1920s, Chinese in the United States had survived exclusion and become discontent with individual successes in the U.S. court system. Their organized efforts to fight for amendment to the 1924 Immigration Act and for the right to continue the practice of Chinese medicine marked a significant development in the transformation of their identity. They were claiming all rights immigrants and ethnic minority groups deserved; they took great pride in their Chinese cultural heritage and tried very hard to protect and continue it; they were being Chinese and becoming Chinese American.

Building Permanent Communities in the United States

Chinese American communities in the 1920s were becoming what James Clifford called "collective homes away from home."[74] "Collective homes away from home" for Chinese in the United States during this period usually took the physical form of Chinatowns. Visible signs of maturation of Chinese American communities lie in the building or purchasing of permanent facilities in various American Chinatowns. In New York City, the Chinese Merchants' Association bought a four-story building on Mott Street in Chinatown in 1920. In the next few years, the building was remodeled, "at a cost of $300,000," with a "red-tiled pago-da roof, restaurant on the first two floors, residential apartments on the next two, and a teak-lined reception hall on the top floor."[75] In February 1929, the CCBA in New York City purchased a three-story building on Mott Street for $91,500. The newly purchased CCBA building met the needs of an expanding Chinese school for local Chinese children.[76]

The Chinatown in Seattle witnessed the erection of several permanent structures in the 1920s. In 1922, a new Chinese Baptist church was finished. The new church became "a magnet for social and religious activities in the community," and "virtually every Chinese child in the city attended the Baptist Church Nursery School." In 1923, Charlie Louie, an owner of sev-eral Chinese restaurants and a Chinese import-export store, built a Chi-nese opera house. In 1929, Louie made further investments and turned the opera house into Louie's Chinese Garden, a restaurant with a dance hall. The establishment attracted Chinese as well as non-Chinese customers. In 1929, the CCBA in Seattle had its own building constructed next to Louie's Chinese Garden. The building housed the local Chinese school on the first floor and a huge auditorium with a stage on the upper floor.[77]

The physical development of San Francisco's Chinatown in the 1920s tells a more detailed story of the maturation of the Chinese Amer-ican community. San Francisco was regarded by Chinese in the United States as Dafu, the number one city. Serving as the port of entry for most Chinese coming into the country, San Francisco had 16,303 Chinese, which was 21.8 percent of the total Chinese American population of 74,959 in 1930.

The Chinese population in San Francisco more than doubled, from 7,744 to 16,303, in the 1920s. This increase naturally created a demand for more living space. The first modern apartment building, completed in 1926 with investment from Chow Fong Low, a widowed Chinese American woman, relieved the crowded housing conditions and demon-strated the American Chinese determination to make the United States their permanent home.

Another major construction project completed in the 1920s in San Francisco Chinatown was the Chinese Hospital. The Chinese in San Fran-cisco had relied mainly on herbal doctors for treatment of medical prob-lems. For the poor, who could not pay for herbal doctors and who were not accepted at local public health care facilities, the CCBA had estab-lished a dispensary, the Tong Hua Dispensary, in 1899 in San Francisco's Chinatown. In the next few decades, this one-room clinic was support-ed by donations from various Chinese associations.[78] With Chinese and Western doctors working together at the clinic, the Tong Hua Dispensary provided the necessary medical facility for local Chinese who were largely kept away from the mainstream medical facilities in the area.

By 1920, the CCBA and other Chinese leaders started to realize that the limited dispensary was no longer able to meet the needs of the local Chinese population. Among the leaders was T. J. Gintjee, who became a member of "the committee to organize and stimulate public opinion in support of the project" to establish a Chinese hospital. Gintjee observed that "maimed and crippled Chinese who . . . , for want of surgical care, were compelled to go through life as sufferers." He believed that "even moderate skill could have made them strong and useful men and women."[79]

In addition, in the first two decades of the twentieth century, a bachelor-dominated Chinese American society was replaced by emerging Chinese American communities of complete families, who intended to stay in the United States permanently. The old concept of returning home when one was sick and old faded away among Chinese. By the early 1920s, with an increasingly large number of children, women, and old people, Chinese communities realized the need for more complete health care facilities.

In 1922, fifteen Chinese organizations headquartered in San Francisco got together and established the Fundraising Bureau for a Chinese hospital, known in English as the Chinese Hospital and in Chinese as *Donghua yiyuan*. These fifteen organizations were the San Francisco CCBA, the seven district associations, the Chinese Chamber of Commerce, the CACA, the Zhigongtang, the GMD, the Constitutionalist Party, the Chinese Christian Church Alliance, and the YMCA. The bureau consisted of fifty-six representatives from the fifteen organizations, with Chen Lesheng, a Chinese church minister, as bureau head and Chen Duanpu, general manager of *Chinese World*, as deputy head.[80]

With representatives from all sections of the Chinese community in the United States, the bureau raised funds to build the hospital from Chinese in the United States and from Caucasian supporters, mostly medical professionals. The three Chinese newspapers published the names of contributors, many of whom donated one or two dollars. There were also many fundraising activities. Several Chinese theatrical performance companies staged fundraising plays. By August 1923, the bureau made the seventeenth report on the status of the fundraising. This report gave a total figure of $130,308.[81]

Soon afterward, the bureau took the first steps toward building the hospital. On August 6, the bureau bought a piece of land at Jackson and Trenton streets with $10,500.[82] The plan to build the hospital at the location encountered resistance from non-Chinese people in the neighborhood. The bureau used CCBA's attorney, John McNab, and organized lobbying efforts to persuade city authorities to grant the permit to build the hospital. In the San Francisco city hall, a meeting was held at which the city officials explained to representatives of the objecting residents that a modern Chinese hospital would not harm them. Actually, the officials said, a hospital was better than leaving the land vacant to vagrants.[83] On August 23, the Health Committee of the Board of Supervisors voted unanimously to grant the permit.[84] The construction of the hospital was carried out by Barret & Hilp Co., who offered the lowest bid, $146,206 for the entire construction.[85]

The fundraising bureau continued its task while construction was under way because the building cost of $146,206 and the land purchase cost of $10,500 went beyond the $130,308 already raised. Furthermore, the hospital was a charity project. Future maintenance depended on charitable contributions from Chinese communities in the United States and from sympathizers and supporters in American mainstream society.

The completed building was an impressive modern structure. It had five floors and a basement. It was equipped with modern facilities such as automatic elevators. The hospital had fourteen private patient rooms, forty cubicles or beds, a surgical department with two operating rooms, a maternity department with a delivery room, a pharmacy, a lab, and an outpatient department.[86]

Widespread support among Chinese in the United States for such a community project was demonstrated by the impressive amount raised for construction. Such support and enthusiasm did not stop at the completion of the structure. On the day of the opening ceremony, Chinese organizations and individuals from all over the United States donated medical equipment, furniture, or money to buy equipment and furniture. Among the donated equipment was an X-ray machine.[87] Indeed, the hospital was run largely as a charitable institution. Except for some wards for paying patients, the hospital provided medical services to the poor.[88] Its maintenance thus depended mainly on community support.

The Chinese community took great pride in the completion of the Chinese Hospital. It organized a grand opening ceremony and invited representatives from various Chinese communities throughout the United States as well as city and state officials to the ceremony. San Francisco mayor James Rolph and lieutenant-governor of California C. C. Young spoke at the ceremony. They praised the admirable effort of the Chinese in contributing to the building of such a community hospital and expressed faith that the hospital would serve the health care needs of men and women, old and young, of Chinese communities in the United States.

The singing of the U.S. national anthem by a group of Chinese children was a noticeable feature of the ceremony.[89] The new hospital was open to all visitors after the opening ceremony. A ten-day celebration with street fairs, a beauty contest, a well-baby contest, big banquets, and street parades followed. Money raised in the ten-day activities went to support the maintenance of the hospital.

The composition of the first hospital staff showed American Chinese people's willingness to accept Western medicine and their determination to make the hospital a Chinese-controlled community asset. The first director of the hospital was Howard H. Johnson, a Caucasian medical doctor. There were five Chinese doctors on the staff, and all were American-educated and licensed to practice medicine in the state of California. All had also adopted English first names. The rest of the hospital staff were white doctors, twenty-two being practicing doctors and ten consulting doctors.[90] The general manager of the hospital was Chen Lesheng, the Chinese man who headed the fundraising bureau, and all four departments in the hospital were headed by Chinese doctors.[91]

The Chinese Hospital was an important indication of the growth and maturation of American Chinese communities. Together with herbal doctors, the Chinese Hospital served the medical needs of the large Chinese population in the San Francisco Bay area in the next five decades. In 1975, the hospital underwent major renovation and expansion. After a brand new building was completed next to the 1925 structure, the old building was turned into medical offices. According to Thomas Chinn, a Chinese American historian, the Chinese Hospital in the 1980s ran "its own state-licensed HMO, the first Chinese-sponsored health plan in America, providing twenty-four-hour health care for the large community it serves."[92] The hospital was rated in March 2000 by the California Board of Health as a top-quality medical institution in the San Francisco Bay area.[93] It continues to provide medical care to the local Chinese communities.

Besides the Chinese Hospital and Chew Fong Low's modern apartment building, two other buildings completed in the mid-1920s stood as material evidence of a maturing Chinese American community. One of these was the Chinese Chamber of Commerce headquarters in San Francisco. The chamber had been in existence for several decades, yet it had been renting its office. Its mission to defend China's economic interests in the world and to develop business relations with non-Chinese communities in the United States had made the chamber an important community organization. In their effort to construct a complete community, the American Chinese decided to build a permanent home for this important organization. In early 1926, a three-story building was completed and dedicated in San Francisco's Chinatown. All the money for purchasing the land and constructing the building was raised among Chinese in the United States. The chamber proudly invited people from all walks of life, Chinese as well as people from American mainstream society, to attend the dedication ceremony.[94]

The new YMCA in San Francisco Chinatown was the other building. As mentioned in chapter 4, the YMCA played an important part in the development of Chinatown youth. At the same time, the YMCA also sponsored lectures on various topics, offered English classes, and provided employment services aimed at opening up job opportunities beyond the Chinatown borders. The YMCA had become so popular that its original building had to be expanded. The need to expand this important community institution was acknowledged by all Chinese in the United States. The fundraising organization for the YMCA building got enthusiastic support from Chinese communities throughout the United States, from American mainstream society, and from the International Committee of the YMCAs. A total of $250,000 was raised, and an entirely new building was completed in early 1926. The new YMCA was equipped with a swimming pool, a gym, game rooms, and dormitory rooms. Attending the dedication of the new building on February 16 were representatives from all major Chinese organizations, including the CCBA, Chinese Chamber of Commerce, GMD American branch, Zhigongtang, and CACA.[95]

By the mid-1920s, American Chinatowns had become homes away from home to Chinese in the United States. China was no longer an attractive place to live. Racial prejudice and discrimination in the United States segregated and isolated Chinese from American mainstream society. Investing in and contributing to building facilities and permanent structures, Chinese in the United States helped create their own communities. The mentality among the American Chinese was no longer "oriented to roots in a specific place and desire to return"; instead, it was oriented "around an ability to recreate a culture in diverse locations."[96] It is to the discussion of Chinese American culture that we now turn.

Chinese American Communities in the 1920s

Compared with the Chinese American communities in 1910, American Chinatowns, especially San Francisco's Chinatown, which had been leading the way in the general development of a Chinese American community and culture, had been transformed by the 1920s. In 1922, Wu

Panzhao, owner of *Chung Sai Yat Po*, noted that San Francisco's Chinatown had been "modernized." He observed,

> The quaint, the picturesque, the Oriental environment and mysterious
> atmosphere which entered so largely into make-up of Chinatown of yes-
> teryear . . . are no longer in evidence.
>
> As one strolls along the street of Chinatown, no longer the sight of
> Chinese children garbed with the pleasing raiments of the Orient, . . .
> chattering in the speech of their fathers, playing the games which were
> by their forebears centuries before in the valley of the Yangtse. But he
> will see the Oriental children closely-clipped hair, in smart American
> clothes, and many in khaki uniforms of the Boys Scouts, playing Amer-
> ican games, mostly delighting in parading with wooden guns carrying the
> Stars and Stripes in martial array, singing "Dixie Land" and "Marching
> Thru Georgia." . . .
>
> One should not be surprised . . . to see the Chinese girl, formerly so
> retiring, so demure, so timid, so modest, suddenly transformed into a
> vivacious, independent, self-assertive, dressed in the latest cut of fash-
> ion as her American sisters are. It is not an infrequent sight to see a young
> Chinese girl wearing high cut skirt, high French heels, low neck dress,
> bobbed hair, beauty spot and carrying vanity bags with the indispensable
> lipsticks and powder puffs. . . .
>
> The younger generation of the Chinese people are so thoroughly Amer-
> icanized. Most of them are well educated, receiving a high school [diplo-
> ma] and many a college education. They are very ambitious and patriot-
> ic in the extreme. They take important parts in everything pertaining to
> the duties of American citizenship. . . . There is nothing Chinese about
> them except their complexion which is only skin deep.[97]

Wu Panzhao wrote this mainly for the American mainstream reader. Combating images of Chinese as unassimilable, he emphasized the
changes and Americanizing aspects of San Francisco's Chinatown. Yet a
careful study of several organizations and of various activities in San
Francisco's Chinatown in the 1920s will give us a more complete picture.
Both Americanizing aspects and enduring Chinese values and China
connections made American Chinatowns centers of a diasporic culture,
where modern American culture converged with traditional Chinese
culture and where American patriotism was accompanied by concerns
for the welfare of China.

A visitor to San Francisco's Chinatown in the 1920s not only would
see fashionable Chinese women but also would notice that Chinese
women had taken upon themselves civic and community responsibilities. The Chinese YWCA, established in 1916, had 699 members and was
"serving an average of 15,000 persons a year in the 1920s." The main

purpose of the Chinese YWCA was "less to convert souls than to Americanize the foreign-born." Members provided their own community with services that included "home visits, English classes," and advice on modern ways of housekeeping and baby care. It also helped Chinese women find employment opportunities and deal with domestic problems. Chinese YWCA members also worked closely with other Chinatown organizations in fundraising activities such as benefits for the Chinese Hospital and disaster relief work for China.[98]

The Chinese YWCA exemplified Americanization and modernization of Chinese American women and the Chinese American community as a whole. Contrary to their traditional roles prescribed by Confucianism, they stepped outside their homes and assumed community and social responsibilities. One of the most important roles played by the Chinese YWCA in the 1920s was to encourage Chinese American women to learn modern ways of raising healthy babies and to get Chinese mothers out of their homes and into the public arena. In 1928, the Chinese YWCA was the co-sponsor of a Well Baby Contest with the San Francisco's City Public Health Department. The contest was "part of a national campaign . . . to lower infant mortality by educating mothers about infant hygiene." Chinese mothers enthusiastically participated in the contest. "Over 60 mothers entered 176 babies in the contest." Physicians from the Chinese Hospital examined all participating babies and finally declared three as the healthiest babies and awarded their mothers with prizes.[99]

The Chinese YWCA played a major role in the upbringing of second-generation Chinese American women. Discrimination and the largely segregated Chinatown community circumscribed the social life of second-generation Chinese Americans. Even the public school Chinese children in San Francisco attended was designated particularly for "Orientals" and was called the Oriental School. The YWCA gave the second-generation girls "a library collection for leisure reading," "access to the swimming pool at the Central YWCA," and "classes in gymnastics, American cooking, dressmaking, and music." Such activities helped to familiarize them with the American way of life. More importantly, as members of the Chinese YWCA, young Chinese girls were given opportunities to run their own recreational clubs, participate in fundraising efforts, "broaden their social life" by interacting with people beyond Chinatown's limits, and even "develop leadership skills."[100]

The Chinese YWCA thus paved the way for second-generation Chinese American girls to grow up and enter the public sphere. The first organization for and by the second-generation American Chinese women was the Square and Circle Club. In 1924, seven American-born Chinese teenage girls in San Francisco read in newspapers that there was a terrible flood in China and that the ensuing famine was causing great human suffering. Their concern for the welfare of their ancestral land and their sense of civic duty prompted the organization of the club. In naming their club, they were inspired by a Chinese proverb, "In deeds be square and in knowledge be all-round." The first activity of the club was a jazz dance to raise relief funds for flood victims in China.[101]

What distinguished the Square and Circle Club from other Chinatown organizations at the time was its American way of carrying out its activities and the boldness demonstrated by its members in asserting their power in the Chinese American community and in the larger society. The jazz dance, commented a non-Chinese newspaper at the time, "combines the characteristics of both peoples—American jazz by Chinese orchestra, and American dancing by Chinese girls in American party frocks and high heels."[102] Unlike other Chinese women's groups who served auxiliary roles in philanthropic or public work such as fundraising events, the club was an independent organization. In 1926, the club organized a "hope chest raffle." The idea of a hope chest raffle was distinctively American, and they carried it out in an American fashion. Club members stood on street corners to sell tickets. They used American music and put on American costumes.[103] Judy Yung, who had access "to the club's past minutes and scrapbooks," found that the club wrote letters "to government officials asking for longer hours and better lighting at Chinese Playground, a dental and health clinic for Chinatown, retention of Chinatown's only Chinese-speaking public health nurse, public housing, and passage of immigration legislation favorable to the Chinese. The club also worked with other community organizations to register voters, clean up Chinatown, [and] protest racist legislation."[104]

Modernization of American Chinatowns was reflected not only in the increasingly visible social roles played by Chinese American women but also in the several activities San Francisco's Chinatown organized in the mid-1920s. Such activities included the 1925 beauty contest to raise money for the Chinese Hospital and to attract visitors to a ten-day street affair, the 1927 Flower and Lantern Festival, and the 1927 fundraising activities, which also included a beauty contest.

Although all these events were organized for the purpose of raising money, they were also widely publicized to American mainstream society to correct the distorted image of American Chinatowns that still prevailed. Despite Chinese efforts to stop exhibitions such as the Chinatown Underground display at the Panama Pacific International Exposition, Chinatowns were still regarded as places filled with underground tunnels of opium dens, gambling joints, and brothels.[105] Or Chinatowns were mysterious places where "heathen Chinese worshipped their gods and divined their fates from fortune sticks" and bloody battlegrounds where barbarian Chinamen fought tong wars.[106] "The horrors and vices of the San Francisco Chinatown" became local tourist attractions. White promoters "created false impressions in the minds of tourists, concerning Chinese habits and life," a Chinese American woman, Esther Wong, complained in 1924.[107]

All these events were also avenues to promote Chinatown businesses and to showcase their cultural heritage. American Chinese in the 1920s still confronted a racist mainstream society and were barred from most lucrative business opportunities. Chinatown businesses exploited differences between Chinese culture and Western culture for profit. *Chinese Digest*, a Chinese-language newspaper run by American-born Chinese, pointed out in the 1930s that tourism had become the economic lifeline of Chinatowns. To keep a Chinatown economy running, Chinese inhabitants should "make tourists want to come; and when they come, let us have something to show them."[108] Despite the fact that the Chinese had been ridiculed for their different customs and practices, they still held deep pride in Chinese culture and civilization. The American-born Chinese were taught to be "proud of China's four thousand years of glorious and continuous history, of her four hundred million population, and of her superior culture and civilization." The younger generation was also told to be "thankful for the traditions and customs you have inherited as a member of the yellow race."[109]

San Francisco's Chinatown organized a beauty contest to raise money for the hospital and to draw visitors to a ten-day street fair celebrating the opening of the hospital. Publicly putting young Chinese women on stage was a symbol of Chinese acculturation into American mainstream norms. In 1921 the first Miss America beauty contest was held in Atlantic City. The idea of a Chinatown beauty contest was also a reflection of the overall modernization of American Chinatowns noticed by Wu Panzhao. Chinese American women had stepped outside their traditional boundaries and entered the public sphere, as the Chinese YWCA and the Square and Circle Club had demonstrated.

Organized by the CCBA and the Chinese Hospital Association, the beauty contest was a fundraising scheme. Sixty Chinese women entered the contest.[110] According to a participant of such a beauty contest, "It wasn't a matter of intelligence or beauty, just popularity."[111] Participants gave public speeches in the streets and went door to door to sell tickets.

The Chinese-language newspapers printed participants' photos. A ticket box was set up at the meeting hall of the CCBA. Everyone, Chinese or not, was welcome to participate in the activity, and they could buy as many tickets as they wanted. Buyers wrote the name of their favorite contestant on the tickets and dropped the tickets in the box. The ticket box was opened every day, and results were announced in the Chinese-language newspapers. The one who received the most tickets was crowned queen.[112]

The beauty contest was a great success in raising money for the hospital and bringing crowds to Chinatown. The winner of the contest sold 70,700 tickets.[113] The crowning of the queen was held outside the new Chinese Hospital. The ceremony attracted so many people that "the street opposite the coronation platform was choked with a mass of people of all races. . . . People filled the windows of surrounding houses and patients and nurses of the hospital watched the proceedings eagerly," the *San Francisco Chronicle* reported.[114]

The crowning of the beauty queen was an occasion of Americanization and modernization. San Francisco mayor James Rolph was invited to crown the queen, Lena Leong, who was twenty-one years old, unmarried, and working in a Chinese business in San Francisco. While crowning the queen, the Caucasian mayor gave her "two kisses." Such behavior was absolutely unacceptable in traditional China, where unmarried women should not be seen by men other than their fathers and brothers, let alone be kissed by a strange man. Yet it was obviously an acceptable act for the Chinese in San Francisco, for all Chinese attending the ceremony greeted the kisses with "thunderous applause,"[115] according to *Young China*. The crowning ceremony was followed by a dance ball "more grandiose than any the San Francisco Chinatown had ever seen," at the Grand Lodge of the CACA. The beauty queen and Chinese American women danced with Chinese and white men.[116]

The ten-day street fair that followed attracted many visitors to Chinatown. The Square and Circle Club, together with Chinese Christian churches, ran a pastry and tea stand that was very successful in raising money for the hospital. The Canton Noodle Factory cooked and sold noodles at the fair, and half of the profit went to the hospital. There were also stands and games at the fair, run by Chinese and non-Chinese alike, whose profits benefited the hospital.[117] John McNab, the CCBA lawyer, petitioned the city government not to charge a $25-per-stand-per-day fee at the Chinatown street fair because the fair was for the purpose of raising funds for a community hospital. He was successful in getting the charge waived.[118] The street fair was thus a great success.

Besides presenting their own image of Chinatowns to counteract distorted portrayals of filthy ghettos with morally depraved people, the Chinese in the United States closely cooperated with Christian churches in building up community facilities and presenting a more positive Chinatown image. In early 1927, St. Mary's Church in San Francisco's Chinatown opened a new English- and Chinese-language school for the Chinese community in the Bay area. To raise money for the school and publicize the school's existence, the church initiated a "Flower and Lantern Festival," with a Chinatown beauty contest as the central and climactic event. The church received support and cooperation from Chinatown organizations. The Chinese-language newspapers carried pictures of Chinese women who volunteered to participate in the beauty contest. The San Francisco CCBA sent out flyers, encouraging all Chinese to welcome and take an active part in the festival. The Chinese Chamber of Commerce officially advised all Chinese businesses to take the opportunity to promote their businesses to mainstream society.[119]

The beauty contest sponsored by St. Mary's Church worked in the same way as the one administered at the opening of the Chinese Hospital in 1925. The contest lasted ten days. Chinese women sold tickets for the festival. The one who sold the most was crowned again by San Francisco Mayor Rolph. The money raised through the sale of tickets went to the church to support the new school.

Because the festival was organized by whites and was aimed at attracting mainstream society to visit Chinatown, the San Francisco CCBA asked all Chinatown businesses to clean up their stores and streets and to light up their store fronts. Chinatown residents were told that the festival would affect the reputation of all Chinese and that non-Chinese visitors to the festival would be very picky about the appearance of the Chinese and Chinatown. All Chinese were also advised to show up at the festival with "neat and tidy clothing."[120]

The festival was a great success. The Chinese actively participated in the festival. Hundreds of thousands of tickets were sold.[121] The Chinese-language newspapers reported with pride that the champion of the beauty contest gave a speech in English and donated the prize, a diamond ring, to the church's new school.[122]

San Francisco Chinatown organized another beauty contest in 1927 as a fundraising scheme for the Chinese Hospital. In early 1927, a fundraising campaign was launched to remodel an old building, property of the hospital, into a medical emergency center for poor Chinese.[123] Later that year, to give the campaign a push, a large-scale American Chinatown beauty contest was staged. Whereas the 1925 beauty contest did not reach places outside California, the organizing committee of the 1927 contest sent flyers to places throughout the United States. Chinese or friends and supporters of Chinese could buy tickets from the participating Chinese women via mail or cable. The San Francisco CCBA was behind the fundraising campaign, and its building served as the general office of the organizing committee. Expensive prizes were set for the first thirty winners of the beauty contest, with the first-prize winner getting an automobile.[124]

Called the "Magnificent Lion," the event caught much attention from the mainstream society. An automobile company in the San Francisco Bay area, the Western Motors Company, cooperated with Chinatown organizations in the event and took the opportunity to promote its own products. Participating Chinese women stood on "the running board of an Oakland All-American Six two-door sedan" that carried a banner reading "Magnificent Lion Oct. 29 to Nov. 6" to attract attention.[125] The *San Francisco Chronicle* carried detailed reports of the event. With an eye-catching headline "'Magnificent Lion' Collects 'Eats' Money Given to Hospital Fund," the *Chronicle* so described the 1927 Chinatown fundraising event: "Strings of currency and little bags of coin dangled in the street from balcony and marquee just above reach of crowds below—thousands of dollars in actual money. . . . It [the money] was fodder for the Magnificent Lion, in whose honor a nine-day celebration opened yesterday, he alone was privileged to go prancing about nibbling on tender $1 and $5 bills and the tougher tens and twenties. . . . All that the lion ate, however, he later disgorged into the coffers of the $25,000 fund needed for the Chinese Hospital. . . . The Magnificent Lion will perform again today in his money-gathering capacity."[126]

The whole event lasted nine days, with lion dances in the streets of San Francisco Chinatown, with the Chinese Hospital decorated in festive colors, and with all kinds of games and performances held to attract and entertain visitors. Young Chinese women enthusiastically participated in the beauty contest. As in the one held in 1925, participants sold tickets to raise money for the hospital. The one who sold the most tickets was honored as queen. Participants in the beauty contest raised $11,000, announced the chair of the organizing committee. Chinese throughout the United States and members of American mainstream society contributed to the amount. Together with the money collected by the Magnificent Lion, the event had raised $23,000 by the seventh day, when the queen of the beauty contest was announced.[127]

"Chinatown [is] no longer sleepy," noted the *San Francisco Chronicle* in October 1927.[128] Women were certainly not the only ones bringing life to Chinatown. American-born Chinese boys were growing up in

Boy Scout khaki uniforms and playing American games with wooden guns, as Wu Panzhao noticed. The Yoke Choy Club, organized by a group of young Chinese men in 1920, was a sports and music club. Combating racial stereotypes that categorized yellow skin as sickly and weak and Chinese men particularly as opium smokers, the Yoke Choy Club helped popularize sports among young Chinese men. Its members participated in various sports and games sponsored by the Chinatown YMCA and won many prizes in the 1920s.[129] The club also played Western music at various public events in Chinatown such as the crowning of the beauty queens in the 1920s.

Chinese sports activities in the 1920s attracted attention from the *San Francisco Chronicle*. It reported, "Not to be outdone by their Occidental brethren in this business of East vs. West New Year's day football games, rival Chinese elevens, representative of San Francisco and Oakland, will clash this afternoon at Ewing Field for the Celestial gridiron championship of the Pacific Coast, an annual feature of the Chinese new year festival."[130] The next day, the *Chronicle* continued the coverage of the Chinese football game between Jun-Kwan, representing San Francisco's Chinatown, and U.C. Club, a team organized by Chinese students at the University of California at Berkeley: "Amid the popping of firecrackers and the cheers of several hundred fans who braved the downpour to root for their favorites. . . . For sixty minutes the rival Oriental elevens battled fiercely on a mud-covered gridiron. . . . It was a real contest, with the winners showing superiority in every department and the losers contesting gamely for every inch of ground."[131] The winner of the 1926 Chinese New Year's game was Jun-Kwan, the San Francisco Chinatown team.

Adding to the picture of San Francisco's Chinatown of this period were China-related activities. Every October 10, the anniversary of the beginning of the revolution that overthrew the Qing dynasty and established the Chinese Republic, Chinese in San Francisco held various formal ceremonies to celebrate the occasion. On October 10, 1926, on the Chinese Playground in San Francisco's Chinatown, a formal ceremony was held that included raising the Chinese and American national flags, singing patriotic songs, giving speeches, and having Chinese school students march in formation. On the same day, across the Bay in Oakland, students of the Chinese Public School celebrated the occasion by marching through Oakland's Chinatown in a festive parade. Students then gathered at a crossroads in Chinatown for the rest of the ceremony, which included singing the Chinese national anthem, displaying Chinese and American national flags, Chinese teachers giving speeches, and students being reviewed by their teachers in marching formations.[132]

There were also gatherings in the evening to commemorate the occasion. There was a parade in the evening on October 10, 1926 in San Francisco's Chinatown. After the parade, students of various Chinese schools gave prepared speeches on patriotism toward the Chinese Republic. Chinese adults, such as local GMD members, spoke on current events in China.[133] At the gathering at the University of California at Berkeley, Chinese college students spoke on ways to contribute to the building up of the Chinese Republic. One of the ways, according to the speakers, was to go back to China after receiving a college education and to help expand modern education in China.[134]

Such activities carried out every October demonstrated the connection between China and the American Chinese. Such activities always involved students and young people, so that they would not grow up in the United States unaware of their ancestral land. The queen of the 1927 Chinatown beauty contest, Ella Dong, a junior taking courses in education at University of California at Berkeley at the time, said that she could not resist the idea of "going to China to teach" when asked what she planned to do.[135]

San Francisco Chinese also grasped every opportunity to promote Sino-American relations. Their October 10 celebrations featured speeches on the current situation in China. Reverend Wu Panzhao was invited in April 1925 to talk at a women's club meeting in Hotel Oakland. He told his audience that China was changing so fast that "greater changes have come about in that nation in a shorter time than in any other nation in the world." Woman, known as "the Liberty girl," "is rapidly achieving recognition in China after centuries of subjugation to man," Wu emphasized. The greatest change, according to Wu, was in the field of education, which had contributed to the improved conditions for Chinese women.[136] In June 1925, CCBA and the Chinese Chamber of Commerce gave a banquet in San Francisco's Chinatown in honor of the new U.S. ambassador to China. Reverend Wu Panzhao spoke at the banquet, praising the United States as the only power that treated China with justice and emphasizing that China at the time needed "friendly support" from the United States.[137] *Chinese World* introduced the new ambassador as "a friend and expert of China" and praised his conviction that communism could not survive in China because it was incompatible with the Chinese family system and with Chinese culture and tradition.[138]

American Chinatowns had changed. To Chinese in China, they represented Americanization and modernization. To American mainstream society, Chinatown was changing, but it was still a strange cultural enclave, and the Chinese were still unassimilable and therefore ineligible for citizenship. Not only was the Chinese Exclusion law still in full force, but Chinese wives of American citizens of Chinese ancestry were still deprived of the right to immigrate into the United States. To American Chinese themselves, the United States had become home. They took pride in being Chinese and shared their Chinese cultural heritage with non-Chinese at all opportunities; they adopted Christian, capitalist, and democratic values and used American democratic institutions to fight for their rights; they identified with American middle-class values and collectively contributed to the building of their own ethnic communities; and they were disappointed in the politics of their homeland yet still continued to help the poor and needy and work for an independent and modern China.

APPENDIX:
POLITICAL EVENTS IN CHINA,
1898–1924

1898

Hundred Days' Reform, proposed by Kang Youwei, a Confucian scholar, carried out by Emperor Guang Xu, suppressed by Empress Dowager Ci Xi. Kang escaped persecution and arrived in North America.

1899

Kang Youwei organized Baohuanghui (Society to Protect the Emperor) in Canada.

1900

Boxer Uprising, an antiforeign rebellion in northern China, was crushed by allied troops from Britain, Germany, France, the United States, Russia, Italy, Austria, and Japan.

1905

Sun Yat-sen organized the Tongmenghui (Revolutionary Alliance) in Tokyo, Japan. Tongmenghui's political platform was "to overthrow the Manchu barbarians, to restore China to the Chinese, to establish a republic, and to distribute land equally."

1906

Empress Dowager Ci Xi issued an edict promising to prepare a constitution, carry out administrative reforms, and convene a national assembly.

1911

Guangzhou Uprising, the ninth failed uprising against the Qing dynasty led by the Tongmenghui, took place in Guangzhou, Guangdong Province.

Wuchang Uprising. Anti-Qing revolutionaries started the uprising in Wuchang, Hubei Province. The uprising was followed by responses in other provinces in southern China and became the trigger of the 1911 Revolution.

1912

Republic of China was founded in Nanjing, and Sun Yat-sen became provisional president of the republic.

Minshe (People's Society) was organized in China to support Li Yuanhong, commander of the military government established as a result of the successful Wuchang Uprising, as provisional president.

The Qing court announced the abdication of the emperor.

Sun Yat-sen resigned the provisional presidency.

Yuan Shikai, premier in the Qing government, was elected provisional president by the National Council in Nanjing.

Minshe merged with the Republican Party, which supported Yuan Shikai as provisional president and acted as the main opposition party to the Tongmenghui.

Tongmenghui merged with other small political groups and became the Guomindang (GMD, or Nationalist Party).

Results of the first election for the Parliament were announced. Guomindang won majority seats in the Parliament.

1913

Song Jiaoren, acting chair of the GMD, was murdered at the Shanghai train station while on his way to participate in the organization of the new government in Beijing.

Yuan Shikai single-handedly took out a "reorganization loan" with the Five-Power Banking Consortium (of Britain, France, Germany, Russia, and Japan) by ignoring the Parliament's role in negotiating treaties with foreign countries.

The Progressive Party was organized by combining the Republican Party with other small parties. The Progressive Party supported Yuan and acted as the main opposition party to the GMD.

Seven provinces in southern China rebelled against the Yuan government, starting the anti-Yuan revolt known as the Second Revolution.

Yuan Shikai was elected president by the Parliament.

Yuan Shikai dissolved the GMD and revoked certificates and badges from more than half of all Parliament members because of their affiliations with the GMD, effectively destroying the Parliament by making it impossible to reach a quorum.

1914

The new constitution, known as the Constitutional Compact, was declared, which extended the presidential term to ten years and made it renewable without limits.

Sun Yat-sen organized the Zhonghua Gemingdang (Chinese Revolutionary Party) in Tokyo, Japan, where he was exiled when the Second Revolution was suppressed.

1915

Japan made the Twenty-one Demands on China.

Yuan Shikai yielded to Japan's ultimatum and accepted the demands.

Chen Duxiu, a veteran revolutionary who returned to China from his exile in Japan as a result of his participation in the Second Revolution, founded the *New Youth* magazine, which started the literary and intellectual ferment and became the forum of the New Culture Movement.

Yuan Shikai declared 1916 the first year of the Hong Xian Empire and prepared himself to be enthroned on January 1, 1916.

The military leader in Yunnan Province declared independence from the Yuan government and launched the movement "to protect the republic." Several other provinces in southern China joined Yunnan in the movement against Yuan's monarchical restoration.

1916

Yuan Shikai announced cancellation of the Hong Xian Empire.

Yuan Shikai died of uremia.

1917

Zhang Xun, a militarist, attempted to restore Manchu Emperor Pu Yi to the throne. The attempt did not get support from other provincial military leaders and was defeated in less than two weeks.

Sun Yat-sen organized a military government with an "extraordinary parliament" in Guangzhou, challenging the government in Beijing.

1919

Beijing students held demonstrations and set fire to the residence of Cao Rulin, a pro-Japanese official in the Beijing government, in response to the news that the Paris Peace Conference had agreed to transfer Germany's rights in China's Shandong Province to Japan.

Sun Yat-sen changed the name of his party, Zhonghua Gemingdang, back to Guomindang (GMD).

1920

Militarists and politicians in southern China launched a campaign for a federalist system, in which each province would adopt its own constitution and provincial representatives would gather to draft a new national constitution, as an effort to end the war between the military government in Guangzhou and the Beijing government. The campaign produced no result.

1921

The Extraordinary Parliament in Guangzhou reorganized the military government and elected Sun Yat-sen Extraordinary President.

The Chinese Communist Party (CCP) was founded in Shanghai.

1922

Radical intellectuals and students organized an anti-Christian movement in Beijing. The movement condemned Christianity as the "instrument of imperialism."

Chen Jiongming, governor of Guangdong Province and commander-in-chief of the provincial army, organized a mutiny against Sun Yat-sen, who narrowly escaped to a gunboat, which took him to Shanghai.

GMD representatives from all provinces gathered in Shanghai and decided to reorganize the party.

1923

Sun Yat-sen and Adolf Joffe, a Soviet envoy, made a joint declaration for an alliance between the Soviet Union and the GMD.

Sun Yat-sen returned to Guangdong after Chen Jiongming was defeated by other militarists in southern China.

Cao Kun, a northern militarist, bribed the majority of the Parliament in the Beijing government with money and had himself elected president.

Sun's Guangdong government demanded that it, instead of the Beijing government, should receive the customs surplus from the port of Guangzhou in September and threatened to seize the customs house in Guangzhou in December.

1924

The reorganized GMD held its first national conference in Guangzhou. At the conference, a decision was made to accept CCP members into the GMD, and CCP leaders were elected to the GMD Central Executive Committee. The Military Government became the Nationalist Government.

The Foreign Diplomatic Corps in Beijing decided to allow the Sun government to keep the customs surplus from the port of Guangzhou.

The Huangpu Military Academy, the GMD party military school in Huangpu, Guangdong Province, was established to train disciplined army officers who understood and were committed to the GMD political platform of defeating warlordism internally and imperialism externally.

The Guangzhou Merchants' Association held a general strike against a law regarding city reconstruction and taxes passed by the Guangzhou municipal government under the control of the GMD.

The Guangzhou Merchants' Association clashed with Sun's government over a purchase of weapons from abroad.

Sun Yat-sen launched a northern expedition from Guangdong to "open a new field" for his nationalist revolution.

NOTES

Introduction

1. The interview tapes are in the author's possession.
2. Preface to *Entry Denied*, x.
3. Sociologist Stanford Lyman's *Chinese Americans* is an example.
4. Siu, "The Sojourner," 34–44.
5. Dillon's *The Hatchet Men, 1880–1906* is an example.
6. Examples include Huang, *Huaqiao yu Zhongguo geming*; Liu, *Meiguo huaqiao shi*; Zhong, *Huaqiao yu Zhongguo guomin geming yundong*; *Huaqiao yu Xinhai geming*; Wu, *Huaqiao shi zhuanji*; Yang, Liu, and Yang, *Meiguo huaqiao shi*.
7. Wang, "The Structure of Dual Domination," 149–69. Wang, Foreword to *Xing, Ma huaren yu Xinhai geming*.
8. Here are some examples. Ma's *Revolutionaries, Monarchists, and Chinatowns* studied the politicization of American Chinatowns in the first decade of the twentieth century as a result of interactions with developments in China. Yu's *To Save China, To Save Ourselves* revealed the struggles put up by New York's Chinese Hand Laundry Alliance for survival in the United States and for China's independence against Japan's control between 1934 and 1953. Yung's *Unbound Feet* and Ling's *Surviving on the Gold Mountain* delved deep into the lives of American Chinese women and told stories of their struggles against racial and sexual discrimination. *Claiming America*, an edited volume, has several articles on the struggle for equal rights by some groups of American Chinese and on the identity formation of American-born Chinese. Chen's *Chinese San Francisco, 1850–1943* described changes in Chinese life and the process of acculturation in the largest Chinese community in the United States. Hsu's *Dreaming of Gold, Dreaming of Home* revealed the process of immigration and continued ties between American Chinese and their homeland.
9. Wong, "The Transformation of Culture," 201–32.
10. According to Him Mark Lai, a leading expert in Chinese American studies, "*Leong Gor Yun* is merely *Liang Ge Ren* (two persons) as pronounced in Cantonese. The book [*Chinatown Inside Out*] was authored by Chinese journalist Zhu Xia (Y. K. Chu) and a white journalist." Personal communication, May 28, 2001.
11. Leong Gor Yun, *Chinatown Inside Out*, 161.
12. Yu, "John C. Young," 5.
13. Leong Gor Yun, *Chinatown Inside Out*, 161.
14. Yung, "Social Awakening," 195–207.

15. Daniels, *Asian America*, 4.
16. Quoted in McCunn, *Chinese American Portraits*, 117.

Chapter 1: A Search for a Modern China and Challenges to Traditional Chinese Identity, 1911

1. Won, "Recollections of Dr. Sun Yat-sen's Stay," 75–80.
2. Chinese in the United States at this time generally called Euro-Americans *xiren*, or Westerners.
3. Smith, *China's Cultural Heritage*, xiii.
4. Huang, "*Shaonian Zhongguo* chenbao chuangkan zhi huiyi," 46–52.
5. *Chinese World*, December 5, 12, 13, 16, 1910 and April 17, 1911.
6. The National Relief Bureau was set up by the Zhigongtang and the Tong-menghui in the United States to raise money for the revolutionary cause, but it was not very successful until after the Wuchang Uprising of October 1911, which dealt a fatal blow to the Qing ruling court.
7. *Young China*, December 30 and 31, 1911.
8. I am borrowing this phrase from Jonathan D. Spence, a well-known histori-an of Chinese studies. His most recent book covering Chinese history from the late Ming dynasty to the student democracy movement of 1989 is titled *The Search for Modern China*.
9. Cohen, "Being Chinese," 88–108.
10. Clifford, "Diasporas," 302.
11. Mei, "Socioeconomic Developments," 398.
12. Bureau of the Census, *Abstract of the 15th Census, 1930*, 80, Table 22.
13. Mei's analysis of the socioeconomic conditions of the San Francisco Chi-nese at the turn of the century provides more details about the limits on economic opportunities the Chinese American community faced. Mei, "Socioeconomic Developments," 378–97.
14. Takaki, *Strangers from a Different Shore*, 239. According to Takaki, 56 percent of the American Chinese population lived in urban areas in 1920, and by 1940 the percentage had increased to 71.
15. Ma, *Revolutionaries*, 13.
16. Chan, *Asian Americans*, 34.
17. From now on I will refer to them as the CCBA and the Chinese Chamber of Commerce, respectively.
18. Liu, *Meiguo huaqiao shi*, 213–20.
19. There were 56,596 Chinese born in China and 14,935 born in the United States. Bureau of the Census, *Abstract of the 15th Census, 1930*, 81, Table 25.
20. Bureau of the Census, *Abstract of the 13th Census, 1910*, 99, Table 24.
21. Lai, Lim, and Yung, *Island*, 84–86.
22. The Six Classics are *Book of Changes, Book of History, Book of Poetry, Book of Rites, Spring and Autumn Annals,* and *Book of Music.* In 1898, to preserve what he believed to be the best of China's cultural heritage, Kang Youwei proposed that Confucianism be established as China's state religion. See Hsiao, *A Modern China and a New World*, 44–45, 532–34.
23. Liang Qichao met Kang Youwei for the first time in the fall of 1890, and

thereafter Liang studied intermittently for four years at Kang's private school, Wanmu Caotang, in Guangzhou. It was during those four years that Liang's "intellectual foundation for his whole life was laid," according to Hao Chang, who studied Liang's development as an intellectual. Chang, *Liang Ch'i-ch'ao and Intellectual Transition*, 58–60.

24. Kang theorized that absolute monarchy was the lowest form of government, whereas "the people's rule," or democracy, the highest form of government, could be achieved only in the future. The republican form of government in the United States and France was only a partial realization of the "people's rule." For China at the end of the nineteenth century, the appropriate form of government, according to Kang and his followers, was constitutional monarchy, a transitional form of government between absolute monarchy and democracy. Hsiao, *A Modern China and a New World*, 85–94.

25. The Baohuanghui-sponsored banking and investment programs usually were transnational cooperations attracting investments and participation from Chinese in southeast Asia, Hong Kong, Europe, and North America. The two large programs in North America were the Compania Banking Chino Y Mexico and Zhenhua Company. The former, based in Mexico, dealt with real estate investment in Mexico and handled Baohuanghui's financial matters in North America. The latter made investments in developing natural resources in Guangxi Province in southern China. Lai, *Cong huaqiao dao huaren*, 181–82. For the Compania Banking Chino Y Mexico and its real estate investment in Mexico, also see Jacques, "The Chinese Massacre in Torreon," 235–36.

26. The Zhigongtang was an extension of a major secret society in China. The principal goal of this secret society was *fanqing fuming*, to overthrow the Qing dynasty and restore the Ming dynasty. Members of this secret society usually were poor peasants and outcasts in Chinese society. In the United States, members of the Zhigongtang usually were small businessmen and wage workers. Their lower economic and social status and the political goal of the organization determined that they were antiestablishment.

27. Lai, *Cong huaqiao dao huaren*, 143.

28. Ma, *Revolutionaries*, 59.

29. The Chinese Exclusion Act of 1882 was made permanent in 1904, and maltreatment of the exempt classes of Chinese immigrants continued, in violation of diplomatic treaties between China and the United States. In 1905, Chinese in the United States petitioned people in China to boycott American goods to pressure the U.S. government to end the exclusion law and stop the maltreatment. The boycott achieved only limited results because the Qing ruling court, under the pressure from the United States, ordered provincial authorities to put down boycott demonstrations and open ports to American goods. For a detailed study of this boycott, see McKee, *Chinese Exclusion versus the Open Door Policy*.

30. Born in 1866 in Xiangshan, Guangdong Province in China, Sun Yat-sen attended Iolani School, an Anglican institution, and Oahu College, an American Congregationalist school, in Honolulu from 1879 to 1883. He returned to Hong Kong and attended the Diocesan Home, another Church of England school, and Government Central School, a Hong Kong secondary school for children of all nationalities, between 1883 and 1884. He then studied medicine for five years, from 1887 to 1892, at the College of Medicine for Chinese, a British institution

in Hong Kong. See Schiffrin, *Sun Yat-Sen and the Origins of the Chinese Revolution*, 10–20.

31. For instance, Sun believed that the United States' political system, a republic with a constitution protecting the rights of its citizens, was the best in the world. Therefore, the United States was the "teacher/model for our new government in the future," according to Sun. After the 1911 Revolution, he declared, "We have finally established a republic and the wonderful political systems of the United States and France are our guiding principles." *Sun Zhongshan quanji*, 4: 332, 1: 20, and 3: 43. For a good analysis of the connection between Sun's revolutionary ideas and the West, see Wang, *Chinese Intellectuals and the West*, 245–46, 335–37; and Schiffrin, *Sun Yat-sen and the Origins of the Chinese Revolution*.

32. The secret organization was named Xingzhonghui, or the Revive China Society. The purpose of the society was "to overthrow the Manchus, restore China, and establish a republican government." Li, *Sun Zhongshan quanzhuan*, 38.

33. Sun said that "the evolution of Europe and America was based on three leading principles, namely nationalism, democracy, and socialism or people's livelihood" in the editorial he wrote for the first issue of *Min Bao* (People's Tribune), Tongmenghui's party paper in Japan. Quoted in Li, *The Political History of China*, 204. Also see Wang, *Chinese Intellectuals and the West*, 248.

34. Li, *The Political History of China*, 201. The phrase *pingjun diquan*, here translated as "distributing the land equally," is also translated as "the equalization of land ownership," "equalization of land rights," "the equitable redistribution of the land," or "the proportionalization of the land." See Schiffrin, "Sun Yat-sen's Early Land Policy," 549.

35. Schiffrin, *Sun Yat-sen and the Origins of the Chinese Revolution*, 308–9, 362.

36. Ma, *Revolutionaries*, 133.

37. Changbai Mountains are in China's northeast, where most Manchu people live.

38. *Young China*, August 19, 1910.

39. The Geary Act not only extended the 1882 Exclusion Act but also required all Chinese in the United States to register. After it was enacted, any Chinese caught without a registration certificate was subject to immediate deportation.

40. Hoexter, *From Canton to California*, 153.

41. Ibid., 163.

42. By 1911, *Chung Sai Yat Po*'s readership went beyond Chinese Christians in the United States. In fact, it had become the most popular Chinese-language newspaper for Chinese in the United States, with a circulation of 3,500, whereas the figure for *Chinese World* was 3,000 and the one for *Young China*, which was only a few months old, was 1,500. Daggett, *History of Foreign Journalism*, 49–57.

43. Hoexter, *From Canton to California*, 171.

44. *Chinese World*, January 13, 1911.

45. *Chinese World*, May 22, 1911.

46. *Chinese World*, May 16, 20, 22, and 26, 1911.

47. The Han and Manchus were of the same race, the Asiatic Mongolian race. Both of them had been considered part of *Huaxia*. *Huaxia*, just like *Zhonghua*, means "Chinese" with a connotation of culture and civilization. To talk about Manchus as aliens was an expedient way for the revolutionaries to arouse hatred

against the ruling class, which happened to be Manchus at the time. If Manchus were considered aliens, then there were other aliens in China, for China consisted of more than fifty different nationalities. Information about race is from Hu, *Zhongguo minzu zhi.*

48. Lo, *Kang Yu-wei,* 213.

49. Chang, *Liang Ch'i-ch'ao and Intellectual Transition in China,* 166–67.

50. *Young China,* May 12, 1911. *Young China* carried a series of editorials continually from May 12 to June 22 attacking Xu's argument. Xu's article was carried in *Chinese Reform News,* the Constitutionalist Party's newspaper in New York.

51. *Chinese World,* October 16 and 17, 1911.

52. *Chinese World,* May 2, 1911.

53. *Chinese World,* May 4, 1911.

54. *Young China,* May 12, 1911.

55. *Young China,* February 2, 1911.

56. *Young China,* February 21, 1911. This line of anti-Manchu argument had been used by radical revolutionaries in China and among Chinese students in Japan since the early 1900s. See Schiffrin, *Sun Yat-sen and the Origins of the Chinese Revolution,* 293–99.

57. *Young China,* February 19, March 10 and 15, April 3, 5, 6, 8, 10, 12, 14, 15, and 23, 1911.

58. *Young China,* May 4, 5, 6, and 7, 1911.

59. *Young China,* May 4, 1911.

60. *Young China,* February 18 and April 1 and 5, 1911.

61. *Young China,* April 4 and 5 and May 12, 1911. Pu Yi, the last emperor, was enthroned at age three in 1908.

62. *Young China,* April 4, 1911.

63. *Young China,* April 1 and 28 and May 6, 1911. It was common at this time for writers for Chinese-language newspapers to use pen names. Although the Tongmenghui was the first sexually integrated Chinese American organization, women who joined it were largely family members of the organization's leaders. When the Tongmenghui American branch was first established, meetings had to be held secretly at homes of the organizers. Female members of these families took upon themselves the task of watching out for intruders and thus were members of the organization. Lilly King Gee Won and her mother (see note 1 of this chapter) were examples of such involvement. For a detailed study of Chinese American women's involvement in community and political activities around this time, see Yung, *Unbound Feet,* 52–105.

64. *Young China,* April 1, 1911.

65. *Young China,* April 18, 1911.

66. *Chung Sai Yat Po,* January 6, 7, 9, 10, and 12, 1911.

67. *Chung Sai Yat Po,* March 16 and April 3 and 19, 1911.

68. *Chung Sai Yat Po,* March 16, 1911.

69. *Chung Sai Yat Po,* April 12, 1911.

70. *Chung Sai Yat Po,* April 8, 1911.

71. *Young China,* April 16 and 17, and *Chung Sai Yat Po,* February 15 and April 18, 1911.

72. *Chung Sai Yat Po,* January 12, 1911. The paper's advocacy for education

reflected a popular desire of many American Chinese. According to Him Mark Lai, it was Yung Wing who was the first to propose fundraising among American Chinese for a school back in the hometown, Xiangshan County, Guangdong Province in 1872. Between the founding of the Republic of China in 1912 and 1920, such fundraising activities played a major role in establishing two secondary schools, 104 primary schools, a professional school, and a girls' school in Taishan County, making it an educationally advanced county in Guangdong Province. *Cong huaqiao dao huaren*, 238.

73. *Chung Sai Yat Po*, January 14, 1911.

74. For a detailed study of the process in which American Chinese communities became politicized in the decade before the 1911 Revolution, see Ma, *Revolutionaries*.

75. Leong Gor Yun, *Chinatown Inside Out*, 161.

76. The Boxer Rebellion, at the turn of the century, was the most recent movement against foreigners, especially Christians in China.

77. Wu Panzhao was a regular lecturer for the Chautauqua program and the Lyceum Lectures, both of which were entertainment and education programs for American mainstream society. Wu thus earned the title "the Oriental Mark Twain" among mainstream Americans and was awarded an honorary doctoral degree by the University of Pittsburgh in 1913. His ability to bridge the gap between American Chinese and mainstream society was recognized and appreciated not only by non-Christian Chinese in the United States but also by the Chinese government. As a result, he was appointed vice-consul for China in San Francisco in early 1913. For more information on Wu, see Hoexter, *From Canton to California*.

78. *Chinese World*, January 2, 1911.

79. *Chung Sai Yat Po*, January 13, 1911.

80. *Chinese World*, January 2, 1911.

81. *Chung Sai Yat Po*, January 13, 1911.

82. *Chung Sai Yat Po*, January 20, 1911.

83. *Chung Sai Yat Po*, January 16, 1911.

84. *Chinese World*, January 26, 1911.

85. *Chinese World*, January 16, 1911.

86. "Chinese Newspaper Prints Joke and Causes a Riot," *San Francisco Chronicle*, January 16, 1911.

87. The Chinese Exclusion Act of 1882 had effectively reduced the Chinese population in the United States by the 1890s. The reduced population meant a smaller consumer market for Chinese goods. In addition, there were more restrictions and barriers on imports and exports to and from China. The Siyi people, who came from poorer backgrounds and were engaged mostly in small businesses and hand laundries, realized the limits of opportunities for them to grow economically and socially in American Chinatowns. Therefore, they boycotted Sanyi businesses, most of which were bigger and engaged in more profitable import and export trade, in an attempt to create opportunities for their own people to engage in larger businesses and in import and export businesses. For further information on American Chinatown business development in the late nineteenth and early twentieth century, see Ma, "The Big Business Ventures," 101–12.

88. *Chinese World*, February 2, 1911.

89. *Chung Sai Yat Po,* March 29 and May 8, 1911.
90. *Chung Sai Yat Po,* February 3, 1911.
91. *Chung Sai Yat Po,* February 8, 1911.
92. *Young China,* February 27, March 3, 4, 15, and 17, and April 21, 1911.
93. *Young China,* March 11, 1911.
94. *Young China,* April 21, 1911.
95. *Young China,* April 17, 1911.
96. *Young China,* April 23, 1911.
97. In China, if a man's wife had an affair with another man, this husband then "wore a green hat," which was one of the greatest marks of disgrace a man could suffer.
98. *Chinese World,* April 10 and 11, 1911.
99. *Chung Sai Yat Po,* May 4, 1911.
100. *Chung Sai Yat Po,* May 23, 1911.
101. *Young China,* May 4, 1911. The Zhigongtang was notorious for its violent means of achieving its goals.
102. *Young China,* May 4, 1911.
103. Lai, *Cong huaqiao dao huaren,* 181.
104. The Mexican revolutionaries under the leadership of Francisco Madero represented the nationalistic bourgeoisie and were rebelling against Porfirio Diaz's government, which they complained was detached from the people, too closely affiliated with European culture, and selling Mexico out to foreign interests. By promising democracy and agrarian reform, Madero's revolutionaries also gathered support from rural masses. The Mexican revolution was similar to the Chinese revolution in 1911 in its complaint against selling out to foreign interests, its promise for democracy and agrarian reform, and its calls for an overthrow of the government. The information on the Mexican revolution of 1911 comes from Hodges and Gandy, *Mexico, 1910–1976,* 5–12.
105. *Chinese World,* June 15, 1911.
106. *Young China,* May 15, 25, and 30, 1911.
107. *Young China,* May 30, 1911. According to Leo M. Dambourges Jacques, hatred toward Chinese stemmed from the "evident prosperity and industry" of the Chinese in Torreon. Before the massacre, there had been anti-Chinese speeches and demonstrations in 1910 and 1911. One of the speeches, delivered ten days before the massacre, specifically "attacked Chinese dominance of the grocery, vegetable, and gardening industries, and called for the expulsion of all Chinese from Mexico." Jacques, "The Chinese Massacre in Torreon," 237.
108. *Young China,* June 6, 1911. This is a Chinese saying. Death "heavier than Mount Tai" means death for a worthy cause, whereas death "lighter than feather" means death for a worthless cause.
109. *Chinese World,* June 22, 1911.
110. Quoted in Schwartz, "The Inconveniences Resulting from Race Mixture," 62.
111. William Jamieson, a U.S. national who happened to be in Torreon as the massacre took place, recorded this observation in a letter to his father. Quoted in Schwartz, "The Inconveniences Resulting from Race Mixture," 62 and Jacques, "The Chinese Massacre in Torreon," 238.
112. *Chinese World,* June 23, 1911.

113. At this time, the terms *Baohuanghui, the Constitutionalist Party,* and *Baohuangdang* were used interchangeably. Reformers preferred the term *the Constitutionalist Party,* whereas Tongmenghui members used *Baohuanghui* or *Baohuangdang* (a society to protect the emperor) for their negative connotations.

114. A team made up of Chinese and Mexican government representatives investigated the question of whether Chinese in Torreon resisted and thus provoked the massacre to establish grounds for official reparations. After extensive interviews with local residents and businesses, the investigation team concluded that the Chinese in Torreon had been peaceful residents and had acquired no arms before the massacre, either through purchase or from the Mexican government troops stationed in the area. Jacques, "The Chinese Massacre in Torreon," 242–43.

115. *Young China,* June 24 and 30 and July 1 and 3, 1911.

116. *Young China,* July 15 and 16, 1911. The Qing government, in this particular case, was able to get the Mexican government to sign a protocol agreeing to pay 3,100,000 pesos for the death of 303 Chinese. Because of the political and financial turmoil in Mexico in the years that followed, the Mexican government never paid the reparations. Jacques, "The Chinese Massacre in Torreon," 244–45.

117. Scott, "A Resynthesis," 167.

118. *Young China,* July 1, 1911.

119. This flyer was carried in *Young China* from September to October 1911.

120. Liu, *Meiguo huaqiao shi,* 578. The information on exchange rate between the Chinese money and United States dollar is from Schneider et al., *Wahrungen der Welt V,* 213.

121. *Young China,* July 5, 1911.

122. *Young China,* July 18, 19, and 20, 1911.

123. *Chung Sai Yat Po,* October 28, 1911.

124. *Chinese World,* October 16, 1911.

125. *Young China,* October 17, 1911.

126. *Young China,* November 26 and 30 and December 27, 1911.

127. *Young China,* December 28, 1911.

128. *Chung Sai Yat Po,* November 28 and December 1, 1911.

129. "Six Companies Agree to Raise Canton Loan," *San Francisco Chronicle,* December 1, 1911.

130. "Chop Suey Cooks Threaten Strike," *San Francisco Chronicle,* December 1, 1911. No result was reported of this threatened strike. Effective labor organizations by American Chinese independent of the CCBA did not become a reality until the 1930s, when the Chinese Hand Laundry Alliance of New York and the Chinese Workers' Mutual Aid Association of San Francisco were established. Wong, Applewhite, and Daley, "From Despotism to Pluralism," 215–33.

131. *Chinese World,* October 16 and 17, 1911.

132. *Chung Sai Yat Po,* November 11 and December 28, 1911.

133. *Chung Sai Yat Po,* February 14, 20, and 26, 1912.

134. *Young China,* November 3, 1911.

135. *Young China,* November 6, 1911.

136. Zhang, "Xinhai qian Meizhuo huaqiao geming huodong jilu," (Notes on Revolutionary Activities Among Chinese in America Before the 1911 Revolution), 50–51.

137. See note 6 in the introduction.

Chapter 2: Defending Chinese Republicanism and Debating Chineseness in the United States, 1912–14

1. *Chinese World*, October 13, 1913.

2. McKeown, "Reconceptualizing Chinese Diasporas," 325.

3. The Second Revolution was waged by the GMD under Sun Yat-sen's leadership to overthrow the Yuan government and to defend democracy and republicanism in China. The GMD accused Yuan of having murdered Song Jiaoren, the most prominent GMD leader in the Beijing Parliament, to suppress political opposition. The GMD also accused Yuan of violating parliamentary procedure in obtaining a multi-million-dollar loan without submitting it to the parliament for approval.

4. Li, *The Political History of China*, 304–5.

5. *Young China*, December 23 and 25, 1911, January 21 and February 16, 1912.

6. *Young China*, January 25, 1912.

7. *Young China*, March 14 and April 15, 1912.

8. *Young China*, March 19, 1912.

9. *Young China*, June 14, 1912.

10. *Young China*, October 6, 1912. The paper's explanation of the *minsheng* principle is a bit stretched. When Sun Yat-sen explained the *minsheng* principle after the establishment of the Republic of China, he emphasized generally the importance of avoiding the social inequities existing in the capitalist world and specifically state control of the land, natural resources, public utilities, transportation, and other large-scale industries. The vague phrase "equal distribution of land" was now explained as a program by which land owners would report to the government the value of their land and the government would put a tax on the land according to its value. Any increase of land value from then on would benefit the country as a whole, not the individual land owner. Sun believed that such taxation of the "unearned increment—the increase in land values resulting from social progress and not from the improvements made by the owner" (Schiffrin's words)—would discourage land speculation and encourage rich people to invest in the development of industry and commerce. It was the lack of industrial and commercial development that had made China a weak nation, Sun believed. Government ownership of national resources and state control over public utilities would prevent exploitation and bring about economic and social justice to all citizens of the republic, Sun pointed out. However, Sun did not speak specifically about confiscation of private property, abolition of rights of inheritance, or confiscation of land. "Response to Reporters from Shanghai's *Wenhui ribao* (Wenhui Daily)," in *Sun Zhongshan quanji*, 2: 332. For Sun's explanation of the *minsheng* principle, see Schiffrin, "Sun Yat-sen's Early Land Policy," 550–57.

11. Immediately after the founding of the Republic of China, the provisional government legislated to abolish physical torture, forbid the sale of human beings, advise not to bind feet, have all queues cut off, wipe out opium smoking, forbid the sale of laborers overseas, protect overseas Chinese, prevent the corruption of government officials, and abolish titles of *daren* and *laoye* among government workers. Quoted in Li, *Sun Zhongshan quanzhuan*, 207.

12. *Young China*, April 7 and 20, 1912.

13. *Young China*, July 3, 1912.

14. The two most important things Chinese in the United States strove for were to build houses and to buy land for their families in China, and by 1910, some of them had already achieved those goals. For more details, see Lai, *Cong huaqiao dao huaren,* 236–48.

15. *Chinese World,* January 3, 1912.

16. *Chinese World,* March 11, 1912.

17. *Chinese World,* April 3, 1912.

18. *Chinese World,* April 13 and May 8, 1912.

19. *Chinese World,* May 18, 1912.

20. *Chinese World,* May 27, 1912.

21. With help from Russia, the "Empire of Mongolia" was declared on December 28, 1911. On November 3, 1912, Russia and Mongolia signed an agreement by which Russia committed itself to help Mongolia "maintain autonomous regime." On November 5, 1913, Russia and China signed a declaration by which Russia recognized China's suzerainty over Outer Mongolia and China recognized Outer Mongolia's autonomous status. Clubb, *China and Russia,* 153–55.

22. *Chinese World,* October 14 and December 27, 1913. Kang Youwei first proposed to the Qing ruling court that Confucianism be made China's state religion in 1898. In 1913, Kang repeated the proposal to the Chinese parliament. Neither time was he successful. Hsiao, *A Modern China and a New World,* 44, 120.

23. *Chinese World,* June 6, 1912.

24. *Chinese World,* June 8, 1912.

25. *Chinese World,* June 17, 1912.

26. *Chinese World,* September 12, 1912.

27. *Chinese World,* July 7–10, 1912.

28. The *minsheng* principle was precisely aimed at ridding the Chinese nation of poverty. Paul M. A. Linebarger pointed out that *minsheng* aimed at "national enrichment" and strove for "economic justice." *The Political Doctrines of Sun Yat-sen,* 128.

29. Sparks, *China Gold,* 152–55.

30. *Chinese World,* November 3 and 4, 1913.

31. Presidents of district associations and CCBA presidents were titled scholars who were sent to the United States by Chinese government as part of its diplomatic corps. This practice continued until 1925, when the United States "objected to giving" such persons "diplomatic status." Lai, "Historical Development of the Chinese Consolidated Benevolent Association," 22.

32. *Confucian Analects,* Book XII.

33. *Chung Sai Yat Po,* February 20 and 21, 1912.

34. *Chung Sai Yat Po,* October 21, 1912 and September 12 and 29, October 23, and November 24 and 25, 1913. It was precisely the opposition offered by leaders representing the Catholic, Protestant, Muslim, Buddhist, and Taoist faiths in China in the form of a Society for Religious Freedom that blocked Kang's campaign for state religion. Hsiao, *A Modern China and a New World,* 121.

35. *Chung Sai Yat Po,* December 27, 1913.

36. *Chung Sai Yat Po,* April 23, 1913.

37. *Chung Sai Yat Po,* July 24, 1913.

38. *Chung Sai Yat Po,* July 2 and 5, 1912.

39. *Chung Sai Yat Po,* May 13, 1913.

40. *Chung Sai Yat Po,* May 6, 1913.
41. *Chung Sai Yat Po,* March 23, 1912.
42. *Chung Sai Yat Po,* August 2, 1913
43. *Chung Sai Yat Po,* June 15, 1912.
44. *Chung Sai Yat Po,* June 3, 1912.
45. *Chung Sai Yat Po,* February 27, 1912.
46. *Chung Sai Yat Po,* May 9, 1913 and September 12, 1912.
47. *Chung Sai Yat Po,* May 5 and 9, 1913.
48. The lunar calendar and the Chinese New Year are discussed in detail later in this chapter.
49. Assimilation is a complicated process, and there are several types of changes that can be called assimilation. If changes are only in the realm of cultural practices, then it is more precisely called acculturation. Through large-scale intermarriage, it can reach amalgamation. The "assimilation" that *Chung Sai Yat Po* is advocating here is more accurately called acculturation, through which process Chinese modify their cultural practices to fit those of the American mainstream society. My definition of *assimilation* is from Gordon, *Assimilation in American Life,* 71.
50. *Chung Sai Yat Po,* April 12 and 27 and November 4, 1912 and March 19 and 20, 1914.
51. *Chung Sai Yat Po,* April 27, 1912.
52. The section on cultural identifications in this chapter discusses the conflict between *Chung Sai Yat Po*'s vision and the prevailing American Chinese mentality.
53. *Young China,* July 21, 22, and 24, 1913.
54. Wang, *Community and Nation,* 145.
55. *Young China,* February 18, 1912.
56. *Young China,* February 15, 1912. The Native Sons of the Golden State (NSGS) was established in San Francisco in 1895. The organization became a national one in 1915, and the English name was then changed to *Chinese American Citizens Alliance* (CACA). The Chinese name, *Tongyuanhui,* remained the same. For more information about the NSGS and CACA, see Chung, "Fighting for Their American Rights," 95–126.
57. *Young China,* February 20, 1912.
58. *Chung Sai Yat Po,* June 28, 1912.
59. From December 27, 1911 to February 24, 1912, *Young China* reported on eleven occasions that Tongmenghui leaders and members went back to China and were taking up government positions: December 27 and 31, 1911 and January 2, 3 (there were two separate reports on the same day), 8, and 9, and February 1, 4, 7, and 24, 1912.
60. *Young China,* February 1, 1912.
61. *Young China,* January 13, 1912.
62. According to Confucius, a gentleman should be a man of humanity (*ren*). When asked what humanity was, Confucius replied, "To subdue one's self and return to propriety is humanity" (*Keji fuli wei ren*). *Confucian Analects,* Book XII.
63. *Young China,* June 17, 1912.
64. *Young China,* September 18, 1912.

65. *Young China*, August 3, 1912. According to the paper, Wang died from inhaling poison gas at home, a tragic accident. *San Francisco Chronicle* also reported Wang's death. According to the *Chronicle*, Wang's "body was lying on the floor near a small gas stove on which was a pan of water and it is thought that he was preparing a meal and was overcome by the fumes before he could turn off the gas jet." The police said that they found no indications that Wang tried to commit suicide, the *Chronicle* reported. "Chinese Editor Meets Death by Suffocation," August 3, 1912.

66. *Young China*, October 29, 1912.

67. *Young China*, April 10, 1912.

68. *Young China*, April 10, 1912.

69. *Chinese World*, September 27, 1912 and "Chinese Catches an Alleged Thief," *San Francisco Chronicle*, September 28, 1912.

70. *Young China*, October 2, 1912.

71. *Chinese World*, May 25, 1912 and *Chung Sai Yat Po*, June 4, 1912.

72. Wu, *Huaqiao shi gaiyao*, 348.

73. *Chinese World*, October 12, 1912.

74. Both Liang Chaojie and Liang Qichao studied in Kang Youwei's private school, Wanmu Caotang, in Canton in the late 1890s. Kang once commented to a friend that "Liang Chaojie was ten times smarter than Liang Qichao." Guan, *Huaqi zhanggu*, 84.

75. *Chung Sai Yat Po*, October 12, 1912.

76. *Young China*, October 28 and 29, 1912.

77. Feng, *Huaqiao geming kaiguo shi*, 122.

78. According to some China specialists, during the first few years of the new Republic, China's economy developed and expanded steadily. For an example, see Chesneaux, Le Barbier, and Bergere, *China from the 1911 Revolution to Liberation*, 22–26.

79. *Chung Sai Yat Po*, May 11 and 12, 1913 and *Chinese World*, June 3, 1913.

80. *Chinese World*, June 3, 1913.

81. *Chung Sai Yat Po*, May 13, 1913.

82. *Chung Sai Yat Po*, June 30, 1913.

83. *Chinese World*, June 14 and 17, 1913.

84. *Chung Sai Yat Po*, July 9, 1913.

85. In 1911, Guangdong *guomin junzhengfu* (the Guangdong People's Military Government) sold bonds worth more than 600,000 Chinese yuan, about U.S. $378,000, to Chinese in the United States. Quoted in Lai, "The Kuomintang in Chinese American Communities," 204. *Chinese World* apparently is referring to these bonds. The information on the exchange rate between the Chinese yuan and United States dollar is from Schneider et al., *Wahrungen der Welt V*, 213.

86. *Chinese World*, June 19, 1913. It would be very hard to support this accusation. Sun was well known for his devotion to public service. His famous motto was *Tianxia weigong* ("All for the public under the heavens"). James Cantlie, Sun's teacher at the medical school in Hong Kong, said that Sun's "revolutionary ambition and the tenacious efforts driven by the ambition can be compared to Christ's spirit in saving mankind. Mr. Sun's principles in establishing himself in society and in handling his relations with others were undoubtedly selfless and with no intention of benefiting himself." Quoted in Li, *Sun Zhongshan quanzhuan*, 196.

Sun was known for living a very frugal life. While acting as provisional president of the Republic of China in Nanjing, he ate mostly vegetables, and each of his meals cost 40 cents, whereas most government officials and employees spent $3 on each meal. Deng, "Sun Zhongshan xiansheng yiwen," 22.

87. *Chinese World*, June 28, 1913. Sun did not give the Japanese any privileges for running a national bank in China while serving as provisional president. However, he did propose to give Japanese interests joint control of the Hanyehping Company to use Japanese investments to make China "as strong as Japan." However, stockholders of Hanyehping Company rejected the proposal, and Yuan Shikai, who succeeded Sun as provisional president, decided not to implement the proposal. Jansen, *The Japanese and Sun Yat-sen*, 147.

88. *Young China*, May 9, 14, and 16, 1913.

89. The Second Revolution was a short-lived military conflict that did not involve mobilization of the Chinese civilian population. The newly emerged Chinese bourgeoisie, consisting of businessmen, financiers, and industrialists, who gave full support to the establishment of the Chinese Republic, did not support the Second Revolution, either. Just like many Chinese in the United States, China's bourgeoisie did not welcome rebellion or military conflict, for they disrupted the business environment and hindered economic development. China's bourgeoisie opted for the strong man, Yuan Shikai, who had been recognized by foreign powers and supported by China's conservative elite and who represented law and order in China. For a detailed study of China's bourgeoisie and the Second Revolution, see Bergere, "The Role of the Bourgeoisie," 229–95.

90. *Young China*, July 25 and 26, August 12, and September 9, 1913.

91. *Chinese World*, June 26, 1913 and *Chung Sai Yat Po*, September 6, 1913.

92. "The Manifesto of the Progressive Party," *Chinese World*, June 12, 1913.

93. *Chinese World*, June 21, 23, and 25, July 1, 3, and 11, and August 5, 1913.

94. *Young China*, June 29, 1913.

95. *Chinese World*, July 30, 1913.

96. *Chinese World*, August 12, 1913.

97. *Chinese World*, September 2, 1913. This accusation stemmed from the fact that Sun Yat-sen and Huang Xing fled to Japan in early August as the government forces succeeded in putting down the Second Revolution. Another factor that could have contributed to such an accusation was Sun's visit to Japan in the spring of 1913. During the visit, Sun, who had been appointed by President Yuan to head the national program for developing a modern railroad system in China, talked extensively with Japanese businessmen and politicians about possible economic cooperation between China and Japan. For details of Sun's spring visit to Japan, see Jansen, *The Japanese and Sun Yat-Sen*, 157–62.

98. *Chinese World*, July 6, 1912; *Young China*, May 29 and June 6, 1912; and *Chung Sai Yat Po*, May 20, 1912.

99. *Young China*, July 14 and 15, 1912; *Chinese World*, July 16, 1912.

100. "Letter to CCBA from (Chinese) Ministry of Finance," *Chung Sai Yat Po*, April 1, 1915.

101. *Young China*, November 22 and December 4, 18, and 23; *Chinese World*, November 19 and December 2 and 30; and *Chung Sai Yat Po*, December 7, 1912.

102. *Young China*, December 28, 1912.

103. *Young China* attacked the Yuan government's compromise "not to send

officials, not to station troops, and not to migrate people" to Mongolia on January 12, 1913.

104. *Chinese World*, July 5, 1913.

105. Clifford, "Diasporas," 307.

106. The Provisional Constitution of the Republic of China, proclaimed on March 11, 1912, stated that "All the peoples of China were to be equal, without racial, caste, or religious discrimination. . . . They were to enjoy freedom of business enterprise, of the press, of assembly, of private correspondence, movement, and worship." Quoted in Li, *The Political History of China*, 272.

107. *Chung Sai Yat Po*, April 23, 1913.

108. *Chung Sai Yat Po*, July 10, 1912.

109. *Chung Sai Yat Po*, January 17, 1912.

110. *Chinese World*, June 22, 1912.

111. *Chung Sai Yat Po*, June 24, 1912.

112. *Chinese World*, November 27, 1912.

113. *Chung Sai Yat Po*, July 10, 1912.

114. Betty Lee Sung, who grew up in New York Chinatown in the first half of the twentieth century, observed that "Chinese-Americans sometimes swallow the stereotyped image of themselves conjured up by the public. They look upon themselves as insignificant, as handicapped and discriminated against." Sung, *The Story of the Chinese in America*, 3.

115. *Chung Sai Yat Po*, November 2 and December 25, 1912 and August 5, 1913.

116. Cohen, "Being Chinese," 92.

117. There were many such recreational societies in American Chinese communities. According to Liu Boji, there were twenty-four such societies in the Americas in 1911. Liu, *Meiguo huaqiao shi*, 453–60. These societies collected couplets from Chinese all over the Americas, read them, and then rewarded the best ones with a prize. These were purely recreational societies for educated Chinese, and they served as channels for preserving Chinese culture and tradition.

118. *Chung Sai Yat Po*, September 18, 1912.

119. *Chinese World*, September 27 and October 3, 1912.

120. *Chinese World*, September 27, 1912.

121. *Chung Sai Yat Po*, October 2, 1912.

122. *Chinese World*, October 14, 19, 23, 26, and 28 and November 9, 1912.

123. *Chung Sai Yat Po*, October 5, 1912.

124. *Chinese World*, October 21, 1912.

125. Some Chinese business leaders in the Chinese Chamber of Commerce were Christians, and they apparently objected to the proposal of making the Chinese New Year an official holiday in Chinatowns. Therefore, the chamber's decision was the result of a compromise. The decision said that the Western New Year's Day would be observed, but it would be up to individual businesses to decide whether to observe the Chinese New Year's Day. *Chinese World*, October 2, 1912.

126. *Chung Sai Yat Po*, January 30, 1913.

127. *Ta Tung Yat Po* is not available for research in this period. This information came from *Young China*, which quoted and criticized *Ta Tung Yat Po*. February 2, 1913.

128. See chapter 4.

129. The term "roots and routes" is James Clifford's. He argued that diaspora discourse articulates "both roots and routes" to construct "forms of community consciousness and solidarity that maintain identifications outside the national time/space in order to live inside, with a difference." "Diasporas," 308.

130. See McClain, *In Search of Equality* and Salyer, *Laws Harsh as Tigers*.

131. Bureau of the Census, *Abstract of the 15th Census, 1930*, 82, Table 26; *Abstract of 14th Census, 1920*, 143, Table 48; and *Abstract of the 15th Census, 1930*, 186, Table 102.

132. Takaki, *Strangers from a Different Shore*, 234.

133. Yung, *Unbound Feet*, 53.

134. Yung, *Unbound Feet*, 294–96, Table 2.

135. Bureau of the Census, *Abstract of the 14th Census, 1920*, 96, Table 21; and *Abstract of the 15th Census, 1930*, 81, Table 25.

136. *Annual Report, 1909, United States Department of Commerce and Labor, Bureau of Immigration*, quoted in Hsu, "Gold Mountain Dreams and Paper Son Schemes," 53.

137. According to one estimate, 90 percent of the Chinese who immigrated to the United States under exclusion entered via false documents. Hsu, "Gold Mountain Dreams and Paper Son Schemes," 52.

138. Senate Committee on Immigration, "An Act to Regulate the Immigration of Aliens and the Residence of Aliens in the United States."

139. *Chinese World*, May 24, 1912 and *Chung Sai Yat Po*, May 27, 1912.

140. *Chinese World*, May 16, 20, and 24; *Chung Sai Yat Po*, May 6, 8, 11, 13, and 16, 1912.

141. *Congressional Record*, 49: 804.

142. *Chinese World*, May 23, 1912.

143. *Chung Sai Yat Po*, June 4, 1912; *Chinese World*, June 4, 1912.

144. The Chinese-American Association was organized by Chinese and their Caucasian sympathizers in Los Angeles after the founding of the Republic of China. The organizers believed that discrimination against Chinese resulted mainly from ignorance. Therefore, the organizers resolved to educate the public with facts about Chinese in the United States. *Chung Sai Yat Po*, March 26, 1912.

145. *Chung Sai Yat Po*, May 28, 1912; *Chinese World*, May 31, 1912.

146. *Chung Sai Yat Po*, March 19, 1914. According to Stanford Lyman's estimate, between 1910 and 1920, 7,167 Chinese succeeded in entering the United States illegally from Mexico and Canada. Lyman, *Chinese Americans*, 106.

147. *Chung Sai Yat Po*, March 20, 24, and 25, 1914.

148. See Yung, "The Fake and the True," 25–56; McCunn, *Chinese American Portraits*, 107–17; and Takaki, *Strangers from a Different Shore*, 236–37.

149. *Young China*, April 4, 5, 6, 9, and 11, 1914.

150. *Memorial: Six Chinese Companies, An Address to the Senate and House of Representatives of the United States*.

151. *Chung Sai Yat Po*, March 30, 1914. In 1925, searches for illegal Chinese immigrants were carried out in cities such as New York, Chicago, Boston, and Philadelphia. In New York alone, about 600 Chinese were arrested, 134 of whom were finally deported. Lai, *Cong huaqiao dao huaren*, 77.

152. Chung, "Fighting for Their American Rights," 98–99.

153. For more information on the role played by American-born Chinese as

bridges between Chinese and the larger society, see Chan, "Race, Ethnic Culture, and Gender," 127–64.

154. Chung, "Fighting for Their American Rights," 101–2.

155. Ibid, 108.

156. *Chinese World*, May 13, 14, and 15, 1914.

157. *Chung Sai Yat Po*, February 7, 1914.

Chapter 3: Constructing a Chinese American Identity, 1915

1. Wang, *Community and Nation*, 142–58.

2. Wang, Foreword to *Xing, Ma huaren yu Xinhai geming*.

3. *San Francisco Chronicle* first reported Japan's demands on February 13, 1915. The report said that "in spite of the effort to keep them secret," *Chronicle's* reporter in Beijing was able to get the "magnitude and international importance of the Japanese demands . . . from a reliable source." Five days later, on February 18, the *Chronicle* and the *New York Times* revealed that the United States adopted a "waiting" policy because America's "Open Door" policy in China was not "adversely affected" by the demands.

4. According to C. F. Remer's 1933 study of the Chinese boycotts, Chinese merchants in San Francisco were the earliest in proposing an anti-Japanese boycott in response to Japan's Twenty-one Demands. When their cable reached Canton, a Chinese trading port, Cantonese merchants disapproved of the idea because they believed it would "embarrass the government and perhaps furnish excuses for extra demands." Remer, *A Study of Chinese Boycotts*, 46–47.

5. *Chinese World*, February 22, 1915.

6. *Chinese World*, February 23, 1915.

7. In the early 1900s, anti-Chinese forces in the United States were pushing for wider interpretations and an indefinite extension of the Chinese Exclusion Act in an effort to exclude all Chinese from coming into the country. Meanwhile, Chinese in the United States wanted the Chinese government to use the 1904 expiration of the Gresham-Yang Treaty, which had allowed American immigration authorities to treat Chinese harshly, to negotiate a treaty that would protect Chinese rights to immigrate into and stay in the United States.

8. Quoted in Lai, *Cong huaqiao dao huaren*, 74–75.

9. America's discrimination against Chinese was not experienced only by Chinese in the United States. Many merchants, students, diplomats, travelers, and others living in China but having had some experience with Americans or having been to the United States remembered being insulted or ridiculed. Delber L. McKee provided detailed information about such connections *Chinese Exclusion versus the Open Door Policy*.

10. Here are some examples. President Theodore Roosevelt instructed that immigration officers treat Chinese more courteously. He urged Congress to return to the original exclusion legislation, which was aimed strictly at Chinese laborers, a class-based approach, and to avoid a racist posture of trying to exclude all Chinese. Approval of visa application by a reformed consular service significantly quickened the process of examining arriving Chinese. In the broadest sense, the boycott "broke the momentum of the intense pressure building up" against

all Chinese in the United States. McKee, *Chinese Exclusion versus the Open Door Policy*, 127–28, 185, 208, and 210.

11. The order was given on March 15, 1915 to Guangzhou authorities, for, despite discouragement of radical actions, on March 2 the Guangzhou Association of Newspapers called a mass meeting and proposed "the use of native goods" as a response to the Japanese demands. Anti-Japanese boycotts were thus carried out, without official announcements, in Guangzhou and along China's east coast. Luo, "National Humiliation and National Assertion," 302.

12. *Chinese World*, February 27, 1915.

13. *Chinese World*, March 3, 1915.

14. This issue is discussed in detail later in this chapter.

15. According to the U.S. Census, there were 7,744 Chinese in San Francisco and 3,821 in Oakland in 1920. Bureau of the Census, *Abstract of the 14th Census, 1920*, 108, Table 30.

16. *Chinese World*, March 4, 5, and 6, 1915.

17. Wong et al., "From Despotism to Pluralism," 215–33.

18. *Chinese World*, March 13 and 16, 1915.

19. CCBAs in American Chinatowns functioned as virtual governments and exercised control over all aspects of life in their local Chinese communities. Declaring an organization unlawful was only one way they exercised their power. For detailed discussions of CCBAs, see Lai's "Historical Development of the Chinese Consolidated Benevolent Association." Also see Wong et al., "From Despotism to Pluralism."

20. *Chinese World*, May 13, 14, and 18, 1915.

21. *Chinese World*, February 26, 1915.

22. According to Sucheng Chan, two-thirds of the Japanese in California were farm workers in the first two decades of the twentieth century. Chan said that in 1917 Japanese in California "produced almost 90 percent of the state's output of celery, asparagus, onions, tomatoes, berries, and cantaloupes." *Asian Americans*, 38. By comparison, "Chinese farm laborers did less than one percent of the harvesting in 1920." Takaki, *Strangers from a Different Shore*, 240.

23. *Chinese World*, February 26, 1915.

24. *Chinese World*, February 26 and March 1 and 4, 1915; *Chung Sai Yat Po*, April 1, 1915.

25. *Chinese World*, March 4, 1915 and *Chung Sai Yat Po*, April 1, 1915.

26. The rules and regulations governing the boycott provided that all businesses stop importing Japanese goods, although they could still sell Japanese goods in stock; Chinese who were bound by contracts with Japanese could continue to honor the contracts until they expired but should present documents to the association for verification; all Chinese must boycott Japanese American services, including taking Japanese-run steamships crossing the Pacific; and violators would be subject to fines. *Chinese World*, March 1 and 2, 1915.

27. *Chinese World*, March 2, 1915.

28. *Chinese World*, March 5, 1915.

29. *Chinese World*, March 2 and 5, 1915.

30. *Chinese World*, March 18, 1915.

31. *Chinese World*, March 2, 13, and 24 and February 26, 1915.

32. *Chinese World*, March 13, 1915.

33. "Advertisement from the Chinese Bath and Barber Business (*Zhonghua muyu lifa suo*)," in *Chinese World*, April 26, 1915.

34. *Chinese World*, March 9 and *Chung Sai Yat Po*, March 9, 17, 19, and 20, 1915.

35. In 1910 there were 72,157 and in 1920 there were 111,010 Japanese in the continental United States. In 1910, the proportion of the total continental Japanese American population living in the Pacific and Mountain states was 94.4 percent; in 1920 it was 93.9 percent. Bureau of the Census, *Abstract of the 13th Census, 1910*, 82, Table 12, and *Abstract of the 14th Census, 1920*, 98, Table 22.

36. *Chinese World*, April 10 and May 5 and 6, 1915.

37. *Chung Sai Yat Po*, April 22, 1915.

38. *Chung Sai Yat Po*, April 22, 1915.

39. The Chinese government's order against anti-Japanese activities was reaffirmed in a speech given on May 5, 1915 to the Chinese Chamber of Commerce in San Francisco by vice-chairman Nieh Chi-cheh of the Chinese Trade Commission to the United States. Nieh said, "You men of China in this country should not act inadvisedly. Your country does not need that you purchase arms and ammunition for it. It needs rather that you educate your children here and at home, for an educated citizenship is one of the essentials of a republic. You will bestow a lasting benefit in doing this." *San Francisco Chronicle*, May 6, 1915.

40. *Chung Sai Yat Po*, April 5, 1915.

41. *Chinese World*, April 2, 1915; *Chung Sai Yat Po*, April 3, 1915.

42. *Chinese World*, March 25, April 8, 9, and 10, and July 2 and 19, 1915; *Chung Sai Yat Po*, November 15, 1915.

43. *Young China*, April 1, 1915.

44. *Chinese World*, March 5, 1915; *Young China*, March 7, 1915.

45. *Young China*, August 8, 1915.

46. *Chinese World*, August 6 and 17, 1915.

47. *Chinese World*, April 6, 1915.

48. Compared with the anti-American boycott of 1905–6, the anti-Japanese boycott staged by American Chinese had little effect on Sino-Japanese negotiations. The limited success of the former rested largely on worries over China's reciprocal measures to close China's door to American businesses. In the latter case, business transactions between American Chinese and Japanese was so negligible that even if every Chinese in the United States had cooperated with the boycott, it could not have produced much impact at the negotiating table. American Chinese learned a negative lesson. When Japan invaded China in the 1930s and 1940s, Chinese in the United States did not organize an anti-Japanese boycott within Chinese communities. Instead, they coordinated with anti-Fascist forces in American mainstream society and actively participated in organizing the American League for Peace and Democracy and China Aid Council, two civic organizations that petitioned the American government to stop Japanese aggression in China and raised relief funds for China's resistance effort. Instead of organizing boycotts within Chinatowns, American Chinese printed English pamphlets urging the American public to boycott Japanese goods. Between 1937 and 1941, many American Chinese served as pickets at docks, barring shipments of scrap iron to Japan. For Chinese American patriotic activities during the 1930 and 1940s, see Yu, *To Save China, To Save Ourselves*, 100–118 and Lai, *Cong huaqiao dao huaren*, 306–11.

49. *Chinese World,* May 13 and 14, 1915.

50. This phrase was used in *Young China,* April 20, 1915.

51. *Young China,* April 7, 1915.

52. *Young China,* April 25, 1915.

53. *Young China,* April 20, 1915. The Yuan government did not lodge any formal protest against the U.S. government concerning anti-Chinese immigration practices in the period between 1912, when Yuan became China's president, and early 1915. The Yuan government needed recognition and support from the United States. See Hunt, *The Making of a Special Relationship,* 216–23. In this period, the U.S. Congress did not pass any major discriminatory laws against the Chinese, nor was there any treaty negotiation, like the occasion that triggered the anti-American boycott of 1905. Congressional proposals and bills attempting to further limit and regulate Chinese immigration, introduced but failed to become laws in this period, are discussed in chapter 2.

54. *Chinese World,* April 21, 1915; *Young China,* April 21, 1915.

55. *Chinese World,* April 26, 1915.

56. *Chinese World,* April 26, 1915.

57. *Chinese World,* April 30, 1915.

58. *Chinese World,* May 12 and 13, 1915.

59. *Chung Sai Yat Po,* May 15, 1915.

60. *Young China,* May 19, 1915.

61. *Chinese World,* July 31, 1915.

62. For details on the operation of the National Salvation Fund in China, see Luo, "National Humiliation and National Assertion," 305–9.

63. *Chinese World,* May 19, 1915. The information on the exchange rate between the Chinese money and U.S. dollar is from Schneider et al., *Wahrungen der Welt V,* 213.

64. *Chinese World,* May 3 and 6, 1915.

65. *Chinese World,* March 19, 1915.

66. *Chinese World,* April 7, 1915.

67. *Chinese World,* June 3, 1915.

68. *Chinese World,* June 9, 1915.

69. *Young China,* July 1, 1915.

70. *Chung Sai Yat Po* kept silent on the issue of the national bonds as well. Such silence could be interpreted only as the paper's refusal to support either bonds or a fund because the paper had been and remained as concerned about affairs in China as the other two papers. To *Chung Sai Yat Po,* the Yuan government was no longer worthy of support. Yet because of its moderate and nonpartisan stand, the paper did not join *Young China* in advocating the overthrow of the Yuan government.

71. *Chinese World,* July 7, 1915.

72. *Chinese World,* July 12, 1915.

73. *Chinese World,* July 5 and 6, 1915.

74. *Chung Sai Yat Po,* December 8, 1915. The announcement was actually made in Shanghai in September 1915. Luo, "National Humiliation and National Assertion," 309.

75. Within two weeks in mid-July, 15,000 Chinese yuan were collected and sent back to the flooded areas in China through the San Francisco CCBA. *Chinese World,* July 16 and 28, 1915.

76. Here are three examples of how the *San Francisco Chronicle* and *San Francisco Examiner* described local Chinese. They were "filthy coolies" whose opium use was "corrupting the youth of the country" (the United States) in 1882. They were "wily sons of the Manchus" engaged in the importation of Chinese slave girls into the United States in 1907. They were "wily Orientals" who were smugglers of illegal immigrants, drunk gunmen, gamblers, or thieves in 1912. Becker, *The Course of Exclusion,* 24, 111, 127.

77. "A letter from Carroll Cook to the CCBA," Box 3, Ng Poon Chew Collection.

78. *Chinese World,* January 2, 13, and 26, 1911; *Young China,* March 14 and 15, 1911.

79. In 1909, Elsie Sigel, a daughter of a Chinese Sunday school teacher in New York City, was found dead in the apartment of a Chinese man known as William Leon, Leong Lee Lim, Leon Ling, Leung Lum, and William L. Lion. The search for this Chinese man went beyond New York City but ended fruitlessly. "The Elsie Sigel case entered the record books as unsolved." Bonner, *Alas! What Brought Thee Hither?* 120–22.

80. Strong, *Chinatown Photographer Louis J. Stellman.*

81. "Letter from Ng Poon Chew to Mr. Louis J. Stellman, June 5, 1917," ibid., 67.

82. "Letter from Ng Poon Chew," "Letter from Look Tin Eli, President and General Manager of China Mail Steamship Co. Ltd., June 8, 1917," and "Letter from Robert Liang Park, Editor of *Chinese World,* June 8, 1917," ibid., 67–68.

83. "Proposal of the Ministry of Industry and Commerce Regarding Participation in the PPIE," *Chinese World,* June 14, 1913.

84. *Chung Sai Yat Po,* March 26, 1912.

85. "Letter from Zhenhuang Company to (Chinese) Council Xu (Shanqing)," *Chinese World,* July 7, 1914.

86. This is the exact translation of the Chinese words *riye shichang.* According to Robert W. Rydell, who wrote a book on all international expositions held in the United States between 1876 and 1916, the section Zhenhuang Company was referring to was named the Joy Zone. Rydell, *All the World's a Fair,* 227–32.

87. Both San Francisco and San Diego wanted to host the exposition. As a compromise, San Francisco was designated by the U.S. Congress to hold the exposition and San Diego was given the authority to sponsor a limited fair focusing on "exhibits from Latin America and the American Southwest." The San Francisco fair ran from February to December 1915, and the San Diego one began in January and concluded in December 1916. For details on the fairs, see Rydell, *All the World's a Fair,* 208–33.

88. "Letter from Zhenhuang to Xu," *Chinese World,* July 7, 1914.

89. Ibid.

90. "Proposal of the Ministry of Industry and Commerce." The Beijing government signed the Reorganization Loan in April 1913. The loan was very much opposed by the opposition party, the Guomindang (GMD). The bitter controversy over the loan, plus the March assassination of Song Jiaoren, chairman of the GMD's executive committee, led to the famous Second Revolution, which started in July 1913. The budget for the participation in the PPIE was thus squeezed out of China's poor financial situation, and China's domestic unrest made Chi-

na's presence at the PPIE an insignificant issue to its government and people at home.

91. *Chinese World*, July 18, 1914.

92. The Chinese government exhibition halls were named "Forbidden City." The halls were prefabricated in China and assembled at the PPIE by Chinese workers sent from China by the Beijing government. *San Francisco Chronicle*, May 2, 1915.

93. *Chung Sai Yat Po*, July 9, 1914.

94. *Young China*, July 10, 1914.

95. *Chung Sai Yat Po*, July 17, 1914. None of the three Chinese-language newspapers reported any measures taken to replace the workers' clothing. Yet such strong criticisms apparently led to some action. According to Frank Morton Todd, who wrote "the official history of the international celebration" at the PPIE, the Chinese workers who put the Chinese exhibition halls together "wore American clothes" and "worked effectively with ineffective tools—the best test of good workmen." Quoted in Rydell, *All the World's a Fair*, 229.

96. Wu, *"Chink,"* 65–66.

97. *Chung Sai Yat Po*, July 16, 1914.

98. *Chung Sai Yat Po*, July 10, 1914.

99. *Chung Sai Yat Po*, July 17, 1914.

100. *Young China*, July 10, 1914.

101. *Chinese World*, February 25, 1915; *Young China*, February 23, 1915. The three Chinese-language newspapers never referred to the Chinese government exhibition structures as the "Forbidden City," the name used by fair visitors.

102. *San Francisco Chronicle*, Sunday magazine, May 2, 1915.

103. *Chinese World*, February 25, 1915; *Young China*, February 22, 1915.

104. *Chinese World*, February 25, 1915.

105. *Chinese World*, March 3, 1915. Chen Qi was crippled in one leg.

106. *Chinese World*, March 6, 1915.

107. *Young China*, March 7, 1915.

108. *Young China*, March 9, 1915.

109. Rydell, *All the World's a Fair*, 40, 227–32, 236. Under different names, most of the world's fairs held in the United States in the late nineteenth and early twentieth centuries had a section devoted to this theme: Midway Pleasance at the Chicago fair (1893), Vanity Fair at the Nashville fair (1897), and Pike at the Saint Louis fair (1904). At the San Diego fair of 1916, there was the Isthmus. For a good historical documentation and analysis of this theme at American fairs, see Rydell.

110. *Chinese World*, March 19, 1915; and Rydell, *All the World's a Fair*, 228.

111. The phrase "the world of tomorrow" is borrowed from Rydell. He convincingly demonstrated that the PPIE projected a world in which race really mattered and natural selection was the mechanism directing the evolutionary process.

112. *Chinese World*, March 19, 1915.

113. *Chinese World*, March 20, 1915.

114. *Chung Sai Yat Po*, March 22, 1915. The letter was written on March 19 by a Chinese living in Los Angeles.

115. *Chung Sai Yat Po*, March 22, 1915.

116. *Chung Sai Yat Po*, March 24, 1915.

117. *Chinese World,* October 2, 1914.

118. *Chinese World,* November 10, 1914.

119. Nee and Nee, *Longtime Californ',* 71.

120. Ibid, 71–72.

121. *Young China,* March 26, 1915.

122. *Chinese World,* March 20, 1915.

123. *Chinese World,* March 27, 1915.

124. "Concession on Zone Is Ordered Closed," *San Francisco Chronicle,* March 27, 1915.

125. *Chinese World,* March 31, 1915.

126. Rydell, *All the World's a Fair,* 229.

127. Ibid., 230.

128. *Young China,* June 16, 1915.

129. *Chinese World* first hoped that the discussion in China about restoring a monarchical system would stop and China would declare that it would uphold the republican system only (September 9, 1915). The paper then argued that monarchical restoration would provide opportunities for Russia and Japan to encroach on China and for the United States to withdraw its official recognition (October 15, 1915). *Chung Sai Yat Po* warned that monarchical restoration would bring disasters to China (August 17, 1915). Later on, it pointed out that monarchical restoration would only attest to the rightness of the prejudice carried by American mainstream society that Chinese people were too inferior to enjoy republican democracy (September 4, 1915). *Young China,* which had been warning Chinese in the United States that Yuan harbored the ambition of becoming emperor one day, carried editorials one after another, exposing the restoration scheme and urging all Chinese in the United States to rise up against Yuan (September 2 and 4 and October 3 and 11, 1915).

130. *Chung Sai Yat Po,* September 16, 1915. Contrary to American Chinese hopes, the Wilson administration regarded the "monarchical question as a domestic matter, the settlement of which is to be left in the hands of the Chinese" (Minister Reinsch to the Secretary of State, November 19, 1915). On December 21, 1915, the secretary of state instructed Minister Reinsch to "recognize new Government of China and say that . . . we recognize right of every nation to determine form of its government." Department of State, *Papers Relating to the Foreign Relations of the United States, 1915,* 78–79.

131. "Pacific Mail Company to Dissolve," *San Francisco Chronicle,* June 11, 1915.

132. *New York Time,* August 4, 1915.

133. The Seamen's Act was an important piece of Progressive legislation aimed at improving the working conditions of sailors and protecting the safety of passengers. Link, *Wilson: The New Freedom,* 269–74.

134. *New York Times,* September 29, 1915. Andrew Furuseth, president of the Seamen's Union, had been a well-known anti-Asian leader in the country. In 1905, he and some other labor leaders in California formed an Asiatic Exclusion League whose "chief weapons were legislation, boycott, and propaganda." For details on the Asiatic Exclusion League, see Daniels, *The Politics of Prejudice,* 27–30.

135. *Chinese World,* August 30, 1915.

136. *Chung Sai Yat Po,* November 15, 17, and 29 and December 11 and 27, 1915.

137. *Chung Sai Yat Po*, July 30, 1915.

138. *Chinese World*, August 18, 1915.

139. *Chinese World*, August 30, 1915.

140. *Chung Sai Yat Po*, September 10 and 11, 1915.

141. Ma, "The Big Business Ventures," 106.

142. *Chung Sai Yat Po*, September 3, 1915.

143. *Chung Sai Yat Po*, September 16, 1915.

144. *Young China*, September 10, 1915.

145. *Young China*, September 12, 1915.

146. *Chung Sai Yat Po*, September 29, 1915.

147. *Chinese World*, August 27 and September 3 and 6, 1915.

148. *Young China*, September 6 and 8, 1915.

149. *Young China*, November 22, 1915.

150. *Chung Sai Yat Po*, October 6 and 7, 1915.

151. *Young China*, September 19, 1915.

152. "Liner China to Be Sent on Voyage to Orient," *San Francisco Chronicle*, October 15, 1915.

153. Lai, *Cong huaqiao dao huaren*, 100.

154. "Steamer China Is Purchased by Chinese to Ply on Pacific," *San Francisco Chronicle*, October 12, and "Liner China to Be Sent on Voyage to Orient," *San Francisco Chronicle*, October 15, 1915.

155. *Young China*, October 12, 15, 20, 28, 29, and 31, 1915.

156. Lai, *Cong huaqiao dao huaren*, 101.

157. Ma, "Big Business Ventures," 108.

158. Lai, *Cong huaqiao dao huaren*, 102.

159. *Chinese World*, June 24, 1918.

160. Ma, "Big Business Ventures," 108.

161. *Chinese World*, January 16, 1923.

162. *Chinese World*, October 1, 1923.

Chapter 4: An Ideological Foundation of the Chinese American Identity, 1916–24

1. *Chinese World*, March 3 and 4, 1916.

2. *Chung Sai Yat Po*, September 4, 1915; *Young China*, September 2 and December 1, 1915.

3. *Chinese World*, May 8, 1916; *Chung Sai Yat Po*, May 27, 1916. The National Protection Army was formed in China in December 1915 to protect the Chinese republic against Yuan's monarchical restoration.

4. *Young China*, October 30, 1911.

5. *Chung Sai Yat Po*, September 4, 1915; *Young China*, November 11, 1915.

6. Frank J. Goodnow made this statement in San Francisco when he arrived from China en route to Johns Hopkins University in early October, 1915. *San Francisco Chronicle*, October 7, 1915.

7. Li, *The Political History of China*, 312–13.

8. *Young China*, July 29, 1915.

9. *Young China*, January 7, 1916.

10. *Young China*, January 5, 1916.

11. *Young China*, January 5, 7, 25, and 28, 1916.

12. *Young China*, January 28, 1916.

13. *Chung Sai Yat Po* editorialized on many American holidays such as Presidents' Day, Independence Day, Thanksgiving Day, and Christmas, praising and admiring its democratic institutions as well as its economic achievements. In the previous chapters, we have also seen the paper's persistent argument that development of capitalism was essential for a strong and modern China.

14. *Chung Sai Yat Po*, January 27, 1916. The paper used the term "a conservative party" to refer to those who supported Yuan's restoration attempt.

15. *Chung Sai Yat Po*, January 27, 1916.

16. *Chung Sai Yat Po*, January 7, 1916.

17. The National Protection Army rose in early January 1916 in China's southwest province of Yunnan. After declaring Yunnan independent from Yuan's control, the army made inroads into the neighboring Sichuan Province. By mid-March, Guangdong and Guangxi had also declared independence. Military leaders in Yuan's Northern Army urged him to declare an end to his monarchical movement to stop the civil war in China. Pressure also came from Britain, France, Russia, and Italy, who preferred to see stability in China under the existing government. Between November 1915 and February 1916, these governments advised Yuan three times to give up his monarchical ambition. Japan, who wanted to keep a divided and decentralized China in order to pursue its interests there, had not only supported the National Protection Army in the south with financial aid and weapons but was reportedly prepared to intervene against Yuan's monarchical movement. Chen, *Yuan Shih-kai*, 216–28.

18. *Chung Sai Yat Po*, March 27, 1916.

19. *Chung Sai Yat Po*, April 5, 1916.

20. *Chinese World*, February 29, 1916.

21. *Chinese World*, March 3, 1916.

22. *Chinese World*, June 29 and 30, 1916.

23. *Chinese World*, July 11, 1916.

24. *Chung Sai Yat Po*, September 16, 1915.

25. *Young China*, October 25 and 29, 1915.

26. *Young China*, October 30 and 31, November 11, 19, and 30, and December 12, 1915.

27. *Young China*, December 11, 1915.

28. "National Chinese Sing New Republic's Hymn," *San Francisco Chronicle*, January 2, 1916.

29. "Chinese in America Raise Big War Fund," *San Francisco Chronicle*, January 5, 1916.

30. *Young China*, May 15 and 16, 1916; *Chung Sai Yat Po*, May 27, 1916.

31. *Chinese World*, May 8, 1916; *Young China*, May 15, 1916.

32. Another such historical moment occurred when the Republic of China was established, which all Chinese in the United States welcomed and celebrated.

33. Yang, Liu, and Yang, *Meiguo huaqiao shi*, 484–85.

34. *Chinese World*, September 22, 1916.

35. *Chinese World*, September 20 and 23, October 2, and November 1, 1916.

36. *Chinese World*, September 22, 1916.

37. Sparks, *China Gold*, 166.

38. Wong, *Fifth Chinese Daughter*, 128.

39. Chinn, "A Historian's Reflections on Chinese-American Life in San Francisco," 32 and 38.

40. Such ceremonies started in December 1913 when the new Chinese constitution failed to make Confucianism China's state religion. All Chinese schools, in China and overseas, were encouraged to have ceremonies worshipping Confucius so that Confucianism would be carried down from generation to generation through the educational channel.

41. *Chinese World*, September 23, 1916, October 6, 1923, and October 9 and 12, 1926.

42. Quoted in Chan, "Race, Ethnic Culture, and Gender," 151.

43. Chow, *The May Fourth Movement*, 46.

44. Chen, *New Youth*. Quoted in Chow, *The May Fourth Movement*, 59.

45. Chow, *The May Fourth Movement*, 45, 273–74.

46. *Chinese World*, January 8 and 9, 1919.

47. *Chinese World*, January 17, 1919.

48. *Chinese World*, November 22 and December 8, 13, and 17, 1919.

49. *Chinese World*, June 10, 11, and 14, 1919 and August 8 and 14, 1920.

50. Germany had a leasehold over Shandong. During World War I, to secure financial support from Japan, the Beijing government signed a secret agreement with Japan, giving Japan the right to station police and establish military garrisons in Jinan and Qingdao, two major cities in Shandong, and the right to build and manage railroads in Shandong. To get Japan's naval assistance against Germany in the war, Britain, France, and Italy agreed secretly to support Japan's claims in Shandong. At the Paris Peace Conference, these secret agreements became public and obtained the support from the American delegation, led personally by President Woodrow Wilson.

51. *Chinese World*, May 5, 6, 9, 19, 20 and 30, 1919; *Young China*, May 4, 5, 6, and 31 and June 1, 1919.

52. *Young China*, June 18 and 28 and July 25, 1919.

53. *Chinese World*, May 22, 1919; *Chung Sai Yat Po*, July 11, 1919.

54. The letter was dated July 25, 1919. House of Representatives, "Petitions and Memorials."

55. Both Cao and Zhang were pro-Japanese officials in the Beijing government. For more details on this incident and the May Fourth Movement, see Chow, *The May Fourth Movement*, 84–116.

56. *Chinese World*, March 12, 1920.

57. *Chinese World*, June 29, 1920.

58. Chan, "Race, Ethnic Culture, and Gender," 132, 135.

59. "Dr. Ng Poon Chew's View on Love and Marriage," from an interview printed in the *Milwaukee Journal* (date not known), Box 3, Ng Poon Chew Collection.

60. *Young China*, June 23 and 24, 1919. Chen referred to Chen Duxue, the founder of *New Youth* and one of the leaders of the New Culture Movement in China. Hu referred to Hu Shi, another leader of the movement. Hu studied at Cornell and Columbia universities and returned to teach at the Beijing University in 1917. He joined Chen in editing *New Youth* and had been a strong advocate of the New Culture Movement.

61. *Young China* remained the voice of the GMD among Chinese in the United States. The GMD at the time was the main force in the southern government in China.

62. *Young China,* August 12, 1919.

63. *Chung Sai Yat Po,* October 15, 1919.

64. *Chung Sai Yat Po,* December 6, 1919.

65. Tu, "Cultural China," 25.

66. Ibid. The term has been used by scholars including Tu Wei-ming.

67. Besides Yuan Shikai's attempt in 1916, there was another very short-lived attempt by Zhang Xun in 1917 to restore the last Manchu emperor.

68. *Chung Sai Yat Po,* March 23, 24, and 25, 1922.

69. *Chung Sai Yat Po,* December 10, 1914.

70. *Chung Sai Yat Po,* October, 16, 1914.

71. Lai, *Cong huaqiao dao huaren,* 145–47.

72. *Chung Sai Yat Po,* March 24, 1922.

73. *Chung Sai Yat Po,* November 2, 1912.

74. *Chung Sai Yat Po,* July 10, 1912.

75. *Chung Sai Yat Po,* December 25, 1912.

76. *Chung Sai Yat Po,* May 6, 1913.

77. *Chung Sai Yat Po,* June 27, 1914.

78. *Chung Sai Yat Po,* July 25, 1914.

79. *Chung Sai Yat Po,* May 5, 9, and 31, June 2, August 5, and September 26, 1913.

80. *Chung Sai Yat Po,* September 19, 1912.

81. Quoted in Yung, *Unbound Feet,* 167.

82. Chinn, "A Historian's Reflections on Chinese-American Life in San Francisco," 25.

83. *Chung Sai Yat Po,* June 22, 1922.

84. Judy Yung documented a story of a widowed Chinese woman who sought help from the Chinatown YWCA to escape from her intolerable mother-in-law in the early 1920s in her book *Unbound Feet,* 96–97.

85. Yung, *Unbound Feet,* 96, 301.

86. Ibid., 93.

87. Ibid., 94.

88. Ibid., 80–82.

89. Chow, *The May Fourth Movement,* 324–25.

90. Lin, *Christianity and China.* For a concentrated study on the anti-Christian movement of this period, refer to Yip, *Religion, Nationalism and Chinese Students.*

91. *Chung Sai Yat Po,* May 13, 1922.

92. *Chung Sai Yat Po,* June 5, 1922.

93. This is discussed later in this chapter.

94. *Chung Sai Yat Po,* May 27, 29, and 30, 1922.

95. *Ta Tung Yat Po* is available for research, with some missing issues, from 1919 to 1923 in the Ethnic Studies Library at University of California, Berkeley.

96. *Ta Tung Yat Po,* April 18, 1922.

97. Quoted in Tseng, "Chinese Protestant Nationalism in the United States," 43.

98. *Ta Tung Yat Po,* April 18, 1922.
99. *Chung Sai Yat Po,* April 28, 1922.
100. Bays, "The Growth of Independent Christianity in China," 310–11.
101. Lai, *Cong huaqiao dao huaren,* 147.
102. Takaki, *Strangers from a Different Shore,* 240.
103. Chan, *Asian Americans,* 34.
104. *Young China,* December 20 and 21, 1918.
105. Preston, *Aliens and Dissenters,* 118–51, 181–237.
106. Xu, *Huaqiao yu diyici guogong hezuo,* 15–20.
107. *Chinese World,* March 15, 1920.
108. *Chinese World,* June 8 and 9, 1920.
109. *Chung Sai Yat Po,* May 17, 1922.
110. *Young China,* August 19, 1919.
111. *A Study of Overseas Remittance* (Taipei: Office of Research and Development of the Overseas Chinese Commission, 1970). Quoted in Lai, *Cong huaqiao dao huaren,* 237.
112. Lai, *Cong huaqiao dao huaren,* 237.
113. Ibid.
114. Ibid., 241–44.
115. Li, *The Political History of China,* 404. Sun Yat-sen had been involved in the Southern government, which called the Northern government unconstitutional because the original constitution of the Republic of China was invalidated by Yuan's monarchical restoration.
116. Zhang, *Zhonghua minguo shigang,* 320.
117. *Chinese World,* May 19, July 13, and August 5, 8, and 26, 1921.
118. *Ta Tung Yat Po,* April 19, 1922.
119. *Ta Tung Yat Po,* April 19 to 28, 1922.
120. *Ta Tung Yat Po,* January 18, 1922.
121. The crime referred to here is Sun's "sabotaging national unity" in China by insisting on waging another revolution.
122. When Yuan Shikai declared the GMD an illegal party after he defeated the Second Revolution, Sun Yat-sen fled to Japan and reorganized his party under the name of the Chinese Revolutionary Party (*Zhonghua Gemingdang*) and required all members to give fingerprints and to pledge allegiance.
123. *Chinese World,* June 24 and September 20 and 21, 1922.
124. At the time when Chen Jiongming rebelled against Sun, Chen was the commander-in-chief of the planned northern expedition army and was able to lead the troops against Sun, who had to flee to Shanghai on a boat.
125. Xu, *Huaqiao yu diyici guogong hezuo,* 41.
126. *Chinese World,* January 9, 1923.
127. When Sun finally launched the Northern Expedition in September 1924, he apologized to the people in Guangdong. He said, "I have troubled many of my fellow elders and brothers in my native province by commanding several armies . . . and by asking all sorts of supplies. . . . The price of commodities is exorbitant and maintaining a livelihood for the people is increasingly difficult. The responsibility of revolution should be borne by the people of the whole nation; instead, a majority of responsibility has been taken by the people of Kwangtung [Guangdong]. That is enough to make Cantonese people feel unjustly treat-

ed." Quoted in Li, *The Political History of China*, 463. Li Chien-nung stated that the Northern Expedition was launched in haste, mostly because Sun realized that the people in Guangdong, especially merchants, had developed ill feelings against his government and army. So he decided to order all troops to leave the province, hoping to win back sympathy and support of the people in Guangdong. Ibid., 464.

128. *Chinese World*, June 27, 1923.

129. *Chinese World*, June 29, 1923.

130. *Chinese World*, February 27, 1924.

131. Sun Yat-sen compared his action to the Boston Tea Party. In his cable to the U.S. government, which had ordered destroyers to Guangzhou to stop Sun's seizing of the customs office, Sun said, "We must stop the money from going to Peking to buy arms to kill us, just as your forefathers stopped taxation going to the English by throwing English teas into Boston harbor." Quoted in Wilbur, *Sun Yat-sen*, 185–86.

132. *Chinese World*, March 8, 1924.

133. *Chinese World*, April 4, 1924.

134. *Chung Sai Yat Po*, January 5, 1923.

135. *Chung Sai Yat Po*, May 17, 30, and 31, June 4, 7, 18, 20, and 29, and July 6, 18, 19, 23, and 24, 1923.

136. *Young China*, February 2 and 3, 1924.

137. Cheng, Liu, and Zheng, "Chinese Emigration." Chen's financial success was itself an example, to all Chinese in the United States, that capitalism was the best way to achieve individual and national development.

138. *Chung Sai Yat Po*, July 31, 1923; Lai, *Cong huaqiao dao huaren*, 211. The information on the exchange rate between Chinese money and United States dollar is from Schneider et al., *Wahrungen der Welt V*, 214.

139. *Chung Sai Yat Po*, July 31, 1923.

140. *Chung Sai Yat Po*, August 1, 1923.

141. *Chung Sai Yat Po*, August 2, 1923.

142. Zhang was a warlord in northeast China and was well known among Chinese in the United States for his pro-Japanese attitude to retain control in the region. Knowing that most Chinese in the United States disliked Zhang, *Young China* explained that Zhang offered to surrender his regional military forces to Sun because Zhang was shrewd enough to realize that Sun's government was the future government of China. April 8 and 9, 1922.

143. *Chung Sai Yat Po*, August 8, 9, and 14, 1923.

144. *Young China*, February 2 and 3, 1924.

145. *Young China*, April 10, 1924.

146. *Young China*, April 12, 1924.

147. Since the May Fourth Incident in which workers went on strike to support students' patriotism, workers in China had been using strikes as a tool against injustice. After the establishment of the CCP in 1921, communists and left-wing GMD members had been helping workers to form unions and organize protests and strikes for better working conditions and higher pay. For details on workers' strikes in the 1920s, see Chesneaux, *Chinese Labor Movement*.

148. John King Fairbank said that Sun's task for national unification was complicated by several different interests. They were "a Cantonese provincialism seeking regional strength," referring mainly to Chen Jiongming, "a Canton-city

merchant element that recruited its own troops," and "South China generals who competed as warlords." Fairbank, *The Great Chinese Revolution*, 210.

149. *Chung Sai Yat Po*, June 28, 1924; *Chinese World*, July 28, 1924

150. The "western houses" with gun holes and the defensive walls around "overseas Chinese villages" were examples of such effort of self-protection.

151. *Chinese World*, July 28 and 29, 1924.

152. *Chinese World*, July 29, 1924.

153. *Chinese World*, August 19, 1924; *Chung Sai Yat Po*, August 16, 1924.

154. *Chung Sai Yat Po*, August 26, 1924; *Chinese World*, August 19, 1924.

155. *Young China*, October 12, 1924.

156. The British authorities in Hong Kong threatened to order their navy to attack the Sun government's forces in the event of a military showdown. Li, *The Political History of China*, 465. The British in Hong Kong also promised to help Chen Lianbo to become "the Washington of China" by overthrowing the Sun government in Guangdong, which the British believed was leading China toward communism unless it was crushed in time. Hu, *Imperialism and Chinese Politics*, 298–99.

157. *Chung Sai Yat Po*, September 1, 1924.

158. Li, *The Political History of China*, 463.

Chapter 5: Building Permanent Chinese American Communities and Displaying American Chinatown Culture, 1920–27

1. Chinn, *Bridging the Pacific*, 104.

2. Ibid., 125.

3. Yung, *Unbound Feet*, 152.

4. Kwong, *Chinatown*. Kwong complained that earlier studies of Chinese American history depicted the period between 1910 and 1950 in terms of American Chinatown life as "silent years." As late as 1991, Sucheng Chan pointed out, "In the existing literature on Asian Americans, the years between the end of World War One and the beginning of World War Two are often depicted as an interregnum about which little is known." Chan, *Asian Americans*, 103. Studies of Chinese American history done by scholars in mainland China and Taiwan usually left the reader with the impression that Chinese in the United States between 1910 and 1930 lived an isolated life in Chinatowns and gave most of their attention to the nationalist revolution in China. For Chinese-language studies, see note 6 in the introduction.

5. Yung, *Unbound Feet*, 294–95; McKenzie, *Oriental Exclusion*, 190.

6. Sucheng Chan estimated that about 400 Chinese merchant wives and 300 wives of American citizens of Chinese ancestry "sought admission each year" in the first three years of the 1920s. Chan, "The Exclusion of Chinese Women," 125.

7. Immigration Act of 1924, 162.

8. McClain, *In Search of Equality*, 70–73

9. Immigration Act of 1924, 155.

10. *Chung Sai Yat Po*, April 15, 16, 19, 22, and 23, 1924; *Young China*, April 21, 1924.

11. *Chung Sai Yat Po*, May 22, 1924.

12. *United States v. Mrs. Gue Lim*, 460.

13. Ibid., 466.

14. *Tsoi Sim v. United States*, 922–25.

15. *Chinese World*, July 25, 1924 and May 7, 1925.

16. *Chinese World*, January 7, 1924.

17. *Chung Sai Yat Po*, April 23, 1924.

18. *Young China*, July 16, 1924; *Chinese World*, July 14 and 17, 1924.

19. The 1880 treaty between the United States and China was a result of a compromise between anti-Chinese elements in California and America's China-oriented business interests. Whereas the former wanted to stop all Chinese from coming to the United States, the latter wanted to exploit the huge Chinese market. The treaty, signed by the weak Qing government, allowed the United States to legislate against Chinese laborers but promised fair treatment of other Chinese immigrants. Since the passage of the 1882 Chinese Exclusion Act, which stopped Chinese laborers from coming into the United States, Chinese merchants and American citizens of Chinese ancestry had enjoyed exempt-class status.

20. *Chung Sai Yat Po*, July 15, 1924; *Young China*, August 17, 1924. Canada was another country that enacted a law in 1923 restricting "entry to or landing in Canada of persons of Chinese origin or descent, irrespective of allegiance or citizenship, other than government representatives, Chinese children born in Canada, merchants and students." Quoted in McKenzie, *Oriental Exclusion*, 16.

21. *Chinese World*, July 25, 1924.

22. *Young China*, August 9, 1924.

23. *Chinese World*, July 22 and September 15, 1924; *Chung Sai Yat Po*, September 8 and 13, 1924; *Young China*, July 25, 27, and 31 and September 3 and 14, 1924.

24. *Chung Sai Yat Po*, July 29, 1924.

25. *Young China*, July 29, 1924.

26. *Young China*, July 19, 1924.

27. Subcommittee of the Senate Committee on Immigration, "Admission as Nonquota Immigrants of Certain Alien Wives and Children of United States Citizens."

28. *Young China*, July 19, 1924. The Americanization program was carried out by the Department of the Interior and Bureau of Education of the U.S. government. An *Americanization Bulletin* was published, in which the commissioner of education, P. P. Claxton, explained the program. He wrote, "To enter into this common heritage of the best of all, to be inspired with these ideals, to learn to understand the institutions which guarantee our freedom and rights and enable us to work together for the common good, to resolve to forget all purely selfish means for the work of the highest welfare of our country and of the world is to become Americanized. To give to the foreign born population in the United States and all others the fullest and freest opportunity for this is what we in the Bureau of Education mean by Americanization. Every part of our program is directed to this end." *Americanization Bulletin* 1, no. 3 (November 1918): 1.

29. *Ex parte Chiu Shee*, 799.

30. *Ex parte Cheung Sum Shee et al.* and *Ex parte Chan Shee et al.*, 997, 998, 999.

31. Ibid.

32. Ibid., 999. Section 9 of the 1924 act is specifically about "issuance of immigration visas to relatives." See Immigration Act of 1924, 157–58.

33. *Chinese World*, February 26, 1925.

34. *Chung Sai Yat Po*, March 30, 1925.

35. *Chinese World*, March 13, 1925. The tong war was between On Leong Tong, a Chinese merchant organization for the protection of their members' interests and with branches throughout the eastern part of the United States, and Hip Sing Tong, another Chinese organization protecting the interests of its members, usually small businessmen, and with branches all over the United States. This tong war was a senseless killing of innocent tong members. A peace treaty between the two tongs was signed on March 25, 1925. Bonner, *Alas! What Brought Thee Hither!* 151–55.

36. *Cheung Sum Shee et al. v. Nagle*, 336–46.

37. *Chang Chan, Wong Hung Jay, Yee Sin Jung et al. v. Nagle*, 346–53.

38. *Chinese World*, February 17, 1926.

39. Subcommittee of the Senate Committee on Immigration, "Admission as Nonquota Immigrants of Certain Alien Wives and Children of United States Citizens," 7; and Chung, "Fighting for Their American Rights," 108.

40. Subcommittee of the Senate Committee on Immigration, "Admission as Nonquota Immigrants of Certain Alien Wives and Children of United States Citizens," 4–5.

41. Ibid, 6.

42. Ibid., 11–15.

43. Affidavit of Tom Wong Hoe Sing, in "A Plea for Relief Together with a Supplement Containing Some Arguments in Support Thereof," ibid., 22.

44. Liu, "The Resilience of Ethnic Culture," 174.

45. Coolidge, *Chinese Immigration*, 70–71.

46. *San Francisco Chronicle*, November 20, 1881.

47. Muench, "One Hundred Years of Medicine," 51–80.

48. Barlow and Richardson, *China Doctor of John Day*, 54–70.

49. The rest of the advertisements were for hotels; banks; grocery, vegetable, and meat stores; Chinese books and stationery; clothes and jewelry; of various Chinese organizations; companies' capital-raising announcements; and so on.

50. Berlant, *Profession and Monopoly*, 234.

51. Muench, "One Hundred Years of Medicine," 70.

52. Barlow and Richardson, *China Doctor of John Day*, 66.

53. Berlant, *Profession and Monopoly*, 235.

54. Liu, "The Resilience of Ethnic Culture," 186.

55. Tisdale, "Chinese Physicians in California," *Lippincott's Magazine* 63 (March 1899). Quoted in Liu, "The Resilience of Ethnic Culture," 185.

56. *San Francisco Chronicle*, February 11 and April 1, 1925 and October 30, 1927.

57. *San Francisco Chronicle*, January 7, 1923.

58. *San Francisco Chronicle*, April 1, 1925.

59. *San Francisco Chronicle*, February 11, 1926.

60. California Legislature, Assembly Bill 440 (1925).

61. *Chinese World*, February 11, 1925.

62. Loo, "San Francisco's Chinatown," 284.

63. *Chinese World*, February 11, 1925.

64. *Chinese World*, February 21 and 25, 1925.

65. *Chinese World*, February 11, 1925.

66. Liu, "The Resilience of Ethnic Culture," 184.

67. *Chinese World*, February 11, 1925.

68. *Chinese World*, March 20, 1925.

69. *Chinese World*, March 20, 1925.

70. *Chinese World*, March 20, 1925.

71. *Chinese World*, April 3, 1925 and Assembly Bill 440.

72. *Chinese World*, February 11, 1925.

73. *Chung Sai Yat Po*, March 23, 1925.

74. Clifford, "Diasporas," 308.

75. Bonner, *Alas! What Brought Thee Hither?* 151.

76. Chen, "The Chinese Community in New York," 41–42.

77. Chew, *Reflections of Seattle's Chinese Americans*, 140, 141.

78. Donghua yiyuan dongshiju, *Donghua yiyuan sishi zhounian jinian zhuan-kan*, 7.

79. Gintjee and Johnson, "San Francisco's First Chinese Hospital," 283.

80. Donghua yiyuan dongshiju, *Donghua yiyuan sishi zhounian jinian zhuan-kan*, 54.

81. *Young China*, August 5, 1923.

82. Donghua yiyuan dongshiju, *Donghua yiyuan sishi zhounian jinian zhuan-kan*, 39.

83. *Young China*, August 24, 1923.

84. Donghua yiyuan dongshiju, *Donghua yiyuan sishi zhounian jinian zhuan-kan*, 39; *San Francisco Chronicle*, August 24, 1923.

85. Donghua yiyuan dongshiju, *Donghua yiyuan sishi zhounian jinian zhuan-kan*, 39.

86. Gintjee and Johnson, "San Francisco's First Chinese Hospital," 284.

87. *Young China*, April 19, 1925.

88. Gintjee and Johnson, "San Francisco's First Chinese Hospital," 285.

89. *Young China*, April 19, 1925; *San Francisco Chronicle*, April 19, 1925.

90. Chinn, *Bridging the Pacific*, 133.

91. Gintjee and Johnson, "San Francisco's First Chinese Hospital," 285.

92. Chinn, *Bridging the Pacific*, 133.

93. *Qiao Bao* (China Press), March 15, 2000.

94. *Young China*. February 11, 1926.

95. *Young China*, February 12, 15, and 17, 1926.

96. Clifford, "Diasporas," 306.

97. Ng Poon Chew, "Chinatown Modernized." A version of this article appeared in *San Francisco Chronicle*, January 18, 1922.

98. Yung, *Unbound Feet*, 96.

99. Yung, *Unbound Feet*, 97–98.

100. Yung, *Unbound Feet*, 152.

101. For a detailed study of the Square and Circle Club, see Wong, "Square and Circle Club," 127–53.

102. Quoted in Yung, *Unbound Feet*, 153.

103. Wong, "Square and Circle Club," 147.

104. Yung, *Unbound Feet*, 155.

105. Takaki, *Strangers from a Different Shore*, 249.

106. Sung, *The Story of the Chinese in America*, 130.

107. Esther Wong, "The History and Problem of Angel Island," March 1924, Survey of Race Relations, Stanford University, Hoover Institution Archives. Quoted in Takaki, *Strangers from a Different Shore*, 249–50.

108. *Chinese Digest*, January 31, 1936. Quoted in Takaki, *Strangers from a Different Shore*, 249.

109. These quotes are from Robert Dunn Wu, the first-prize winner of the 1936 Ging Hawk Club essay contest on "Does My Future Lie in China or America?" See Chinn, *Bridging the Pacific*, 139.

110. *San Francisco Chronicle*, April 14, 1925.

111. Yung, *Unbound Feet*, 148.

112. *Chinese World*, April 3, 1925.

113. *Young China*, April 28, 1925; *San Francisco Chronicle*, April 30, 1925.

114. *San Francisco Chronicle*, April 30, 1925.

115. *Young China*, April 30, 1925.

116. Ibid.

117. *Chung Sai Yat Po*, May 3, 1925.

118. *Chung Sai Yat Po*, April 30, 1925.

119. *Chinese World*, January 16 and 17 and February 14 and 15, 1927.

120. *Chinese World*, January 11 and February 14, 1927.

121. *Chinese World* reported four days before the crowning of the beauty queen that almost 100,000 tickets had already been sold. February 14, 1927.

122. *Chinese World*, February 11 and 18, 1927.

123. *Chinese World*, January 15 and 17, 1927.

124. *Young China*, October 22, 1927.

125. *San Francisco Chronicle*, October 30, 1927.

126. Ibid.

127. *Young China*, October 30 and November 4, 1927; *San Francisco Chronicle*, November 4, 1927.

128. *San Francisco Chronicle*, October 30, 1927.

129. Chinn, *Bridging the Pacific*, 125–28.

130. *San Francisco Chronicle*, February 13, 1926.

131. *San Francisco Chronicle*, February 14, 1926.

132. *Young China*, October 12, 1926.

133. *Chinese World*, October 11, 1926; *Young China*, October 12, 1926.

134. *Young China*, October 12, 1926.

135. *San Francisco Chronicle*, November 4, 1927.

136. *San Francisco Chronicle*, April 14, 1925.

137. *Chinese World*, June 12, 1925.

138. *Chinese World*, June 11, 1925.

SELECTED BIBLIOGRAPHY

Chinese-Language Sources

NEWSPAPERS CONSULTED

China Press (僑報)
Chinese World (世 界日報)
Chung Sai Yat Po (中西日報)
Ta Tung Yat Po (大同日報)
Young China (少年中國)

SECONDARY MATERIALS

Deng Muhan (鄧慕韓). "Sun Zhongshan xiansheng yiwen" 孫中山先生逸聞 (Anecdotes of Mr. Sun Yat-sen). In *Xinhai geming shiliao xuanji xubian* 辛亥革命史料選輯續編 (Sequel to selection of historical materials concerning the 1911 revolution). Changsha: Hunan renmin chubanshe, 1983.

Donghua yiyuan dongshiju 東華醫院董事局 (Board of Directors of the Chinese Hospital). *Donghua yiyuan sishi zhounian jinian zhuankan* 東華醫院四十周年紀念專刊 (The Chinese Hospital: 40th anniversary, 1923–63). Hong Kong: Yongansheng, 1963.

Feng Ziyou (馮自由). *Huaqiao geming kaiguo shi* 華僑革命開國史 (History of the role of overseas Chinese in the revolution and establishment of the republic). Taibei: Taiwan shangwu chubanshe, 1953.

Guan Chunru (關春如). *Huaqi zhanggu* 花旗掌故 (Anecdotes of America). Hong Kong: Caise shijie chuban gongsi, 1991.

Hu Naien (胡耐恩). *Zhongguo minzu zhi* 中國民族志 (Annals of China's nationalities). Revised edition. Taibei: Taiwan shangwu chubanshe, 1974.

Huang Boyao (黃伯耀). "Shaonian Zhongguo chenbao chuangkan zhi huiyi" 少年中國晨報創刊之回憶 (Recalling the founding of *The Young China Morning Paper*). In *Shaonian Zhongguo chenbao sanshi zhounian jiniance* 少年中國晨報三十周年紀念冊 (Commemorative album of the thirtieth anniversary of *The Young China Morning Paper*). San Francisco: Shaonian zhongguo chenbaoshe, 1940.

Huang Zhenwu (黃珍吾). *Huaqiao yu Zhongguo geming* 華僑與中國革命 (Overseas Chinese and the Chinese revolution). Taibei: Guofang yanjiuyuan, 1963.

Huaqiao yu Xinhai geming 華僑與辛亥革命 (Overseas Chinese and the 1911 revolution). Beijing: Zhongguo shehui kexue chubanshe, 1981.

Lai, Him Mark (麥禮謙). *Cong huaqiao dao huaren: Ershi shiji Meiguo huaren shehui fazhan shi* 從華僑到華人 : 二十世紀美國華人社會發展史 (From overseas Chinese to Chinese American: A social history of the Chinese in the United States in the twentieth century). Hong Kong: Sanlian shudian youxian gongsi, 1992.

Li Fan (李凡). *Sun Zhongshan quanzhuan* 孫中山全傳 (Biography of Sun Yat-sen). Beijing: Beijing chubanshe, 1991.

Liu Boji (劉伯驥). *Meiguo huaqiao shi, 1848–1911* 美國華僑史, *1848–1911* (A history of the Chinese in the United States of America, 1848–1911). Taibei: Liming wenhua shiye gongsi, 1976.

Sun Zhongshan quanji 孫中山全集, 1–4卷 (Complete works of Sun Yat-sen, vols. 1–4). Beijing: Zhonghua shuju, 1986.

Wang Gungwu (王庚武). "Qianyan" 前言 (Foreword). In *Xing, Ma huaren yu Xinhai geming* 星，馬華人與辛亥革命 (Overseas Chinese and the 1911 revolution, with special reference to Singapore and Malaya). By Yan Qinghuang; trans. Li Enhan. Taibei: Lianjing chuban shiye gongsi, 1982.

Wu Lehua (巫樂華). *Huaqiao shi gaiyao* 華僑史概要 (An outline history of overseas Chinese). Beijing: Zhongguo huaqiao chubanshe, 1994.

Wu Ze, ed. (吳澤編). *Huaqiao shi zhuanji* 華僑史專集 (A collection of studies on the history of overseas Chinese). Shanghai: Huadong shifan daxue chubanshe, 1984.

Xu Xiaosheng (許肖生). *Huaqiao yu diyici guogong hezuo* 華僑與第一次國共合作 (Overseas Chinese and the first GMD-Communist cooperation). Guangzhou: Jinan daxue chubanshe, 1993.

Yang Guobiao, Liu Hanbiao, and Yang Anyao. (楊國標，劉漢標，楊安堯). *Meiguo huaqiao shi* 美國華僑史 (A history of overseas Chinese in the United States). Guangzhuo: Guangdong gaojiao chubanshe, 1989.

Zhang Aiyun (張靄蘊). "Xinhai qian Meizhou huaqiao geming huodong jilu" 辛亥前美洲華僑革命活動紀錄 (Notes on revolutionary activities among the Chinese in America before the 1911 revolution). In *Sun Zhongshan yu Xinhai geming shiliao zhuanji* 孫中山與辛亥革命史料專輯 (Special collection of historical materials concerning Sun Yat-sen and the 1911 revolution). Guangzhou: Guangdong renmin chubanshe, 1981.

Zhang Xianwen, ed. (張憲文編). *Zhonghua minguo shigang* 中華民國史綱 (An outline history of the Republic of China). Zhengzhou: Henan renmin chubanshe, 1985.

Zhong Guangxing, ed. (鐘廣興編). *Huaqiao yu Zhongguo guomin geming yundong* 華僑與中國國民革命運動 (Overseas Chinese and the Chinese nationalist revolution). Taibei: Haiwai chubanshe, 1981.

English-Language Sources

NEWSPAPERS CONSULTED

San Francisco Chronicle
San Francisco Examiner
New York Times

GOVERNMENT DOCUMENTS

Bureau of the Census. *Abstract of the 12th Census, 1900*. Reprint. New York: Arno Press, 1976.

Bureau of the Census. *Abstract of the 13th Census, 1910*. Reprint. New York: Arno Press, 1976.

Bureau of the Census. *Abstract of the 14th Census, 1920*. Reprint. New York: Arno Press, 1976.

Bureau of the Census. *Abstract of the 15th Census, 1930*. Reprint. New York: Arno Press, 1976.

California Legislature, Assembly Committee on Medical and Dental Laws. "An Act to Regulate the Manufacture, Sale and Use of Herb Roots or Other Nature Products Used in the Administering of Sickness or Treating Diseases of a Human Being and Providing a Penalty for the Violation Thereof." Assembly Bill 440 (1925).

Chang Chan, Wong Hung Jay, Yee Sin Jung et al. v. Nagle. *United States Report*, 268 (1925).

Cheung Sum Shee et al. v. Nagle. *United States Reports*, 268 (1925).

Congressional Record, 62nd Congress, 3rd Session (1912), Vol. 49.

Department of State. *Papers Relating to the Foreign Relations of the United States, 1915*. Washington, D.C.: Government Printing Office, 1924.

Ex parte Chan Shee et al. *Federal Reporter* 2d, 2 (1924).

Ex parte Cheung Sum Shee et al. *Federal Reporter* 2d, 2 (1924).

Ex parte Chiu Shee. *Federal Reporter*, 2d, 1 (1924).

House of Representatives. Record Group 233. Box HR66A-H6.3. "Petitions and Memorials." National Archives, Washington, D.C.

Immigration Act of 1924. *United States Statutes at Large*, 43 (1924).

Senate Committee on Immigration. "An Act to Regulate the Immigration of Aliens and the Residence of Aliens in the United States." Hearings on S. 3175, 62nd Congress, 2nd session (1912).

Subcommittee of the Senate Committee on Immigration. "Admission as Non-quota Immigrants of Certain Alien Wives and Children of United States Citizens." Hearings on S. 2271, 70th Congress, 2nd session (1928).

Tsoi Sim v. United States. *Federal Reporter*, 116 (1902).

United States Census Office. *Abstract of the 11th Census, 1890*. Reprint. New York: Arno Press, 1976.

United States v. Mrs. Gue Lim. *United States Reports*, 176 (1900).

SECONDARY MATERIALS

Americanization Bulletin 1:3 (November 1918).

Barlow, Jeffrey, and Christine Richardson. *China Doctor of John Day*. Portland, Ore.: Binford and Mort, 1979.

Bays, Daniel H. *Christianity in China: From the Eighteenth Century to the Present*. Stanford, Calif.: Stanford University Press, 1996.

———. "The Growth of Independent Christianity in China, 1900–1937." In *Christianity in China: From the Eighteenth Century to the Present*. Ed. Daniel H. Bays. Stanford, Calif.: Stanford University Press, 1996. 307–16.

Becker, Jules. *The Course of Exclusion: San Francisco Newspaper Coverage of the Chinese and Japanese in the United States, 1882–1924*. San Francisco: Mellen Research University Press, 1991.

Bell, Colin, and Howard Newby. *Community Studies: An Introduction to the Sociology of the Local Communities*. New York: Praeger, 1974.

Bergere, Marie-Claire. "The Role of the Bourgeoisie." In *China in Revolution: The First Phase, 1910–1913*. Ed. Mary C. Wright. New Haven, Conn.: Yale University Press, 1968. 229–95.

Berlant, Jeffrey Lionel. *Profession and Monopoly: A Study of Medicine in the United States and Great Britain.* Berkeley: University of California Press, 1975.

Board of Directors of the Chinese Hospital. *Chinese Hospital: 40th Anniversary, 1923–1963.* Hong Kong: Wing On Shing, 1963.

Bonner, Arthur. *Alas! What Brought Thee Hither?: The Chinese in New York, 1800–1950.* Cranbury, N.J.: Associated University Press, 1997.

Chan, Sucheng. *Asian Americans: An Interpretive History.* Boston: Twayne, 1991.

———. "The Exclusion of Chinese Women, 1870–1943." In *Entry Denied: Exclusion and the Chinese Community in America, 1882–1943.* Ed. Sucheng Chan. Philadelphia: Temple University Press, 1991. 94–136.

———. Preface to *Entry Denied: Exclusion and the Chinese Community in America, 1882–1943.* Ed. Sucheng Chan. Philadelphia: Temple University Press, 1991. vii–xv.

———. "Race, Ethnic Culture, and Gender in the Construction of Identities among Second-Generation Chinese Americans, 1880s to 1930." In *Claiming America: Constructing Chinese American Identity during the Exclusion Era.* Ed. K. Scott Wong and Sucheng Chan. Philadelphia: Temple University Press, 1998. 127–64.

Chang, Hao. *Liang Ch'i-ch'ao and Intellectual Transition in China, 1890–1907.* Cambridge, Mass.: Harvard University Press, 1971.

Chen, Jerome. *Yuan Shih-kai, 1859–1916: Brutus Assumes the Purple.* Stanford, Calif.: Stanford University Press, 1961.

Chen, Julia I. Hsuan. *The Chinese Community in New York: A Study in Their Cultural Adjustment, 1920–1940.* San Francisco: R. and E. Research Associates, 1974.

Chen, Yong. *Chinese San Francisco, 1850–1943: A Trans-Pacific Community.* Stanford, Calif.: Stanford University Press, 2000.

Cheng, Lucie, Yuzun Liu, and Dehua Zheng. "Chinese Emigration: The Sunning Railroad and the Development of Toisan." *Amerasia* 9:1 (1982): 59–74.

Chesneaux, Jean. *Chinese Labor Movement, 1919–1927.* Trans. H. M. Wright. Stanford, Calif.: Stanford University Press, 1968.

Chesneaux, Jean, Francoise Le Barbier, and Marie-Claire Bergere. *China from the 1911 Revolution to Liberation.* Trans. Paul Auster, Lydia Davis, and Anne Destenay. New York: Pantheon Books, 1977.

Chew, Ron, ed. *Reflections of Seattle's Chinese Americans: The First 100 Years.* Seattle: University of Washington Press, 1994.

Chinn, Thomas W. *Bridging the Pacific: San Francisco Chinatown and Its People.* San Francisco: Chinese Historical Society of America, 1989.

———. "A Historian's Reflections on Chinese-American Life in San Francisco, 1919–1991." Oral history conducted in 1990 and 1991 by Ruth Teiser, Regional Oral History Office, Bancroft Library, University of California at Berkeley, 1993.

Chow Tse-tsung. *The May Fourth Movement: Intellectual Revolution in Modern China.* Cambridge, Mass.: Harvard University Press, 1960.

Chung, Sue Fawn. "Fighting for Their American Rights: A History of the Chinese American Citizens Alliance." In *Claiming America: Constructing Chinese American Identity during the Exclusion Era.* Ed. K. Scott Wong and Sucheng Chan. Philadelphia: Temple University Press, 1998. 95–126.

Clifford, James. "Diasporas." *Cultural Anthropology* 9:3 (1994): 302–38.
Clubb, O. Edmund. *China and Russia: The "Great Game."* New York: Columbia University Press, 1971.
Cohen, Myron L. "Being Chinese: The Peripheralization of Traditional Identity." In *The Living Tree: The Changing Meaning of Being Chinese Today.* Ed. Tu Wei-ming. Stanford, Calif.: Stanford University Press, 1994. 88–108.
Confucian Analects, Book XII. In *Confucian Analects, the Great Learning, and the Doctrine of the Mean.* Trans. James Legge. New York: Dover Publications, 1971. 248–62.
Cook, Carroll. Letter to the CCBA. Box 3, Ng Poon Chew Collection, Ethnic Studies Library, University of California at Berkeley.
Coolidge, Mary R. *Chinese Immigration.* 1909. New York: Arno Press, 1969.
Daggett, Emerson (supervisor). *History of Foreign Journalism in San Francisco.* San Francisco: United States Works Progress Administration, 1939.
Daniels, Roger. *Asian America: Chinese and Japanese in the United States since 1850.* Seattle: University of Washington Press, 1988.
———. *The Politics of Prejudice: The Anti-Japanese Movement in California and the Struggle for Japanese Exclusion.* 1962. Gloucester, Mass.: Peter Smith, 1966.
Dillon, Richard H. *The Hatchet Men, 1880–1906: San Francisco's Chinatown in the Days of the Tong Wars.* New York: Ballantine Books, 1962.
Fairbank, John K. *The Great Chinese Revolution, 1800–1985.* New York: Harper and Row, 1986.
Gintjee, T. J., and Howard H. Johnson. "San Francisco's First Chinese Hospital." Vertical File, Ethnic Studies Library, University of California at Berkeley.
Gordon, Milton M. *Assimilation in American Life: The Role of Race, Religion, and National Origins.* New York: Oxford University Press, 1964.
Hodges, Donald, and Ross Gandy. *Mexico, 1910–1976: Reform or Revolution?* London: Zed Press, 1979.
Hoexter, Corinne K. *From Canton to California: The Epic of Chinese Immigration.* New York: Four Winds Press, 1976.
Hsiao, Kung-chuan. *A Modern China and a New World: Kang Yu-wei, Reformer and Utopian, 1858–1927.* Seattle: University of Washington Press, 1975.
Hsu, Madeline Y. *Dreaming of Gold, Dreaming of Home: Transnationalism and Migration between the United States and South China, 1882–1943.* Stanford, Calif.: Stanford University Press, 2000.
———. "Gold Mountain Dreams and Paper Son Schemes: Chinese Immigration under Exclusion." In *Chinese America: History and Perspectives, 1997.* San Francisco: Chinese Historical Society of America, 1997. 46–60.
Hu, Sheng. *Imperialism and Chinese Politics.* Beijing: Foreign Language Press, 1955.
Hunt, Michael H. *The Making of a Special Relationship: The United States and China to 1914.* New York: Columbia University Press, 1983.
Jacques, Leo M. Dambourges. "The Chinese Massacre in Torreon (Coahuila) in 1911." *Arizona and the West* 16 (1974): 233–46.
Jansen, Marius B. *The Japanese and Sun Yat-sen.* Stanford, Calif.: Stanford University Press, 1970.
Kwong, Peter. *Chinatown, New York: Labor and Politics, 1930–1950.* New York: Monthly Review Press, 1979.

Lai, Him Mark, Genny Lim, and Judy Yung. "Historical Development of the Chinese Consolidated Benevolent Association/Huiguan System." In *Chinese America: History and Perspectives, 1987*. San Francisco: Chinese Historical Society of America, 1987. 13–51.

———. *Island: Poetry and History of Chinese Immigrants on Angel Island, 1910–1940*. Seattle: University of Washington Press, 1991.

———. "The Kuomintang in Chinese American Communities before World War II." In *Entry Denied: Exclusion and the Chinese Community in America, 1882–1943*. Ed. Sucheng Chan. Philadelphia: Temple University Press, 1991. 171–212.

Leong Gor Yun. *Chinatown Inside Out*. New York: Barrows Mussey, 1936.

Li Chien-nung. *The Political History of China, 1840–1928*. Trans. and ed. Ssu-yu Teng and Jeremy Ingalls. Stanford, Calif.: Stanford University Press, 1956.

Lim, Genny, ed. *The Chinese American Experience: Papers from the Second National Conference on Chinese American Studies*. San Francisco: Chinese Historical Society of America and Chinese Culture Foundation, 1980.

Lin, Peter. *Christianity and China*. Taipei: Universal Light Publishing House, 1975.

Linebarger, Paul Myron Anthony. *The Political Doctrines of Sun Yat-sen: An Exposition of the San Min Chu I*. Westport, Conn.: Hyperion Press, 1973.

Ling, Huping. *Surviving on the Gold Mountain: A History of Chinese Women and Their Lives*. Albany: State University of New York Press, 1998.

Link, Arthur S. *Wilson: The New Freedom*. Princeton, N.J.: Princeton University Press, 1956.

Liu, Haiming. "The Resilience of Ethnic Culture: Chinese Herbalists in the American Medical Profession." *Journal of Asian American Studies* 1:2 (June 1998): 173–91.

Lo, Jung-pang, ed. and trans. *Kang Yu-wei: A Biography and a Symposium*. Tucson: University of Arizona Press, 1967.

Loo, Chalsa. "San Francisco's Chinatown: Findings from a Survey on Life Quality." In *The Chinese American Experience: Papers from the Second National Conference on Chinese American Studies*. Ed. Genny Lim. San Francisco: Chinese Historical Society of America and Chinese Culture Foundation, 1980. 282–85.

Loo, Chalsa, and Connie Young Yu. "Pulse on San Francisco's Chinatown: Health Services Utilization and Health Status." *Amerasia* 11:1 (1984): 55–73.

Luo, Zhitian. "National Humiliation and National Assertion: The Chinese Response to the Twenty-one Demands." *Modern Asian Studies* 27:2 (1993): 297–319.

Lyman, Stanford M. *Chinese Americans*. New York: Random House, 1974.

Ma, L. Eve Armentrout. "The Big Business Ventures of Chinese in North America, 1850–1930." In *The Chinese American Experience: Papers from the Second National Conference on Chinese American Studies*. Ed. Genny Lim. San Francisco: Chinese Historical Society of America and Chinese Culture Foundation of San Francisco, 1980. 101–12.

———. *Revolutionaries, Monarchists, and Chinatowns: Chinese Politics in the Americas and the 1911 Revolution*. Honolulu: University of Hawai'i Press, 1990.

McClain, Charles J. *In Search of Equality: The Chinese Struggle against Discrimination in Nineteenth-Century America.* Berkeley: University of California Press, 1994.

McCunn, Ruthanne Lum. *Chinese American Portraits: Personal Histories, 1928–1988.* San Francisco: Chronicle Books, 1988.

McKee, Delber L. *Chinese Exclusion versus the Open Door Policy, 1900–1906.* Detroit: Wayne State University Press, 1977.

McKenzie, R. D. *Oriental Exclusion: The Effect of American Immigration Laws, Regulations, and Judicial Decisions upon the Chinese and Japanese on the American Pacific Coast.* 1927. New York: Jerome S. Ozer, 1971.

McKeown, Adam. "Reconceptualizing Chinese Diasporas, 1942–1979." *Journal of Asian Studies* 58 (May 1999): 306–37.

Mei, June. "Socioeconomic Developments among the Chinese in San Francisco, 1848–1906." In *Labor Immigration under Capitalism: Asian Workers in the United States before WWII.* Ed. Lucie Cheng and Edna Bonacich. Berkeley: University of California Press, 1984. 370–401.

Memorial: Six Chinese Companies—An Address to the Senate and House of Representatives of the United States. 1877. San Francisco: R. and E. Research Associates, 1970.

Miller, Stuart C. *The Unwelcome Immigrant: The American Image of the Chinese, 1785–1882.* Stanford, Calif.: Stanford University Press, 1969.

Muench, Christopher. "One Hundred Years of Medicine: The Ah-Fong Physicians of Idaho." In *Chinese Medicine in the Golden Mountains: An Interpretive Guide.* Ed. Henry G. Schwarz. Seattle: Wing Luke Memorial Museum, 1984. 51–80.

Nee, Victor G., and Brett de Bary Nee. *Longtime Californ': A Documentary Study of an American Chinatown.* New York: Pantheon Books, 1972.

Ng Poon Chew. "Chinatown Modernized." Box 3, Ng Poon Chew Collection, Ethnic Studies Library, University of California at Berkeley.

———. "Dr. Ng Poon Chew's Views on Love and Marriage." Box 3, Ng Poon Chew Collection, Ethnic Studies Library, University of California at Berkeley.

Preston, William, Jr. *Aliens and Dissenters: Federal Suppression of Radicals, 1903–1933.* New York: Harper and Row, 1966.

Remer, C. F. *A Study of Chinese Boycotts: With Special Reference to Their Economic Effectiveness.* 1933. Taipei: Cheng-wen chuban gongsi, 1966.

Rydell, Robert W. *All the World's a Fair: Visions of Empire at American International Expositions, 1876–1916.* Chicago: University of Chicago Press, 1984.

Salyer, Lucy E. *Laws Harsh as Tigers: Chinese Immigrants and the Shaping of Modern Immigration Law.* Chapel Hill: University of North Carolina Press, 1995.

Schiffrin, Harold Z. *Sun Yat-sen and the Origins of the Chinese Revolution.* Berkeley: University of California Press, 1968.

———. "Sun Yat-sen's Early Land Policy: The Origin and Meaning of 'Equalization of Land Rights.'" *Journal of Asian Studies* 16 (August 1957): 549–64.

Schneider, Jurgen, Oskar Schwarzer, and Markus A. Denzel, eds. *Wahrunger der Welt V: Asiatische und australische Devisenkurse im 20. Jahrhundert* (Currencies of the World 5: Asian and Australian Exchange Rates in the Twentieth Century). Stuttgart: Franz Steiner, 1994.

Schwartz, Larissa N. "The Inconveniences Resulting from Race Mixture: The Terreon Massacre of 1911." In *Chinese America: History and Perspectives, 1998.* San Francisco: Chinese Historical Society of America. 1998, 57–65.

Scott, George M., Jr. "A Resynthesis of the Primordial and Circumstantial Approaches to Ethnic Group Solidarity: Toward an Explanatory Model." *Ethnic and Racial Studies* 13:2 (April 1990): 147–71.

Siu, Paul C. P. *The Chinese Laundryman: A Study of Social Isolation.* 1953. New York: New York University Press, 1987.

———. "The Sojourner." *American Journal of Sociology* 58 (July 1952): 34–44.

Smith, Richard J. *China's Cultural Heritage: The Ch'ing Dynasty, 1644–1912.* Boulder, Colo.: Westview Press, 1983.

Sparks, Theresa A. *China Gold.* Fresno, Calif.: Academy Library Guild, 1954.

Spence, Jonathan D. *The Search for Modern China.* 2d ed. New York: W. W. Norton, 1999.

Strong, Gary E., ed. *Chinatown Photographer Louis J. Stellman: A Catalog of His Photograph Collection, Including a Previously Unpublished Manuscript, "Chinatown: A Pictorial Souvenir and Guide Written by Louis J. Stellman in 1917."* Sacramento: California State Library Foundation, 1989.

Sung, Betty Lee. *The Story of the Chinese in America: Their Struggle for Survival, Acceptance, and Full Participation in American Life—From the Gold Rush Days to the Present.* New York: Collier Books, 1967.

Takaki, Ronald. *Strangers from a Different Shore: A History of Asian Americans.* New York: Penguin Books, 1990.

Trauner, Joan B. "The Chinese as Medical Scapegoats in San Francisco, 1870–1905." *California History* 57 (Spring 1978): 70–87.

Tseng, Timothy. "Chinese Protestant Nationalism in the United States, 1880–1927." *Amerasia* 22:1 (1996): 31–56.

Tu Wei-ming. "Cultural China: The Periphery as the Center." In *The Living Tree: The Changing Meaning of Being Chinese Today.* Ed. Tu Wei-ming. Stanford, Calif.: Stanford University Press, 1994. 1–34.

Wang, L. Ling-chi. "The Structure of Dual Domination: Toward a Paradigm of the Study of the Chinese Diaspora in the United States." *Amerasia* 21:1–2 (1995): 149–69.

Wang, Y. C. *Chinese Intellectuals and the West, 1872–1949.* Chapel Hill: University of North Carolina Press, 1966.

Wang Gungwu. *Community and Nation: Essays on Southeast Asia and the Chinese.* Kuala Lumpur: Allen and Unwin, 1981.

Wilbur, C. Martin. *Sun Yat-sen: Frustrated Patriot.* New York: Columbia University Press, 1976.

Won, Lilly King Gee. "Recollections of Dr. Sun Yat-sen's Stay at Our Home in San Francisco." Trans. Ellen Lai-shan Yeung. In *Chinese America: History and Perspectives, 1990.* San Francisco: Chinese Historical Society of America, 1990. 67–82.

Wong, Jade Snow. *Fifth Chinese Daughter.* Seattle: University of Washington Press, 1995.

Wong, K. Scott. "The Transformation of Culture: Three Chinese Views of America." *American Quarterly* 48 (June 1996): 201–32.

Wong, K. Scott, and Sucheng Chan. *Claiming America: Constructing Chinese*

American Identity during the Exclusion Era. Philadelphia: Temple University Press, 1998.

Wong, Paul, Steven Applewhite, and J. Michael Daley. "From Despotism to Pluralism: The Evolution of Voluntary Organizations in Chinese American Communities." *Ethnic Groups* 8:1 (1990): 215–33.

Wong, Victoria. "Square and Circle Club: Women in the Public Sphere." In *Chinese America: History and Perspectives, 1994.* San Francisco: Chinese Historical Society of America, 1994. 127–53.

Wu, Cheng-tsu, ed. *"Chink!": A Documentary History of Anti-Chinese Prejudice in America.* New York: World Publishing, 1972.

Yip, Ka-che. *Religion, Nationalism, and Chinese Students: The Anti-Christian Movement of 1922–1927.* Bellingham: Center for East Asian Studies, Western Washington University, 1980.

Yu, Connie Young. "John C. Young: A Man Who Loved History." In *Chinese America: History and Perspectives, 1989.* San Francisco: Chinese Historical Society of America. 1989, 3–14.

Yu, Renqiu. *To Save China, to Save Ourselves: The Chinese Hand Laundry Alliance of New York.* Philadelphia: Temple University Press, 1992.

Yung, Judy. "The Fake and the True: Researching Chinese Women's Immigration History." In *Chinese America: History and Perspectives, 1998.* San Francisco: Chinese Historical Society of America, 1998. 25–56.

———. "The Social Awakening of Chinese American Women as Reported in *Chung Sai Yat Po,* 1900–1911." In *Unequal Sisters: A Multicultural Reader in U.S. Women's History.* Ed. Ellen Carol DuBois and Vicki L. Ruiz. New York: Routledge, 1994. 195–207.

———. *Unbound Feet: A Social History of Chinese Women in San Francisco.* Berkeley: University of California Press, 1995.

INDEX

Ah-Fong, Chuck, 157–58, 159
All American Chinese National Salvation Association, 80, 82, 86, 100, 105, 107, 201n
All American Overseas Chinese Military Fundraising Bureau, 112, 118
Americanization, 170, 173, 177; program of, 152, 214n
anarchism, 125, 126, 132
Angel Island Immigration Station, 14
Annam, 24
anti-American boycott, 78–79, 187n, 200n, 202n
anti-Christian movement, 8, 113, 132, 182
Anti-Christian Student Alliance, 131–32
antifeudalism, 125
anti-imperialism, 125
anti-Japanese boycott, 7, 76, 87, 105, 107, 109, 200n; effect of, 202n; organized and implemented, 78–86, 201n
anti-Manchuism, 17, 20, 24, 26, 31
Arkansas, 146
assimilation, 53–54, 155, 195n
Atlantic City, N.J., 172
Atlantic Transport Company, 109
Austria, 179

Bakersfield, Calif., 83
Bank of China, 91
Baohuangdang, 35, 192n. *See also* Baohuanghui
Baohuanghui (Society to Protect the Emperor), 5, 26, 30, 31, 187n, 192n; and Chinese tragedy in Torreon,

Mex., 33–36; and *Chinese World,* 19, 27–28; establishment of, 15, 179
Baoshanghui (Society to Protect Commerce), 15
Baptist Church Nursery School, 164
Bayside Cannery, 79
beauty contest, 146, 167, 171, 172–75, 177
Beijing, 4, 58, 61, 75, 89, 124–25, 126, 180, 182
—government of, 80, 109, 110, 182, 183, 209n; decline of confidence in, 144; and militarists, 145. *See also* Chinese government; northern government; Yuan government
Beijing University, 122
Boise, Idaho, 158
Boise Businessmen's Association, 158
Bolshevik, 134
Boston, Mass., 84, 151, 153
Boxer Uprising, 179
Bureau Resisting the New Immigration Act, 151, 153
Butler, Nicholas M., 155

California State Assembly, 160
Caminetti, Anthony, 75
Canada, 15, 58, 79, 118, 119, 134, 159, 214n
Canton Bank, 79, 107
Canton Noodle Factory, 173
Cao Kun, 183
Cao Rulin, 124, 183, 209n
capitalism, 2, 25, 113 208n; in China, 52–53; and Chinese American identity, 133–45
capitalist ideology, 13, 103

141–42; and Tongmenghui, 10, 21, 33; and traditional Chinese identity, 26, 27, 47; and Yuan Shikai, 45–46, 88–89
Young China Public Speech Society, 85
Young Men's Christian Association (YMCA): in New York City Chinatown, 128; in Oakland Chinatown, 128; in Seattle Chinatown, 128
—in San Francisco Chinatown, 176; building of, 147, 168; and Chinese Hospital, 165; proposed and opened, 63–64; roles of, in Chinatown life, 129–30
Young Women's Christian Association (YWCA): in San Francisco Chinatown, 130, 147, 169–71, 172
Yu ling, 78, 107
Yuan government, 43, 88, 90, 181, 203n; support of, 44, 51, 55–56; and Twenty-one Demands, 79, 81, 86. *See also* Beijing: government of; Chinese government
Yuan Shikai, 43, 54, 180, 181, 197n; abolition of parliament, 87, 88; appeal to, 75; confidence in, 79; a dictator, 60; monarchical restoration,

45, 46, 105, 112–19, 208n; a practical leader, 59; and republican form of government, 45; and Sun Yat-sen, 55, 56; support of, 85
Yunnan, 22, 116, 118, 181, 208n
YWCA. *See* Young Women's Christian Association

Zhang Xun, 181, 210n
Zhang Zongxiang, 124, 209n
Zhang Zuolin, 141, 212n
Zhenhuang Company, 95–96, 100–104
Zhigongtang, 15, 32, 37, 187n; change to Chinese Republic Association, 56; and Chinatown YMCA, 168; and Chinese Hospital, 165; among Chinese in Torreon, Mex., 35; and "Citizen Donation," 61; and National Protection Army, 118; political aim of, 17, 24; as rebels, 38; support of, for Yuan government, 56; and Tongmenghui, 32–33, 37, 40–41, 56. *See also* Chinese Republic Association
Zhongguo, 20
Zhonghua, 20, 188n
Zhu Zhaoxin, 58

SHEHONG CHEN is an assistant professor of history at the University of Massachusetts at Lowell. She received her Ph.D. from the University of Utah.

THE ASIAN AMERICAN EXPERIENCE

*The University of Illinois Press
is a founding member of the
Association of American University Presses.*

---

*University of Illinois Press
1325 South Oak Street
Champaign, IL 61820-6903
www.press.uillinois.edu*